A SEASON OF DARKNESS

A SEASON OF
DARKNESS

Douglas Jones and **Phyllis Gobbell**

BERKLEY BOOKS, NEW YORK

THE BERKLEY PUBLISHING GROUP
Published by the Penguin Group
Penguin Group (USA) Inc.
375 Hudson Street, New York, New York 10014, USA
Penguin Group (Canada), 90 Eglinton Avenue East, Suite 700, Toronto, Ontario M4P 2Y3, Canada
(a division of Pearson Penguin Canada Inc.)
Penguin Books Ltd., 80 Strand, London WC2R 0RL, England
Penguin Group Ireland, 25 St. Stephen's Green, Dublin 2, Ireland (a division of Penguin Books Ltd.)
Penguin Group (Australia), 250 Camberwell Road, Camberwell, Victoria 3124, Australia
(a division of Pearson Australia Group Pty. Ltd.)
Penguin Books India Pvt. Ltd., 11 Community Centre, Panchsheel Park, New Delhi—110 017, India
Penguin Group (NZ), 67 Apollo Drive, Rosedale, North Shore 0632, New Zealand
(a division of Pearson New Zealand Ltd.)
Penguin Books (South Africa) (Pty.) Ltd., 24 Sturdee Avenue, Rosebank, Johannesburg 2196,
South Africa

Penguin Books Ltd., Registered Offices: 80 Strand, London WC2R 0RL, England

The publisher does not have any control over and does not assume any responsibility for author or third-party websites or their content.

A SEASON OF DARKNESS

A Berkley Book / published by arrangement with the authors

PRINTING HISTORY
Berkley mass-market edition / December 2010

Copyright © 2010 by Phyllis Gobbell and Douglas E. Jones.
Cover photos: *Lawn* by Douglas Jones; *House* © Linda Johnsonbaugh/Shutterstock; *Girl* by Shutterstock: *Headline* by the *Tennessean.*
Cover design by Jane Hammer.
Interior text design by Tiffany Estreicher.

ISBN: 978-0-425-23915-5

BERKLEY®
Berkley Books are published by The Berkley Publishing Group,
a division of Penguin Group (USA) Inc.,
375 Hudson Street, New York, New York 10014.
BERKLEY® is a registered trademark of Penguin Group (USA) Inc.
The "B" design is a trademark of Penguin Group (USA) Inc.

PRINTED IN THE UNITED STATES OF AMERICA

10   9   8   7   6   5   4   3   2   1

Most Berkley Books are available at special quantity discounts for bulk purchases for sales, promotions, premiums, fund-raising, or educational use. Special books, or book excerpts, can also be created to fit specific needs.

For details, write: Special Markets, The Berkley Publishing Group, 375 Hudson Street, New York, New York 10014.

PART 1

A Parent's Worst Nightmare

1

February 25, 1975

It was the kind of late-winter day in Nashville that promised spring. On the heels of brutal temperatures, sleet, ice, and light snow, here was a sun-splashed afternoon with billowy clouds sailing across blue skies. A few more days like this, and jonquils would start to poke their heads through the ground. Spring was not far away now.

On that bright Tuesday, February 25, 1975, nine-year-old Marcia Trimble came home from school, watched *Gilligan's Island*, and ate a snack before she went out to deliver Girl Scout cookies. It was Marcia's first year as a Scout. Her mother, Virginia, was the leader of her troop, no. 802. Parents, kids, everyone in the neighborhood liked blond-haired, freckle-faced Marcia. She was a great ambassador for the Girl Scouts, enthusiastic about selling cookies. It made her feel like an adult operating a real business. Girl Scout cookies were an easy sale in Nashville. Folks were glad to help the Scouts. The sinful Tagalongs and Samoas came in small boxes, just a slight indulgence.

The Trimbles lived in a ranch-style redbrick house with three bedrooms, at 4009 Copeland Drive, near the edge of a prominent residential area, fashionable Green Hills, which bordered elegant, historic Belle Meade, where Nashville's "old money" lived. Marcia Trimble's neighborhood was a setting of quiet streets and wooded areas, a place where yards were tended with care and mature trees were good for climbing, where children rode bikes and came home at dark, and neighbors looked out for one another. There were no leash laws in 1975, and Copeland Drive had its share of family dogs that played in the street along with the youngsters. For Marcia and the many other children who roamed freely through the pleasant neighborhood, it was a comfortable, safe place.

Marcia went out with her cookie carton and met March Egerton coming from his house, a few doors down from the Trimbles. The ten-year-old boy with light brown hair and dark-rimmed glasses was a classmate at Julia Green Elementary School and a friend to both Marcia and her twelve-year-old brother, Chuck. Like Marcia, March had been watching *Gilligan's Island*. He bought two boxes of cookies, one of Samoas and one of Thin Mints, and munched on them while Marcia made some deliveries down the street. When she came back, he bought another box of Thin Mints. For a while, March accompanied Marcia through the neighborhood—to the O'Connors, who were not at home, to the Collinses, and to the Womacks' house at 4102 Copeland. Fifteen-year-old Jeffrey Womack said he didn't have the cash to pay for the cookies his mother had ordered but promised to bring the money to Marcia later.

Marcia and March walked toward the Maxwells' house, but from a distance they could see that Mrs. Maxwell's car was not there. Charles Trimble, Marcia's dad, came driving down Copeland and saw the children. He called to Marcia and asked her about coming home. "I'll be on in a few minutes," she said. But she was in no hurry. She and March sat down at the edge of the street in front of the Rolfe house, next to the Trimbles. Marcia's mother, Virginia Trimble, saw them from her window. She called to her daughter and asked what they were doing. "Waiting for them to come home," Marcia said. She told March she still had to deliver to the Maxwells, O'Connors, Thompsons, Brooms, and Whites.

By now, shadows were falling across the yards and the street. There was a chill in the air. The winter wind had scoured the trees and ground, leaving the yards of Copeland Drive stark and bare. Under her coat, Marcia wore new blue jeans and a blue and white checked blouse trimmed in red. She wore black patent leather boots that she had bought with Christmas money. She carried a cardboard carton containing boxes of cookies and a white envelope with $15 collected from her sales.

A car turned into the Trimble driveway. Grandmother Eunice Trimble had arrived—another customer who had bought cookies. Marcia jumped up and sprinted toward the house, calling back, "Oh, Grandmother, I have your cookies!" She came out with four boxes of cookies and put them in her grandmother's car, receiving a $5 bill for payment, then helped Eunice carry some things inside. Marcia's brother, Chuck, was shooting baskets in the driveway, and March Egerton joined him in a game of HORSE.

Inside the house, Marcia shed her coat and went to her room. Charles fixed a drink for himself and his mother. Virginia was busy with supper.

A few minutes later, Marcia bounced back into the kitchen with her cardboard carton.

"I'm going to take Mrs. Maxwell her cookies," she said.

"Put your coat on, honey," Virginia Trimble told her daughter.

"Oh, Mom, I won't need my coat. I'll be right back," Marcia called as she darted out the back door, carrying the cookies.

She saw March and Chuck. "Want to play HORSE?" one of the boys called.

"I'll be back in a few minutes," she said.

Marcia cut through the Rolfe yard and crossed the street to Mrs. Howard's driveway, next to the Maxwells' house. It was about 5:25 P.M. The winter sun dropped like a stone behind the western hills.

The Howard and Maxwell houses were across the street from the Rolfes and the Trimbles, and the backyards of both houses were on a slight hill with a thicket of woods behind the properties. Twenty-six-year-old Marie Maxwell and her husband, Porter, had lived on Copeland Drive for three years. They had two small children. The driveway of their neighbor, Mrs. Howard, ran parallel to theirs, separated by a tall privet hedge.

That afternoon, Marie and her eleven-month-old daughter, Jenna, had attended a birthday party on Chickering Road, then ran some errands before going home. Marie turned into her driveway at about 5:30 P.M., pulled around to the back of the house, and parked near the door. As she walked around the station wagon to take Jenna from her car seat, she glanced through the hedge toward the Howard house. Marie saw three figures standing in the shadows by the Howard garage. One she recognized as Marcia Trimble, facing away from her. One of the others appeared to be a smaller figure, perhaps a child, and the third was a tall figure in a long, dark overcoat. For an instant Marie Maxwell wondered if the taller one was Mrs. Howard, but she knew that Mrs. Howard did not buy Girl Scout cookies and did not allow children in her yard. Marie had never seen Marcia in the Howard yard before.

Assuming that Marcia Trimble would be over shortly with the cookies she'd ordered, Marie Maxwell picked up the baby, went into the house, and located her checkbook in preparation to pay Marcia. She kept the baby dressed in her party clothes for a little while, so Marcia could see Jenna dressed up; Marcia, like a lot of little girls, was fascinated by babies and enjoyed being around Jenna. Marie didn't know the other Trimble family members very well, but she was well acquainted with Marcia.

When Marie heard their family dog, Daisy, barking furiously at the rear of their property toward the woods, she figured that Marcia must have walked up the path through the woods to the Thorpe house to deliver their cookies first.

But she wondered why the dog was making such a fuss. She'd never heard Daisy bark like that at Marcia.

2

Where Is Marcia?

Night was coming fast. Supper was ready, and Marcia was not home.

Virginia Trimble walked out to the front yard sometime between 5:45 and 6:00 P.M. "Marcia!" she called, looking up and down the street. "Marcia!" Hadn't Marcia said she'd be *right back*?

Chuck told his mother that he and March had asked Marcia to play HORSE. That was the last time he saw her. After the game was over, he rode his minibike for a few minutes and then came inside. Charles Trimble had a meeting with the Boy Scouts scheduled that night. The family needed to have supper. Where was Marcia?

Several boys were playing basketball up the street in the Egertons' driveway, but Virginia saw no sign of her daughter. She went to the backyard and then to the front yard again. She stood by the light pole at the street, calling, "Marcia!" Virginia shivered, remembering Marcia had gone out without her coat.

She went inside and telephoned Marie Maxwell, since the

last thing Marcia had said as she ran out was that she was headed to the Maxwells' house. "Marie, have you seen Marcia?" she asked.

"Yes, a few minutes ago," Marie said. "She was talking to somebody in Mrs. Howard's driveway."

"Are you sure it was Marcia?" Virginia knew Mrs. Howard, a widow who was about seventy years old, didn't like children in her yard.

Marie was sure. "I got out my checkbook and waited for her to bring my cookies, but she never came over. I think she went through Mrs. Howard's backyard, toward Estes."

Virginia called around to the other neighbors. Several people had seen Marcia earlier, delivering cookies, but not since she'd headed out to Marie Maxwell's.

Another trip to the yard, and Virginia saw the family dogs, Popcorn and Princess, on the opposite side of the street. They scampered home, to the front porch. If Marcia were at a neighbor's house, the dogs would likely be with her. So why were the dogs back home?

Virginia saw Mrs. Harris and her two girls up the street. Marcia played with seven-year-old Meredith and her little sister Hayden. A few weeks ago, Meredith, a Brownie, had gone around the neighborhood with Marcia, taking cookie orders, learning from her.

The little girls came running into the Trimbles' yard, and Virginia asked them if they'd seen Marcia.

"Isn't she home?" Meredith asked. The neighborhood children were free to roam during daylight hours, but it was widely understood that everyone should go home when the streetlights came on, which had already happened.

"No. She should have been home by now," Virginia said. She went back inside and told her husband, "Why don't you go out in the car and see if you can find her?" It was unusual for Marcia to be out like this. She always responded when her mother called. Charles first went outside and called for his daughter, as Virginia had done. Still no answer, and now dark was settling in. It was 6:30 P.M.

Charles and twelve-year-old Chuck got in the car and drove around the neighborhood; it took less than five minutes to drive the circular route. The only outlet from Copeland was at Hobbs Road, a main thoroughfare through the Green Hills community. Sometimes Marcia went to Geddes-Douglas Nursery at the corner of Hobbs and Estes Road to buy soft drinks. All the neighborhood kids did. Estes was another main access road through Green Hills. The street sat on a ridge above the valley and ran parallel to Copeland. Charles widened his search, circled back to Hobbs, and turned onto Copeland. He could not think of anywhere else to look.

Today, spring was in the air, but dark had brought a chill that seeped into the skin, a reminder that it was still winter. Charles remembered that his daughter had left without her coat.

Where was Marcia?

Virginia continued to contact neighbors. She made a call to the Thorpes on Estes Road. John Thorpe answered, and Virginia asked, "Have you seen Marcia?"

"No, but let me ask Marie." John came back on the line after speaking to his wife. "Marie hasn't seen her, either. Is she selling cookies?"

Virginia repeated what she'd told everyone else: Marcia had gone out saying she'd be right back. She was just going to deliver cookies to Mrs. Maxwell.

Virginia called Sue Myrick, whose daughter, Kellye, was also selling Girl Scout cookies. Neither Sue nor Kellye had seen Marcia that afternoon.

Anita Collins, who lived across from the Womacks, hadn't seen Marcia since about 4:40 P.M. She remembered Charles stopping the car to talk to Marcia and March.

Close to 7:00 P.M. Virginia called Marie Maxwell again. "What time was it when you saw Marcia?" she asked. "I want to get the time straight."

"It must have been about 5:30," Marie said. She thought about it. "Yes, it was around 5:30 when I pulled in the driveway."

"I'm worried," Virginia said, finally putting into words the feeling that had been nagging at her ever since she first went outside and called for her daughter. "Marcia always comes home when she says she'll be home, and she's always back by dark."

Marie suggested a couple of the neighbors who might have bought cookies.

"Yes, I've called them. I've tried everywhere," Virginia said.

Charles and Chuck returned, without any news of Marcia. She had been gone since about 5:20 P.M., more than an hour and a half. It was dark, getting colder. Virginia and Charles could think of nowhere else to look, no other neighbors to call. They waited a few minutes longer. Surely their pretty little girl would come through the door any minute. But she didn't.

They could think of only one other call to make.

Metro Intelligence sergeant Sherman Nickens was at home when the phone rang. Nickens was an old friend of Charles and Virginia's. He had not only attended their wedding; he'd even been at the hospital when both Chuck and Marcia were born.

His wife, Dot, answered the telephone at about 7:15 P.M. and spoke briefly with Charles.

"Sherman," she called to her husband, "something's happened to Marcia."

When Charles told him Marcia was missing, Nickens didn't take it lightly. He asked the standard questions: Could she have run away? Had anything upset her? Charles insisted that Marcia had not run away. She went out to deliver Girl Scout cookies to a neighbor across the street and said she would be right back.

Charles told him he'd been out in the car looking for her, and they had called everyone they knew. He choked up. "What can I do?"

Nickens told him to call the Metro police dispatcher. He gave Charles the number. "Tell the dispatcher to send a patrol officer and someone from Youth Guidance," he said. Then Nickens called the police dispatcher himself. His last call before rushing out of the house was to Sergeant R. C. Jackson from Homicide.

He was sure something was terribly wrong.

When the call came in about the missing child, Officers Richard McKee and Kerry Bissinger from the Patrol Division were dispatched to the scene. They arrived at 7:47 P.M., spoke with the Trimbles, and made out the initial report. Officer Arlene Moore and Sergeant Doug Dennis from Youth Guidance also responded to the missing child call, appearing at the Trimble house at 8:15 P.M. In the meantime, the dispatcher had called Major George Currey, commander of the Youth Guidance Division. Currey had just come home when he received the call. Though he lived across town, it took only about twenty minutes to make the trip to the Green Hills address.

Currey himself had designed the Youth Guidance Division in 1970, and he was well qualified to command the unit. With a background in the military, a BA from Peabody College, and experience teaching school, he became a Juvenile officer for the sheriff's office in 1958. He went on to become an investigator for the district attorney's office. He was appointed assistant director of the Tennessee Law Enforcement Training Academy and later graduated from the FBI National

Academy. When Mayor Beverly Briley set about to establish a Juvenile Division in Nashville-Davidson County with jurisdiction over youthful offenders, he recognized George Currey's unique credentials and asked him to take on the task of designing the unit. By 1975, Currey had some fifty officers under his command. Tonight, he had called some of his best people to Copeland Drive.

Major Currey and Judy Bawcum, another Youth Guidance officer, arrived about the same time. Currey took charge of the operation. His instincts, based on years of experience with missing children, told him this wasn't a child who'd fought with her parents and run off. This wasn't a child who had just lost track of time. The major began calling in all the help he could get.

As police cars lined the street, more neighbors came out. The word spread quickly throughout the neighborhood and beyond: Marcia Trimble was missing.

3

The First Long Night

A silver moon rose, full and bright, in the clear, cold sky.

On the ground, police officers, Civil Defense, and county rescue workers converged at the Trimble residence. By 9:00 P.M. an intense search of the neighborhood was under way. Neighbors on Copeland and residents of the wider area who had heard about Marcia joined the search. The ground was soggy from rain over the weekend. Searchers trudged through the mud, shining flashlights under every bush, calling, "Marcia! Marcia!" Dogs barked at the noises officers and volunteers made roaming through the streets and yards. Two Metro police helicopters hovered just above the treetops, directing a spotlight as police canine units searched dense thickets, fields, and an abandoned rock quarry.

Civil Defense director Robert Poe and his rescue workers operated out of a white panel truck in the Trimbles' front yard. Searchers taking a break warmed their hands over big barrels of fire. Police cars continued to pour into the neighborhood. Before the night was over, more than a hundred cars would line both sides of Copeland Drive and spill over to adjacent streets.

Major George Currey and his officers took statements from the neighbors, made calls, answered calls, and followed leads. Youth Guidance was in charge of the investigation since the missing person was juvenile. Civil Defense directed the physical search, but everyone on the scene participated in the search as the night wore on. The temperature, in the high 50s that afternoon, was now plunging toward freezing. If Marcia was outside, she might not survive through the night.

Inside the Trimble home, the mood grew more somber, hour by hour. It was not likely now that Marcia would come bouncing into the house any minute. The window of time for that possibility had closed. Something had happened to her. Had she been kidnapped? Hit by a car?

Virginia prayed that her little girl was still alive. She was a profoundly religious woman who'd had a life-changing religious experience two years earlier. Sometime during the night that Marcia disappeared, Virginia went into her daughter's bedroom and knelt by her bed. Marcia's room was a quintessential nine-year-old girl's room, with white furniture, a canopy bed, a yellow and blue flowered bedspread, and a girl-sized dressing table. Virginia later told reporters that she prayed: "I'm going to put my cards on the table. Lord, Marcia's missing, and you know where she is. God, please take care of her and keep her warm and dry."

Friends from the Lord's Chapel, the interdenominational church that the Trimbles attended, came to support Charles, Virginia, and Chuck. Faye Seals stayed with the family. Faye, who had driven the carpool for the kids that day, had delivered Marcia to her home after school. "We know Jesus knows where Marcia is," she told reporters. "We know He's looking after her." Bill Moore, pastor of the church, also came to the house. Charles and the pastor embraced, and Charles wept.

Martha Warfield, a cousin of the Trimbles, stayed most

of the night. Martha was also president of the Cumberland Valley Girl Scout Council. According to the council's policy for cookie sales, the girls could go door-to-door in their own neighborhoods but were required to have an adult accompanying them if they went anywhere else. Charles and Virginia Trimble did not place any blame on the Girl Scouts for Marcia's disappearance. Marcia and the thousands of other little girls who sold cookies were supposed to be safe in their own neighborhoods. But the policy on Girl Scout cookie sales was just one of the changes that Nashville would experience after February 25, 1975.

Reporters arrived from the *Tennessean*, the morning paper, and the *Nashville Banner*, the evening paper. Printed on the same presses, the newspapers were fiercely competitive when it came to news and politics. The *Tennessean* was considered a liberal voice, the *Banner* a conservative one. The missing child from Green Hills and the extensive search under way in the area was big news for both papers. Charles refused to let the photographers take pictures of him and his family, but he provided photos of Marcia. He hoped someone would see his daughter's picture in the next day's newspapers.

The local television stations also sent reporters and cameras. In 2001, the *Nashville Scene* published "The File on Marcia Trimble," a two-part article by Matt Pulle that examined the high-profile case. In the article, Pulle told how a young reporter from WTVF Channel 5 knocked on the Trimbles' door, hoping to get an interview with the family. Charles answered and told her no, they were not granting interviews. But Virginia, a true Southern lady, did not want to seem rude. "Please excuse us," she said. "Understand, our child is missing."

The rookie reporter, Oprah Winfrey, politely withdrew.

Marcia Trimble's disappearance made the ten o'clock news. The story touched a chord with the public unlike any missing person's case in Nashville before or since. After the news reported the missing nine-year-old, more private citizens joined the search. The neighborhood, so quiet a few hours earlier, was in a frenzy. Volunteers and men and women in an official capacity—more than two hundred before the night was over—left millions of footprints in the muddy ground.

As officers took statements from the Trimble family members and other witnesses, including children from the neighborhood, Jeffrey Womack's name kept coming up as someone who might have seen Marcia. Virginia Trimble told Detective Tommy Jacobs from Homicide that Marcia had told her mother, "Watch out for Jeffrey," who would be down to bring money and pick up the cookies his mother had ordered. Youth Guidance officer Anita Lowrance spoke to the neighbors that were out in the street looking for Marcia. One of the girls told the officer, "I know where she probably is—she was supposed to meet Jeff about 5:30 buy some Girl Scout cookies."

Sergeant R. C. Jackson, the Homicide detective who had accompanied Sergeant Nickens to the scene earlier in the evening, later wrote in a report, "Everyone seemed to be interested in locating a Jeffrey Womack to see if in fact she had delivered the cookies to the Womack residence and if Jeffrey had seen her or took the cookies from her in an attempt to pinpoint a time."

The police and neighbors had been to the Womack house, but Jeffrey was not there. Then at around 9:45 P.M., he appeared at the Trimble house. He said he'd heard police were looking for him. Shortly thereafter his mother, Christine Womack, and Peggy Morgan arrived at the house. Jeffrey worked part-time for Peggy, a divorced woman in her early thirties who ran a day care on the street. As the two women entered the room and faced Sergeant Nickens and Sergeant Jackson, Peggy said, "He couldn't have done it. He's been with me." Sergeant Jackson thought the woman's statement was strange, considering that at that time they were investigating a missing person. What was she saying Jeffrey couldn't have done? Police later learned that Peggy Morgan had been out bowling that evening, while Jeffrey stayed with some of the children at the day care.

Jeffrey was a skinny fifteen-year-old with long brown hair. Reports would vary as individuals later described how he was dressed. Sergeant R. C. Jackson said he was wearing a long army green jacket, jeans, and tennis shoes. Another report stated he was wearing a light beige hunting jacket and green checked pants. Jeffrey's mother said he was wearing a khaki jacket and red checked pants. But everyone noticed his shoes, even if they weren't consistent about whether he wore tennis shoes or Wallabees. He had written "FUCK YOU" on them. Detective Jacobs told reporters, "That made us think he was someone we needed to talk to."

Sergeant Nickens, Sergeant Jackson, and Detective Jacobs took Jeffrey into one of the bedrooms in the Trimble house and conducted an interview. They explained his rights to him and told him they needed all the information he could give them about Marcia. Jeffrey agreed to empty his pockets. He placed on the bed a $5 bill, some change, and a partial roll of pennies in a red wrapper. Detective Jacobs checked the coat pockets with Jeffrey's consent and also removed a package of condoms.

The officers asked where he'd been, and Jeffrey said he'd been out searching for Marcia at the nearby rock quarry. They asked about the condoms. He said he'd bought them for a Saturday night concert at the Municipal Auditorium. They asked about the $5 bill and the pennies. He said he'd gotten the money from Peggy Morgan earlier that evening.

Jeffrey confirmed that Marcia came to his house about 4:30 P.M. with cookies, but he hadn't had any money then, so she'd left, and he didn't know where she went.

The interview ended, but it was just the beginning of police interest in Jeffrey Womack.

* * *

Around 3:15 A.M., Wednesday, February 26, Robert Poe, Civil Defense director, told weary volunteers to go home and rest, and come back later. "But the search will not end—we can't afford to do that," he told reporters.

The police were treating the matter as a missing person's case, but as the dark hours ticked away, hopes for Marcia's safe return foundered.

The next day's *Banner* ran the headline, "Full Moon's Brilliance Casts No Light on Missing Girl."

4

Not in a Town Like Nashville

Nashville in the mid-1970s was still a little sleepy, still a little sheltered.

Not that Nashvillians were isolated from national and international events, but most residents weren't thinking about the Watergate trials, OPEC prices, and fighting in Cambodia. Nashville was a little insulated.

Nashville sits in the heart of Middle Tennessee, with mountains to the east, and broad, flat farmland to the west. By 1975, the population of the entire metropolitan area was just under 450,000, but for the mostly middle-class residents, Nashville didn't *feel* like a midsize metropolitan city. City and county governments had consolidated in 1963, making Metropolitan Nashville-Davidson County a national pioneer in metropolitan government. Government and business leaders who grappled with the complex issues created by a population shifting *outward* from a once vital urban core still drove home at the end of the day to subdivisions with shade trees and expansive lawns. City leaders envisioned a progressive Nashville that would become a major hub in the New South, but for the most part, in the long-established neighborhoods and even in the flourishing suburbs, life in 1975 went on at a leisurely pace.

All in the Family, Happy Days, and *The Waltons* were popular TV shows among the city's hardworking, family-oriented residents. Nashvillians also watched *The Streets of San Francisco,* but for families who lived in the traditional neighborhoods and the tranquil subdivisions, it was easy to imagine that the crimes Karl Malden solved would never happen here, not in *most* streets of Nashville. Families went to church on Sundays and ate at Shoney's and Lovelace Café. They shopped in new enclosed shopping malls, and Opryland USA was the premier venue for family entertainment. Built around a country music motif, Opryland had the rides and games typical of amusement parks, coupled with high-energy musical shows, all in a pleasant and protected environment on the banks of the Cumberland River, just nine miles from downtown Nashville.

The Grand Ole Opry was about to celebrate its fiftieth anniversary. First broadcast in 1925 with announcer George D. Hay, billed as the "solemn old judge," with bands such as the Possum Hunters and the Fruit Jar Drinkers, the weekly radio program had defined country music for America and beyond. In 1974, the Opry moved from the Ryman Auditorium, the "gospel tabernacle" that had been its downtown home for thirty-one years, to a modern new performance hall at Opryland, but relocation did little to alter the repertoire of the old-timey radio show. Audiences still delighted in the traditional features: Cousin Minnie Pearl, with her gentle "hillbilly" humor, Bill Monroe and his Blue Grass Boys, Little Jimmie Dickens in his rhinestone-studded outfits, the Grand Ole Opry square dancers, fiddle and banjo music, the Dobro, a harmonica wailing. The 1970s brought newcomers to the Opry stage, future country icons such as Dolly Parton, Barbara Mandrell, and Tom T. Hall whose music attracted younger listeners, but the program's huge appeal to the wide radio audience was never just about the chart-toppers of the moment. The Opry obeyed George D. Hay's mandate: "Keep 'er down to Earth, boys!"

But country music was by no means the only music in Nashville. "Music Row," the area that included 16th and 17th Avenues South, near Vanderbilt University, Belmont College, and Hillsboro Village, was known internationally as a center for recording studios and record labels. Music legends such as Elvis and the Beatles had recorded on Music Row. "Music City USA" embraced music in all its forms, from pop to honky-tonk, from rhythm and blues to gospel, from folk to rock and roll. By the mid-1970s, Nashville's profits from the music industry were estimated at one hundred million dollars annually.

Likely, the man on the street would not know much about the music *business* in Nashville. He wouldn't know, for example, that the movement led by Willie Nelson and Waylon Jennings and other "outlaws" was shaking up Music Row, with many artists choosing not to record in the label-owned studios, and that some of the major labels were closing their studios while independent studios flourished. But he might actually know Waylon Jennings, because their sons went to school together. Maybe his daughter took ballet lessons from Jim Ed Brown's wife, Becky. Maybe he lived down the road from Johnny Cash and June Carter Cash, or his wife was working a charity event with Sarah Cannon, a.k.a. Minnie Pearl. That's how it was in Nashville in the 1970s.

Nashvillians listened to WSM radio—the "Air Castle of the South"—which broadcasted the Grand Ole Opry every Saturday night. The station was known nationwide, and its signal was able to reach audiences in many states, especially late at night. The National Life and Accident Insurance Company owned the Grand Ole Opry and Opryland as well as WSM radio and WSM-TV. The company's motto was "We Shield Millions"; hence, the call letters WSM.

Teddy Bart was host of an afternoon talk-radio show on WSM when Marcia Trimble disappeared. He recalled for the *Nashville Scene* the developments that followed. "Never before or after have I witnessed an event which so infused the totality of this town like the Marcia Trimble case," Bart said.

Even decades later, it was clear that in the minds of many of its residents, Nashville was still a *town*.

Nashville dates back to 1779, when James Robertson and a party from East Tennessee established a settlement in the folds and bends of the Cumberland River. In a short period of forty years, Nashville grew into a unique Southern city, with large estates, excellent restaurants along gaslit streets, Protestant churches, a Catholic diocese, and a small Jewish community. Four railroads converged on three different connections.

At the start of the Civil War in 1861, Union generals considered Tennessee a gateway to the South. The Confederate government built Fort Henry on the Tennessee River and Fort Donelson on the Cumberland River. Both forts were lost to Union forces, representing a catastrophe for the South. The Confederate army withdrew from Nashville, and the Union army occupied the city for the next two and a half years.

In late 1864, a fierce battle was fought in the town of Franklin, thirty miles south of Nashville. The Confederate army suffered terrible casualties. Even so, the Confederate general John Bell Hood ordered his 22,000 weary troops, many without boots and blankets, to advance to Nashville. He stopped the army south of the city. The Union commander had 60,000 fresh, well-armed men. Hood understood his army had no chance to overrun the Union force, so he constructed his own defense line, including a series of small forts called "redoubts," on his west flank. Five of the redoubts occupied ground along Hillsboro Pike. Another brutal battle followed, and the Confederate army was forced to retreat south. This ended the serious fighting in Tennessee.

Years later, Estes Road was built on the ridge the Union army used when attacking the redoubts. Copeland Drive was built parallel to Estes at the foot of the ridge.

The Civil War did not settle the dilemma of race for Nashville. The complexities of race relations were woven throughout Nashville's history.

The U.S. Supreme Court decision of 1954 was the beginning of the end of legalized segregation in Nashville schools. But the process of implementing the court-ordered desegregation plan was slow and painful. For Nashvillians, black and white, desegregation and bussing were highly charged emotional issues.

Like other Southern cities, Nashville experienced racial clashes over issues other than education. The 1960s were a decade of protests, physical attacks, and nonviolent sit-in demonstrations. Though the law settled many of the civil rights grievances, the deep wounds between blacks and whites continued to exist.

A new desegregation plan for Metropolitan Nashville Schools was ordered in 1970. Again, it met with protests. Bussing was the explosive issue. In predominantly white areas, such as Green Hills, children attended neighborhood schools through fourth grade and then were bussed to the inner city, while in predominantly black areas, first graders left schools within walking distance of their homes to ride busses across town. It was not a perfect plan.

The conflict over bussing resulted in "white flight" that continued through the 1970s. Many white families moved to Williamson and other perimeter counties or enrolled their children in private schools. Marcia Trimble was scheduled to be bussed in the fifth grade, but as a fourth grader, she was still attending Julia Green Elementary School in her quiet, pleasant, "safe" neighborhood.

* * *

The February 26, 1975, *Tennessean* landed on Nashville door-
steps that Wednesday morning with a soft thud, and kitchen
lights blinked on. Throughout the city, coffee perked and ba-
con sizzled. Nashville woke up early—and not just the old-
timers, early to bed and early to rise. High schools opened
at 7:00 because busses had to make another route for middle
school and yet another for elementary school. Winter mornings, teenagers stood at bus stops in the dark.

Early morning radio and TV updated news and weather
every few minutes. The forecast for that day was mild and
breezy, with another high in the 50s, after an overnight low
of 35. Reports of the nine-year-old Girl Scout who had disappeared from her Green Hills neighborhood dominated the
news.

As the cold night gave way to bright streaks in the morning
sky and Nashvillians left home for jobs and school, Marcia
Trimble's name began to echo across the city. For the next
thirty-three days, the most asked question in Nashville would
be "Where is Marcia Trimble?" And for a long time people
would shake their heads and lament that things like this just
weren't supposed to happen here, not in a town like Nashville.

Tired searchers welcomed the morning and the fresh faces that
appeared on the scene at Copeland Drive. Police and rescue
workers came to replace the fatigued group who had remained
throughout the night—or join those who would not leave. Volunteers poured in. Some were friends and acquaintances of
the Trimbles, but many were strangers who had learned about
Marcia's disappearance from TV, radio, or the *Tennessean*.
Fresh coffee arrived from neighbors and friends. The search
revved up again.

Virginia and Charles Trimble, who'd slept little during the
night, looked out on a sight that was almost inconceivable, so
unlike anything that had ever occurred in their peaceful, se-

cluded neighborhood. Portable toilets had been set up in their once tidy front yard. The news media were also camped in the yard, where friends of Marcia and Chuck so often gathered. WSM-TV's truck used for live broadcasts was parked on the street, with its colorful sign: "Opryland Productions." WLAC's live-action camera and WNGE's cameras were on the scene, as were a host of radio recorders. Huge TV spotlights glared through the windows of the Trimbles' living room.

Reporters wandered through the crowds questioning police, rescue workers, and neighbors. Police radios squawked. The street was a jumble of people and cars. Besides those present in an official or volunteer capacity, there was a steady stream of curious spectators. The newspapers would describe it as a "carnival atmosphere."

As astonishing and heartbreaking as the scene was, the Trimbles were encouraged by all the attention that was being given to their daughter's disappearance and gratified by the outpouring of concern by Nashvillians. Surely, with so many people looking for Marcia, she would soon be found.

Around noon, Charles, wearing a blue shirt and blue jeans, came outside for a brief meeting with reporters. Tall, thin, with dark circles around his eyes and worry etched in his face, he spoke in a quiet voice, thanking those who were trying to find Marcia, pleading for his little girl's safe return. "If anyone is holding her, please release her, unharmed," he begged. "Marcia, if you can hear me, call the police, call the house, or anybody—just let us know." With TV and print media documenting his pain, he said, "We have been terribly worried and we have worked all night to find her." According to the *Tennessean*, he "seemed especially worried that Marcia had left without her coat."

Throughout the previous night, as Civil Defense continued to work from the white panel truck in the yard, police set up a command post in Charles and Virginia's bedroom. They tapped the Trimbles' line and even put in their own phone line, drilling a hole in the wall. They had to consider kidnapping as a real possibility. The extensive search of the neighborhood had provided no clues. Authorities feared the girl had been picked up by somebody in a car.

The search extended to remote areas where investigators thought a kidnapper might take a child. Search teams went out on horseback in Percy Warner and Edwin Warner parks, where trails and narrow roads wound through more than 2,500 acres of woodlands, fields, and picnic areas. On Highway 100, at the edge of Percy Warner Park, a small lake was the site of dragging operations after a piece of clothing was found in the area. Searchers plodded through isolated areas, from Radnor Lake, a few miles from Green Hills, to the huge Percy Priest Lake region, east of the city. Railroad police at Radnor Yard conducted a search of their premises.

Volunteers brought sandwiches, snacks, and drinks in the afternoon. The streets around Copeland were clogged. Teenagers from nearby Hillsboro High joined in, after school was dismissed. Before the day was over, an estimated one thousand people would participate in the search. With two hundred police officers also involved, it was an operation of unprecedented proportions in Nashville. Major Currey made an appeal to the public that went out on radio and TV, asking Nashvillians to check drainage ditches, culverts, and wooded lots. The entire city was involved in the mission to find Marcia Trimble.

Among the searchers was a family heading home to Memphis from Pennsylvania, who happened to be passing through Nashville on Wednesday. The Kaplan family heard about the search on their CB radio, and soon the couple and their three children had joined the effort.

"I thought of my own kids, like a lot of other people out here, I bet," Howard Kaplan told reporters, "and I decided we had time to stop and help if we could."

His sentiments were echoed throughout the city. *This could be my child.*

The more people looking for Marcia, the better—or so it seemed to the well-intentioned officials and volunteers.

But the sheer numbers of people combing the immediate neighborhood and beyond, and the number of official units involved, each with its own command structure, created a scene that "verged on chaos," in the words of reporter Matt Pulle. In his 2001 *Nashville Scene* retrospective on the Marcia Trimble case, he quoted Russell Hackett, a sergeant in the Homicide unit in 1975, who said, "You had some turf wars going on; one element wouldn't tell the other element what was going on." Several Metro Police divisions such as Youth Guidance, Patrol, and Intelligence came under Field Operations, but each was headed by its own major. The Davidson County Civil Defense was joined by rescue squads from thirteen other counties, each with its own captain. But even the Field Operations divisions under the command of Assistant Chief Barton were not communicating with one another. The Nashville Police Department (NPD) had no central database, only Central Records. Individual detectives kept the case files. The lack of cooperation among various entities was due in part to logistical difficulties, but also due to an unwillingness to share information with other units.

Another agency joined the mix. On Wednesday, the FBI appeared at the Trimble house. The agents were not impressed by the chaotic scene. Special Agent Richard Knudsen was quoted in Pulle's article as saying, "You had way too many people—too many media, way too many search people."

The FBI team had their work cut out. They began another round of interviews with the family and neighbors.

Mrs. Howard, the widow who lived across the street from the Trimbles, had not been at home Tuesday afternoon when Marcia disappeared. Marie Maxwell's statement that she'd seen

Marcia in Mrs. Howard's driveway at about 5:30 P.M. was of particular interest to investigators.

FBI agent Jim Callahan interviewed Marie Maxwell. According to his report, Marie said, "I noticed three individuals standing on the other side of the hedge by Mrs. Howard's garage between the east edge of the garage and the garage windows." Besides the individual she identified as Marcia, she said another was nearly the same size as Marcia, in the "same age group." She was unsure if this person was male or female. The third individual was taller, "dressed in a long coat below the knees, mod length or like an older woman would wear." She never heard any talking.

Marie Maxwell also reported seeing a cardboard box with a handle—"the type used by Girl Scouts"—sitting on the ground on Marcia's right side. She saw Marcia hand something "shiny, and light colored" up to the taller person. She believed it was one of the small boxes of cookies.

As she was apparently the last person to see Marcia, Marie Maxwell would be interviewed many times. On April 2, five weeks after the interview with Agent Callahan, she would state that she had been questioned on ten separate occasions: six times by police, four times by the FBI. The interviews would continue for months, even years.

Who were the two individuals that Marie Maxwell saw with Marcia? In her statement to the FBI, less than twenty-four hours after Marcia's disappearance, her identification was sketchy. That would all change as the pressure mounted to identify the two people who surely knew what happened to Marcia, what happened in those moments around 5:30 P.M. on February 25.

With the missing person's case headlining the news and so many people in Nashville searching for the child, it was not surprising that the police were inundated with reports of sightings and false leads. Nothing came of the report that someone heard a girl's faint scream on Sneed Road or the report that four boxes of cookies had been found in a mailbox on Estes. A man informed police that he saw a girl fitting Marcia's description jogging south on Estes Road near the Hobbs intersection at about 5:40 on Tuesday evening. Someone else said he saw a girl he believed to be Marcia walking away from Copeland, near Geddes-Douglas Nursery. An announcer for WSM-TV told police she saw a young girl near Julia Green Elementary School at about the time Marcia disappeared.

Disturbing calls sent authorities twice to North Nashville, a predominantly black area of the city. The first caller said Marcia was alive, being held at a Batavia Street address. The informant wanted Charles Trimble to pay him for his information. Police, heavily armed, picked up the informant and took unmarked cars to the area. Charles was in contact with Virginia the whole time via walkie-talkies. Police realized that the address was that of Muhammad's Temple of Islam—Black Muslims. Nickens told the informant to go inside to see if Marcia was there, and at that point, the informant said he had made up the story to get money, and police backed off.

A few hours later, another call came in with the caller saying Marcia had been "abducted" by black militants armed with machine guns. Police responded with a tactical squad, but again, they concluded the lead was false. Fearful it was an attempt by someone trying to provoke a shoot-out, police left. Race relations in Nashville were precarious. Police were careful not to make any moves that would cause a confrontation.

Police also received a call from the Tennessee Highway Patrol (THP). They were calling from Brownsville, a town in West Tennessee. The THP, in response to a BOLO (Be On the Lookout), had stopped a black man, Phillip A. Wilson from Memphis, driving a white Chevrolet. The THP dispatcher stated the man was a member of the Black Muslims. Someone put out the call: "Above car wanted for kidnapping." Nashville Police could not determine who had issued the BOLO. A report stated that the THP sergeant "was informed by our people that the car wasn't actually wanted," and the driver was allowed to leave.

The calls kept coming in. One reported that the missing child had been spotted near the B&W Cafeteria in Green Hills, and another said she was seen near Bavarian Village in Green Hills. Police and FBI agents rushed to the Green Hills Church of Christ on Hillsboro Road when someone had found the words "Marcia Is Caught" scribbled on the pavement in the parking lot. Amid speculation that a kidnapper had left the message, authorities investigated but never discovered anyone associated with the writing. It appeared the message was a cruel prank.

None of the tips brought police any closer to finding Marcia.

Still, each report brought a renewed flurry of activity among officials. Wednesday afternoon spirits were high because police had heard of a possible sighting in Jackson, Tennessee, 120 miles from Nashville. But like the other leads, this one proved false.

By the time the *Nashville Banner* came out on Wednesday afternoon, a South Nashville man had already been arrested for giving a false report. Next to the main article on Marcia Trimble's disappearance and the massive search operation was the sidebar with the headline, "Police Arrest Man in False Broadcasting." The man had transmitted over his CB radio a report that Marcia had been sighted at I-24 and Haywood Lane.

Bogus reports, false leads, and rumors necessitated the use of valuable manpower, but police were groping for clues. That afternoon, FBI and Youth Guidance officers conducted a second door-to-door canvass of the neighborhood, talking with residents.

A young man who lived in Marcia's neighborhood was

said to have "an affinity for young girls," according to a report submitted by FBI agent Knudsen. The young man gave children candy, and Marcia had visited him. But the report added that nothing had "been developed" associating the young man with any improprieties.

Some of the neighbors had seen a man with "bushy black hair" driving a white 1965 Chevrolet in the Copeland Drive area on Tuesday. Since it was unusual to see a stranger in the neighborhood, police followed up by working on a composite drawing of the man that would come out in the Sunday paper.

It would appear no stones were left unturned, as night descended on the neighborhood, twenty-four hours after Marcia's disappearance. The operation continued, with five hundred searchers remaining after dark. Police continued to track leads.

But at 6:35 P.M. on Wednesday, Agent Knudsen sent a Teletype to the FBI director, reporting on the possible kidnapping: "Metro PD has developed as possible suspect Jeffrey Womack (phonetic), age approximately 15, who resides in neighborhood. Womack interviewed evening of February 25, 1975, and provided alibi. However, Womack has now refused to provide additional statements and refused to submit to polygraph test. Womack's parents have contacted Nashville attorney."

Jeffrey Womack's name had rocketed to the top of the suspect list.

5

An Ordinary Family

Major George Currey, in hat and topcoat, spoke with reporters as the search entered its second morning: "There's been no significant changes." It was becoming harder for officials to convey a sense of optimism. The extensive search Tuesday night and Wednesday had yielded nothing. "The longer it goes, the worse it is," said the weary Youth Guidance commander.

The kidnapping theory provoked the question of why a kidnapper would target the Trimbles. They were not a wealthy family. They were not celebrities. The Trimbles were an ordinary family living in a modest redbrick house. Virginia Trimble, born in Virginia, had left home at fifteen. She moved into her sister's home and worked in a drugstore, at the soda fountain. In time, she finished high school and eventually moved to Nashville, where she met and married Charles Trimble. Charles, a graduate of Montgomery Bell Academy, Nashville's most prestigious prep school for boys, and Vanderbilt University, worked in sales at Keith-Simmons, an industrial supply company. Virginia taught kindergarten at Westminster

Presbyterian Church School. Major Currey told reporters, "It would not appear the family's income would be attractive enough for a kidnapper to abduct the child for money." He agreed that it looked like Marcia had been kidnapped, but not for a ransom. He feared the abduction had sexual implications.

Chief of police Joe Casey was still hoping for a ransom call, an indication that Marcia was alive.

Chief Casey had been on the scene since early in the search. Major Currey described Casey as a man who "did what he said he'd do—nothing wishy-washy about him." Casey was named acting chief of police in 1973, after twenty-two years on the force. He immediately called for an increase of 125 officers to the 800-member police force. In 1974 he became the permanent chief. He'd earned a reputation for taking charge of situations and putting himself in harm's way when the circumstances demanded it. In 1968 he was shot in the arm and side while trying to make an arrest. In 1969 he went to the scene of a downtown beauty salon where a man was holed up with six sticks of dynamite rigged as a bomb, and convinced the man to give up the explosives.

A graduate of North High School, Casey was an imposing figure with a commanding presence in athletic competition. In addition to having made the All-City baseball team, he later played five years of professional baseball. After joining the police force, he coached the Nashville Police Department Babe Ruth League team, and in 1959 he coached the Babe Ruth All-Star team, the first amateur team to compete for a national championship. But baseball was not even his only sport; Casey had also played two years of professional basketball and was a basketball referee at the junior high, high school, and college levels. He officiated at the first interracial basketball game in Nashville. In 1968, he refereed games at A&I University, Nashville's all-black university, which would become Tennessee State University. At the time of some of the racial demonstrations, Casey was present in police uniform during the day, only to return at night to referee a basketball game.

He was a family man, too, married since 1948, the father of five children. And here was a possible kidnapping of a Nashville child.

When Casey spoke with reporters on Thursday, he had spent most of the previous afternoon and night with the Trimbles. He described them as "being under a tremendous strain and very heartbroken."

The *Banner* quoted the chief: "If it's money they want, let us know. These people are ready to raise the money."

There was, in fact, already money on the table. Rewards totaling $30,000 were offered for information that could help in locating Marcia—or lead to the arrest and conviction of the person who had harmed her. The *Nashville Banner*'s "Secret Witness" program posted the first $10,000. This program assured anonymity of anyone who made contact by telephone or mail, giving information that helped solve a crime. The Trimble family added another $10,000 to the reward, and the governor of Tennessee offered the final $10,000 on behalf of the State.

In a press conference at the state capitol, Governor Ray Blanton announced he was suggesting the $10,000 come from money being collected to buy a $25,000 Lincoln Continental for the governor's use. Country music artist Charlie Rich had been soliciting contributions for the car. Governor Blanton said, "We feel that the money being taken up to buy the governor a limousine could be used for a more meritorious service. We hope Charlie Rich and his people see fit to offer their money in lieu of the state's money."

Tennessee first lady Betty Blanton visited the Trimbles' home, offering her support to the family. "We have a son that is nine," she said, "and when you have children you are more concerned." She was just one of several notable visitors to the modest house on Copeland Drive where Marcia's family passed the long, anxious hours. Elbert Brooks, director of Metro Schools, visited the Trimbles, as did Mayor Beverly Briley, who told reporters that he promised the family Metro Government would "continue to offer any service at its disposal until the search is brought to a conclusion."

The community established routines that would continue for days. Girl Scout leaders arrived each morning with boxes of food and jugs of coffee and tea. At noon, members of the Metro Schools Mothers Patrol from the West Nashville and Hillsboro areas brought sandwiches, fried chicken, homemade pies, cakes, and cookies. A Red Cross truck was on-site with coffee and doughnuts, soup, and aspirin. Shoney's, a popular chain with many restaurants across Tennessee, sent urns of coffee, more than a thousand sack lunches, and one hundred gallons of chili during the first three days of the ordeal.

People came from miles away to help. Volunteers joined the search from the National Guard and the Army Infantry, Ft. Campbell, Kentucky. The Hickman County Rescue Squad, one of the many squads from surrounding counties, was joined by their auxiliary, the Hickman County Crewettes, who came to be "on standby if they need us," according to the wife of the Hickman County captain.

Children and adults alike participated in the search. Reporter Thomas Wood was an eleven-year-old Boy Scout in 1975. His troop searched the grounds near the airport. He remembered asking the scoutmaster, "What are we supposed to do if we find her?" Wood said he was sure he believed she was alive; he could not imagine otherwise.

Never had Nashville seen such an outpouring of aid in connection with a missing person—not even when the missing person was a child. What was it about Marcia Trimble's disappearance that triggered such a phenomenal response? What was it about the sunny, blue-eyed nine-year-old that made her seem to belong not just to her family, but to the entire city?

Marcia Trimble's picture appeared in every edition of the newspapers and on the TV news, morning, noon, six o'clock, and ten o'clock. Her description: four feet ten inches tall and weighing eighty pounds, freckles on her nose, a chicken pox scar between her eyes, long blond hair, blue eyes, wearing new blue jeans, black boots, and a blue and white checked blouse with red trim.

People who knew Marcia described her as a happy and tenderhearted girl who was well liked. She enjoyed childhood pastimes such as riding her bike, roller-skating, playing with Barbie dolls, and watching *Little House on the Prairie*. For Christmas a couple of months earlier she'd received a tape recorder, and she had already made several tapes of her and her friends asking riddles, being silly, making up games.

She played with neighborhood children such as ten-year-old March Egerton, seven-year-old Meredith Harris, and Meredith's five-year-old sister Hayden. Marcia's cousin, twelve-year-old Rhonda Allen, often spent the night at her house. She also played with ten-year-old Teresa Seals, whose mother was Virginia's close friend from church, the Lord's Chapel. Marcia had many friends from church.

Marcia and her mother talked a lot about religion. Officer Arlene Moore of Youth Guidance wrote in a report that Marcia "became religious" a few months earlier.

She liked to polish her fingernails. Her smile was bigger recently, since her braces had been taken off. Virginia had explained to her about menstruation and some of the basics about how babies were made, but Marcia had not started her period. She wasn't even developed enough to wear a training bra. Just weeks away from her tenth birthday, she was a still a little girl, but on the brink of puberty, beginning to learn that the world was not always kind.

In December, Marcia, Meredith Harris, and another younger girl from the neighborhood had been out roller-skating on Copeland when a car stopped and a young man exposed himself, masturbating in front of them. Marcia grabbed the younger girls and ran. Meredith recalled the incident in 2008. She told WSMV Channel 4's Demetria Kalodimos, "Marcia in this big voice, take-charge voice, said, 'Mom's got cookies, let's all go inside.'" The girls weren't sure what Marcia meant—she was heading toward a house that was not hers—but she got them to the house. They were safe. "She was pretty level headed," Officer Arlene Moore wrote in her report after Virginia Trimble told her about the incident.

At Julia Green Elementary School, where Marcia was a fourth grader, the librarian, Mrs. Betty Berry, described her as "a dear little girl . . . very bright." Marcia served as a student librarian. Each morning she and another little girl went to all the rooms and collected library books, took them to the library, and carded them for Mrs. Berry. Marcia's last class on Tuesday was in the library.

Mrs. Naomi Deere, Marcia's teacher, described the uneasy atmosphere in the fourth-grade classroom after Marcia's disappearance. Students wanted to find Marcia. They were trying to think of anything that might help police. Mrs. Deere let them listen to the news in class. It was hard to keep a routine, with policemen and reporters around, and the recent events on everyone's mind. One little boy admitted to *Banner* reporter Valerie Marks that he was afraid to go outside after school since Marcia disappeared. On Wednesday, a police ID officer had dusted Marcia's desk for fingerprints. Taking nothing for granted, the police needed a record of prints on her desk before it was contaminated. Mrs. Deere said the children seemed even more unsettled on Thursday. "Two of them cried today," she said.

A little girl named Ina said, "It's been a long time since Tuesday."

Years later, Meredith Harris would also recall in a WSMV Channel 4 interview that "children were pulled out of class to talk to police or look at mug shots without parents' knowledge. Children were asked to think carefully and told they may be the one who saw something important that could solve the mystery of the disappearance."

Charles and Virginia, interviewed first by Youth Guidance officer Arlene Moore and Sergeant Doug Dennis at about 8:15 that first Tuesday evening, gave statements to detectives, to the FBI, and to any of the investigating authorities who asked for their cooperation. They repeated the litany of events from that evening, and they disclosed personal information about their family. Both Charles and Virginia stated they had been separated for about six months in 1973 and that the separation had upset Marcia. But there had been no family problems since their reconciliation. They insisted Marcia would not have run away.

"She had a good relationship with her mother and father," Officer Moore wrote, "but she was concerned about her father's drinking."

Charles told investigators that the afternoon before Marcia disappeared, he went to King's Inn, had three or four beers, then went to Nero's bar for about twenty minutes and had two mixed drinks. Later, he'd fixed a drink at home for himself and for his mother.

Agent Knudsen explained in one of his reports, "Father had history of excessive alcohol usage, which was a contributing factor in referenced separation. However, there is no indication of domestic violence. Even during the separation, daily family interaction was maintained between all family members, including overnight visits with Mr. Trimble at his apartment."

Knudsen's assessment was that the Trimble family was a "stable domestic environment."

The agent pointed out that the family attended church together and "the reunion of the family was attributed to Mrs. Trimble's 'new-found faith,' which influenced her 'tolerance and forgiveness.'"

The Trimbles assisted with the investigation in every way possible, even though it meant peeling back the curtain on their private lives—anything that might help in finding Marcia. Meanwhile, police conducted operations from the command post set up in Charles and Virginia's bedroom. By Friday they had installed yet an additional phone line, bringing the total to four, because of the hundreds of calls police were receiving.

Larry Brinton wrote in the *Banner*, "Their modest residence has been converted into a police command post, a house of worship, a delicatessen of sorts, and a press room for the media. There is a feeling of warmth and compassion inside the three bedroom home, but there's an eerie type of uncertainty in everyone's eyes."

Charles, chain-smoking, his eyes nearly black-rimmed from lack of sleep, had met with reporters again on Thursday. The afternoon paper, the *Nashville Banner*, published a second appeal from Marcia's father, this one a handwritten note: "Please someone help us. Someone has the information we so badly need. Won't you share it with us so our little daughter can share her life with her parents and brother. We need and love her very much. She is only 9 years old and is one who trusts in Jesus. We hope and pray someone will help us." Signed, Charles Trimble.

On this second full day of the intensive search, Charles spent more time with reporters, answering questions, describing the "different moods of anxiety" he had experienced since he and Virginia first began looking for Marcia at dusk on Tuesday evening. Brinton's *Banner* article quoted Charles as saying, "At the very beginning, it's like when any little girl goes out and you yell for her to come home. Then you get in your car and drive down the street looking for her. You come back home and say to yourself, she'll be home in a few minutes. Then, it isn't long before you're back outside yelling for her again. Then you begin the wait." He went on to say that even before the police came, "I knew she wasn't in the neighborhood." The dogs would have been with her, he said, but they had come home.

The Trimbles had planned a summer vacation in Florida. Charles's manner seemed to indicate that he didn't think that would happen, though he said, "Have hope and have strength . . . We four might all be together again."

Larry Brinton described the emotional scene as Marcia's father spoke: "Tears swell in his eyes and hardened policemen turn their heads to look the other way."

Marcia's brother Chuck Trimble could not just sit in the house and wait. The twelve-year-old student at Stokes Middle School was out in the thick of the search.

The last time Chuck saw his sister, she had been crossing the street with her carton of Girl Scout cookies as he and March Egerton were playing HORSE. When they'd asked if she wanted to play, she'd said, "I'll be back in a few minutes." Those were the last words anyone had heard Marcia say—at least anyone who was speaking up. The two individuals whom Marie Maxwell reported having seen with Marcia in Mrs. Howard's driveway had not come forward.

Chuck rode in a police cruiser Tuesday night, searching the neighborhood. He could be spotted waiting in line for chili or sandwiches, with the other searchers, but most often he "religiously followed [Civil Defense director Robert] Poe's every step," according to the *Tennessean*, "doing all he could to find his sister."

Here was an ordinary family, typical of families all over Nashville—working parents, two children in public schools, churchgoers. Here was this extraordinary thing that had happened to these ordinary people.

How could a little girl simply vanish?

About the time Thursday's search was suspended for the night, a report came in that a girl resembling Marcia had been seen that morning at a truck stop in Dickson. The "sighting" was only one of many reports and rumors that police continued to manage, but this one—from Dickson, about thirty miles away—created a stir at the end of a long, tedious day. Civil Defense director Robert Poe "bounded from the Trimble home," telling reporters that he had "stronger hope" because of the "hot new lead," according to the *Banner*. He told them about the report from Dickson, and the media was quick to quote him.

But Major Currey of Youth Guidance "emerged to dampen the new enthusiasm," according to the *Banner* article. He pointed out that the "information is now 14 hours old." He said, "We sent the THP [Tennessee Highway Patrol] to check it, but I see no need to get excited."

The strain of the past two days was showing.

On Friday, Director Poe said he had more than three hundred searchers working in a thirty-mile radius. Major Currey said his people were focusing on the area around the Copeland neighborhood. Civil Defense was clearly in charge of the physical search, while Youth Guidance managed the investigative efforts. But coordination was still an issue.

The rookie class of police cadets was transported to the scene by bus from the Metro Police Academy. More than forty recruits came to search around the houses and in the woods.

Meanwhile, skin divers navigated murky creeks and ponds. Several hundred persons had been questioned, including about thirty known sex offenders. The Dickson sighting was investigated, but nothing came of the lead that seemed so promising at first.

Banner reporter Frances Meeker best explained the change in the mood on Copeland. In her Saturday piece, "Crowd's Spirits Falling," she wrote, "Hope began to dwindle Friday afternoon after reports that Marcia had been seen alive proved to be just another of the many unconfirmed reports clouding the investigation." She went on to say, "Much of the carnival atmosphere has gone from the street but the food provided by various groups increases as the search for Marcia goes on."

Officials began another round of questioning, interviewing family members and neighbors who had already given statements. Police continued to administer polygraphs.

Both Currey and Poe agreed on one thing: They were not giving up.

Late Saturday morning, March 1, Virginia Trimble appeared with her husband on their front porch. It was a disagreeable day, with a light rain that later turned to snow. The search was hampered by the weather. The Trimbles faced a smaller crowd today—mostly reporters and photographers, rescue workers and investigators.

It was Virginia's first time to face the TV cameras and reporters. She was nearly as tall as her husband, and compared to his sorrowful demeanor, Virginia's expression was more resolute. With an all-weather coat draped around her shoulders, a scarf at her neck, and her short light brown hair neatly coiffed, she spoke with "great poise," according to the *Banner*. "I feel better and stronger every day," she said. "I'm just waiting for that call saying, 'Here she is.'"

From that point forward, Virginia was often the one who

spoke to reporters, while Charles remained in the background, looking bewildered.

Virginia's smile was serene as she told reporters, "I have been praying, and today as I sat in the living room, I had a real strong idea to get Marcia's personal Bible." She held up the Bible and showed that Marcia had underlined a certain verse in pencil. "The verse is Luke 10:19, and Jesus is talking," she said.

Virginia was composed as she read the Scripture:

"Behold, I give unto you power to tread on serpents and scorpions and over all the power of the enemy: and nothing shall by any means hurt you."

6

The Neighborhood Holds the Key

"It was light when the girl left and we feel like somebody must have seen something," Chief Joe Casey told reporters. "We just feel like somebody in the neighborhood has got to know something."

Though the search had fanned out well beyond Copeland Drive, authorities held on to the hope that someone would identify the two individuals reported to have been with Marcia in Mrs. Howard's driveway. No one except Marie Maxwell had provided any information about the shadowy figures, and they had not come forward. Had one or both of these persons harmed Marcia? Had they parted company with her after buying cookies in the driveway? Had they witnessed her leaving with someone else?

Civil Defense director Robert Poe said, "Let's be sensible . . . it seems reasonable to think she might have known the person she left with."

Poe continued to tell reporters he believed Marcia was alive, "if we can only find her in time." Police were not as optimistic. Metro Homicide lieutenant Tom Cathey met with the Trimbles, FBI agents, and other investigators on Friday, discussing details of the case. After the meeting, he told reporters, "It doesn't look good. The longer an investigation like this goes on, the worse the chances that the case will be solved."

Authorities continued to look for the "bushy haired" man that several neighbors had seen driving an old-model white Chevrolet or Oldsmobile. The fact that he was a stranger in the neighborhood, his car not recognized by the residents, was reason enough to try to locate and question him. A commercial artist who lived in the area reported having seen a stranger before daybreak Wednesday morning near Harpeth Hall School, just across from the intersection of Copeland and Hobbs. The artist, who was one of the searchers, said he was approached by a man who asked if he'd heard anything about a white car. The artist worked with police for several hours Wednesday on a sketch. His description was similar to other reports from people in the neighborhood: man with bushy hair, large nose, and dark complexion. But even as police attempted to put together a sketch for newspapers and the media to release, Police Chief Casey and Major Currey were skeptical, after so many false leads, so many disappointments. The *Banner* reported that both Chief Casey and Major Currey "discounted the importance of a composite drawing of a 'bushy haired' man seen in the vicinity of the Trimble home."

Meanwhile, officials continued to go door-to-door, interviewing and re-interviewing the neighbors. There, among the people who knew Marcia Trimble, were clues yet to be discovered that would lead them to the child, investigators believed.

Officials had interviewed ten-year-old March Egerton, who'd gone with Marcia as she'd delivered cookies the afternoon she disappeared, and who was also playing HORSE with her brother Chuck when Marcia last left her house. Police would continue to interview other neighborhood boys who were involved in a basketball game at the same time, and they would conduct interviews with neighbors on Marcia's list who had ordered cookies from her.

"The neighborhood holds the key to the mystery," said Chief Casey. Several of the neighbors passed lie detector tests administered by police. But the person of most interest to authorities was one Copeland neighbor in particular. Police were asking a lot of questions about Jeffrey Womack.

Fifteen-year-old Hillsboro High School student Jeffrey Glenn Womack lived with his parents and two older brothers: Tommy, age twenty, and Jonathan, seventeen. His father, Thomas, worked at Parkview Hospital Operations. Christine Womack did not work outside the home. Until the night Marcia Trimble disappeared, the Womacks looked like any other ordinary neighborhood family.

Jeffrey had had his first encounter with investigators at about 9:45 Tuesday night, when he'd come to the Trimble house after hearing that police were looking for him. But he'd made an unusual impression on the police, since he'd arrived wearing tennis shoes with "FUCK YOU" written on them, and police had found a package of condoms, a $5 bill, and a partial roll of pennies in his pockets. When Major Currey briefed FBI agent Knudsen on the case the next day, he told about the interview with Jeffrey Womack. Knudsen's report stated that "when WOMACK was interviewed, he was less than cooperative with the interviewing officers, who determined WOMACK was carrying a contraceptive, which he had no explanation for."

Actually, Jeffrey *did* provide an explanation, improbable as it might have sounded to the interviewers, Detective Tommy Jacobs, Sergeant Sherman Nickens, and Sergeant R. C. Jackson. He said he had the condoms for a concert at the Municipal Auditorium on Saturday night. He later told his mother he'd bought them to sell at school. Jeffrey had a habit of changing his stories. Police noted that he'd told Marcia he didn't have any money to pay for the box of Girl Scout cookies his mother had ordered, but a few hours later he had about $6, counting the pennies. And then there was Peggy Morgan, whose story didn't quite ring true when she came rushing to Jeffrey's defense. He worked part-time for her at her day care, but she appeared more protective of him than that relationship warranted. She said Jeffrey hadn't done anything, and he'd been with her, but Peggy had just returned from an evening of bowling when she came to the Trimble house to provide an alibi for Jeffrey.

Another day care employee, Amy Norvell, was questioned the next day regarding her knowledge of Jeffrey Womack's whereabouts. Amy was a full-time assistant at the day care. She stated that Jeffrey helped care for the children when he came home from school each day. On Tuesday, he had arrived at the day care early in the afternoon and remained there throughout the afternoon, except when he went to his house for "a short period of time," which matched what police knew about Jeffrey being home when Marcia and March arrived to deliver cookies at about 4:30.

Amy told authorities that around 5:10 or 5:15 P.M., she and Jeffrey left the day care to go to McDonald's for hamburgers to feed the children. According to Amy, they arrived at McDonald's at about 5:30, ordered hamburgers, and were back at Peggy Morgan's by 5:45.

Amy and Peggy always bowled on Tuesday nights, leaving Jeffrey in charge at the day care. They left that evening at about 6:15 for the Strike-and-Spare Bowling Alley on White Bridge Road. Jeffrey remained at the Morgan residence until the children were picked up.

Police were interested in the "short period of time" after Marcia went to the Womack house and before Jeffrey and Amy went to McDonald's. Was Jeffrey one of the two individuals Marie Maxwell had seen in Mrs. Howard's driveway?

It was not possible if both Amy Norvell and Marie Maxwell were accurate about the timelines they gave. But if Marie had actually come home earlier than 5:30, and if Amy and Jeffrey had left for McDonald's later than 5:15, there might have been a window of time that allowed Jeffrey to speak with Marcia and another person in Mrs. Howard's driveway.

Officials needed more details from Jeffrey Womack, but they didn't get far with further questioning.

The *Tennessean* reported that a "15-year-old boy was asked to take a polygraph (lie detector) test. Police said he was not a suspect in the case but that he had been seen with Marcia the afternoon of her disappearance." His parents had hired an attorney, John Hollins, because they believed police were "'leaning' too heavily on the youth." Hollins arranged for Jeffrey to take a private polygraph test on Wednesday at the downtown law firm Schulman, McCarley, Hollins and Pride. Reports indicated he passed. On Thursday, Jeffrey went to police headquarters, where Captain Noble Brymer administered a second lie detector test. Detective Tommy Jacobs wrote in a report on February 28: "Captain Brymer ran Womack on the polygraph and definitely eliminated him as a suspect."

Other officials were not convinced.

As *Tennessean* readers opened their newspapers on Sunday morning, March 2, they were able to see composite drawings of two men police were looking for: the "bushy haired man" seen in the neighborhood around the time of Marcia's disappearance, and the man who'd been seen with a young girl at the Dickson truck stop early Thursday morning. The sketches, first aired Saturday night by local TV stations, drew the attention officials might have expected from a city that was following every detail of the case. "Police were deluged with calls from people who said the drawings look like someone they know," the *Tennessean* reported. More leads—but none viable.

On that cold Sunday morning, Virginia and Charles Trimble left the house for the first time since Tuesday. Their son Chuck had been staying with friends, including one of the rescue workers. Charles and Virginia attended church services at the Lord's Chapel, among their fellow church members who had been their mainstay of support. More than five hundred people attended the emotional service, where they prayed for Marcia. Later, Mrs. Trimble told reporters, "All our friends said they are praying without ceasing and that they know Marcia will be found safe. They all feel exactly as I do."

While the Trimbles were at church services, officials on the scene began dismantling the headquarters at the house. The police command post, headquartered in Virginia and Charles's bedroom, was moved to the Youth Guidance Division on Elm Hill Pike, at the old Mt. Nebo School. "We felt we needed to move from the Trimble home for their convenience and also for ours," Major Currey told reporters. "We would have done this the first day but we had no idea it would go on so long." He emphasized that the move should not be construed as a scale-down of the search. "We're not going to slow down a single bit in our efforts to investigate this case," he added.

Civil Defense operations were also moved from the Trimble yard to the Green Hills Church of Christ on Hillsboro Road.

Monday's *Banner* ran a photograph of the family dogs sitting in the Trimble yard, facing the street. The dogs that followed Marcia everywhere had been kept inside until Sunday. The caption under the photo read, "After the crowds have gone from the Trimble home [. . .] the family dogs, Popcorn and Princess, take up the vigil for nine-year-old Marcia Trimble."

The *Tennessean* showed a photo of Charles and Virginia returning from church. The headline ran, "Trimbles Try for Semblance of Normality."

But "normality" was something the Trimbles—and their neighborhood—would never experience again.

* * *

In conjunction with moving their command post from the Trimble house, police discontinued roadblocks limiting access to Copeland Drive. Curiosity seekers once again flooded the area, as if an excursion to the home of the missing Girl Scout was a typical Sunday afternoon outing. The disappearance of Marcia Trimble was the biggest news story in Nashville.

Police and FBI were no longer present at the Trimble house, and the crowds of reporters that had filled the yard for nearly five days were gone. A couple of portable toilets remained, but they would soon be removed. The yard, once nicely manicured, had been churned into mud.

But the search continued. In spite of the cold, damp, dreary weather on Sunday, between three hundred and four hundred people showed up once again to go over areas that had been searched repeatedly by both officials and volunteers.

"In the 18 or 19 years that I've been in police work, we've never had a search this extensive in Davidson County," Major Currey said.

Civil Defense director Robert Poe remembered another search, in 1934, when he was a member of the National Guard. He had helped look for missing six-year-old Dorothy Ann Distelhurst, though that child was "found dead, her eyes burned out and her face disfigured with acid," according to the *Banner*. But after recalling the shocking event, Poe was quick to add, "I feel like Marcia can still be alive and I don't want to give up hope."

Though no leads had brought police closer to discovering what had happened to Marcia Trimble, they were soon able to exclude the suspect referred to as the "bushy haired man." On Saturday, following a telephone tip received by Sergeant Nickens, police picked up a twenty-four-year-old man near

Highway 100. He drove a 1950 white Oldsmobile and fit the description neighbors had given. Following questioning of the man Saturday night and Sunday, officials administered a lie detector test on Sunday night. The man said that he'd been visiting someone who lived near the Trimbles on the day in question, but he'd left the neighborhood before the time that Marcia went out to deliver cookies. Around midnight, he and two other men left Nashville and drove to Texas. Authorities administered polygraphs to all the people in the house he visited and the men who went to Texas with him. The suspect and all others involved passed the polygraphs. He was not, however, the person whom the commercial artist had seen near Harpeth Hall School early Wednesday morning.

One suspect eliminated. It was naturally disappointing that he was not able to add anything of substance to the investigation, but at least police did not have to waste further efforts looking for the "bushy haired man." At this point, no one seemed to hold out much hope for results from the other composite drawing released by police, a long-haired man that some witnesses had seen in Dickson. Though over five hundred calls had come in due to the sketches, none had resulted in viable leads. No substantial information at all had surfaced in recent days.

Reporters were always eager to get a statement from Chief Joe Casey. It was not common for a chief of police to become so wrapped up in the investigation of a missing person, but this case was unlike any other Chief Casey had experienced on his watch. He was deeply involved, and he was baffled. In Sunday's paper, he was quoted as saying, "This is the toughest one I've seen."

The newspapers continued to run Marcia Trimble's photograph and description into the next week. Each edition included several articles on the case. Daily and nightly TV news reported the latest developments, and even when there were no new details to report, the TV stations would flash the photo of the freckle-faced girl and announce that the investigation was continuing. Typical media coverage for a missing person's case was only a fraction of the coverage this one received, but the Marcia Trimble case was a wildfire of a story that had even drawn in the mayor of Nashville and the governor of Tennessee. Conversations about Marcia Trimble began at breakfast tables and continued until the last late-night establishments closed their doors.

Though the city had opened its heart to Marcia Trimble's family, some Nashvillians reacted negatively to her mother Virginia's stoic demeanor. She appeared so composed, so confident, so strong in her faith—not the distraught mother whom the public expected. Her calm smile, under these most grueling circumstances, was disarming to those who could not understand the nature of her religious beliefs.

And then there were the rumors, including a persistent one that circulated widely, claiming that Marcia had actually been adopted, and she had been abducted by her real parents. Major Currey felt the need to make a statement to quash that particular report: "The Trimbles are her natural parents and people who spread rumors like this are doing these people a disservice."

Authorities maintained that the Trimbles cooperated fully in the investigation. On Monday, March 3, both Virginia and Charles were given routine polygraphs. Both passed the tests, as expected. The *Banner* reported that a "police official said there had been no question as to the truthfulness of the Trimbles during the lengthy probe."

Still, rumors circulated that Virginia knew more about Marcia's disappearance than she admitted. FBI agent Richard Knudsen, who stayed in the Trimble house much of the time during the search, described Virginia as "a woman of great faith who expected her daughter to come back." He said, "She wasn't the sobbing, hysterical mother that some expected to see." Indeed, Monday's *Banner* ran a photo of Virginia, smiling her placid "trademark" smile. She looked rested, in stark contrast to the previous week's photos of Charles when he'd made an appeal for his daughter's safety, his face lined with agony, eyes set in black circles.

"We have the most intelligent men in the state and the country looking for my daughter and the Lord will let them know where Marcia is," Virginia said. "I am becoming more positive every day that she's all right and will be back home." Virginia told reporters that she and Charles prayed together before they went to sleep at night and she was sleeping well. "It's a peaceful sleep," she said.

Her manner, unsettling to some, spurred others on to keep searching and hoping. The *Banner* stated, "The Trimbles' deep religious faith his been the central theme of the search."

Hope was not dead—but police were desperate for a break in the case.

Tuesday marked a week since Marcia Trimble had disappeared. The largest manhunt in Nashville history had not resulted in locating the missing child, and police knew no more about the two individuals in Mrs. Howard's driveway than they'd known when Marie Maxwell gave her report. All the searching, interviewing, and lead-chasing had yielded no valuable clues for Metro Police. FBI involvement in the investigation had not helped to crack the case. Momentum was dwindling when police reported a reason for renewed optimism. A dog handler and his specially trained search dogs were being flown into Nashville to join the operation.

Late Tuesday afternoon, Philadelphia dog trainer Tom Mc-Ginn and two German shepherds arrived at the Nashville airport, Berry Field, by private plane. The newspapers reported that Charles and Virginia Trimble had employed McGinn upon the recommendation of the FBI. One of the FBI agents called the dogs "the finest of their kind in the country, if not the world."

Since McGinn opened his training school the year before in 1974, his dogs had won many awards for their work. The same year, the German shepherds had participated in the search for Patty Hearst, and one of the dogs had been wounded in the gun battle between law enforcement and members of the radical Symbionese Liberation Army who'd abducted Hearst. McGinn's most famous dog, King, ultimately helped to trace more than five hundred people and was wounded six times before he died of cancer.

McGinn brought two of his dogs, Wied and Drux, to the Trimble home, where they spent five hours in Marcia's bedroom. Police stripped the bed and put the bedclothes and mattress on the floor, along with Marcia's clothes. While the search dogs familiarized themselves with Marcia's scent, the Trimbles kept their family dogs, Popcorn and Princess, in the garage.

At 9:15 that evening McGinn took Wied and Drux out into the neighborhood. The night was cold and clear. Exactly one week earlier, searchers had gone out on a similar night to begin an operation that they never imagined would still be ongoing. That night, hundreds of officials and volunteers had searched the neighborhood, and helicopters hovered over yards and wooded areas, shining spotlights. This night, the streets were deserted. Police had sealed off the area when the animals arrived, knowing that spectators would surely flock to the scene, but it was vital that no distractions hinder the dogs' work.

McGinn unleashed the dogs, and as they immediately started off through the yard, crossing the street to Mrs. Howard's driveway, things looked promising. This was the route police believed Marcia had taken. But where had Marcia gone after she was seen in the driveway? Where would the dogs head next? Despite so much hope resting on the dogs' noses, all at once the animals lost their initial certainty. They proceeded no further. McGinn worked with them for a while, but he said the lighting was inadequate to finish. He took them back inside to spend the night sleeping on Marcia's bedclothes.

Wednesday morning at 10:00, Wied and Drux were back at work. McGinn took them out for two hour-long excursions through the neighborhood. The *Tennessean* reported that on both outings the dogs "showed signs of recognizing the scent" at a "wooden-fenced backyard on Estes Road." The article noted, "The yard borders on a thicket-filled wooded area across the street from the Trimble home."

As the dogs slept on Wednesday night, a new tip came from Dickson, the outlying community where the other "sighting" had surfaced the week before. Tennessee Highway Patrol reported that at about 9:00 Wednesday night four men had forced a young girl into their gold Chevy Vega at a roller-skating rink. Witnesses said they covered her with a blanket. A man with a CB radio was reportedly following the car. Two Youth Guidance officers and a Metro police helicopter were immediately sent to the scene. Dickson Police stopped the car, bearing Michigan license plates, at a market inside the city limits. There was no girl in the car.

When the report first came in that Marcia Trimble had been located, it sounded like the real thing. A surge of optimism ran through the Youth Guidance office. According to the *Banner*, FBI agent Knudsen said, "If it's *that* girl and she's alive, I'm buying a case (of beer) for everybody!"

The Marcia Trimble case made even jaded FBI agents want to believe.

The dogs worked Thursday, and on Friday they were taken to the truck stop in Dickson where waitresses had reported seeing Marcia more than a week earlier. The THP had followed up on the report, but although nothing had come of it, investigators held on to the slight hope that Wied and Drux might pick up a scent. But McGinn's canine team gave no positive readings on their visit to the truck stop.

McGinn and his dogs had an impressive track record of finding lost children in several states, but the dogs were usually on the trail soon after the child was missing. A week later was a long time for the German shepherds to pick up a scent. In a cloud of disappointment all around, the search dogs were called off after Friday yielded no results. Even the ever optimistic Civil Defense director Robert Poe told reporters on Friday that his "hope is fading as far as finding the girl alive." And Major Currey told reporters, "I wish I could report something, but there's nothing new to tell. It's just like she went across the street and vanished."

A *Banner* headline on Tuesday, March 11, 1975, read, "After 2 Weeks: Where's Marcia?"

Reporter Bruce Honick wrote, "If Marcia is found dead, a possibility uttered only in whispers among police officers, the thick case file will fall on the desk of Homicide Lieutenant Tom Cathey, who would then hand the case over to Homicide Detective Tommy Jacobs."

Though Marcia Trimble was still considered a missing person, Homicide had been involved since the night she had disappeared. Lieutenant Cathey assigned Detective Jacobs to Major Currey the following Friday morning, and Jacobs interviewed neighbors, searched the area, and followed leads with other officers. Police were under tremendous pressure to solve the case, and with each day the possibility increased that they were dealing with a homicide. "For Metro Police Chief Joe Casey, finding the girl—dead or alive—has become almost an obsession," the article stated. The newspapers ran photos of the chief in a boat, wearing his orange life jacket, and watching the tracking dogs from Philadelphia. His solemn expression showed the great weight he carried.

A few telephone tips continued to come in. Police had received more than a thousand calls and conducted about twenty lie detector tests, all to no avail.

"The use of a psychic may be the next step," the *Banner* reported. "It has reached the point where Metro police and FBI agents have played all their cards and now are desperate to try almost anything."

Several individuals professing to have psychic gifts of one sort or another had volunteered their assistance, and police received their information with varying degrees of skepticism. One young psychic claimed Marcia was being held in a room with "a concrete floor, bricks in the walls and with random bricks lying on the floor." She said there were three people with her and that she had been sexually abused. The psychic went on to say that Virginia Trimble, without knowing it, "may have the key" to the abductor's identity.

A man dressed in overalls came to Mt. Nebo School, to the Youth Guidance office, and announced that he was a "dowser." He brought a "divining rod," a device that looked like two sticks, used in the past to seek water. The man said he had "dowsed" for people, too, and he believed he could locate Marcia Trimble. He spread a map of Tennessee and held the rod over the map. The rod shook until at last the device came down at a point on the map: McMinnville, a small town about ninety miles southeast of Nashville. Major Currey went along with the man. He placed a newspaper over the map and asked him to do his "dowsing" again, and if the rod indicated the same place, he might have something. The dowser tried, but his divining rod didn't find McMinnville the second time. He left, disappointed, but his visit gave Major Currey a light moment that day, in the midst of the bleak case.

It was not widely known that one psychic had actually been

invited to Nashville by police. A private citizen put police in contact with M. B. Dykshoorn from the Bronx, who flew to Nashville and met with Major Currey, Chief Casey, and Sergeant Nickens in an obscure motel on Dickerson Road. "He had these abilities," Major Currey said. "He did a remarkable reading on everyone." Dykshoorn identified Major Currey as a teacher, his profession prior to law enforcement, and he was correct in readings on the other two men.

What he had to say about Marcia Trimble was disturbing, however, whether or not he had a gift of clairvoyance. He stated that she was murdered by strangulation, sexually molested, but "not in the normal way."

"He appeared credible," the Youth Guidance commander recalled, "and we were desperate." But Dykshoorn's readings did not aid in finding Marcia.

Spirits were low at the two-week mark. Only thirteen Youth Guidance officers were now assigned full-time to the Marcia Trimble case, compared to the forty-five who'd worked the case at the height of the search. This special investigative team, headed by Sergeant Doug Dennis, followed all leads that came in, but what had been an intense and extensive search effort had lost its momentum.

Still, incredibly, the Marcia Trimble case continued to dominate the news. Though all official activity had ceased at their home on Copeland Drive, the Trimbles had become accustomed to the influx of motorists into their once peaceful neighborhood. Cars crept along the street, passengers staring at the Trimble house, eager to see where the biggest news story in Nashville's history had originated. Virginia said it didn't bother her. "Everybody just loves Marcia and wants to know her a little better."

Charles and Virginia returned to work. Chuck returned to school. Virginia saw a hypnotist. She didn't really believe in hypnosis, but she submitted to hypnosis hoping to recall some detail of the evening Marcia disappeared that might be a clue for police. She still believed he daughter was alive.

On March 17, nearly three weeks into the investigation, Marie Maxwell also submitted to hypnosis at the office of Dr. Vergel Metts, psychiatrist. It was the first of several sessions for Marie. A psychologist, Dr. Charles McDonald, was also present, as were Metro Police officers Judy Bawcum and Shirley Davis. Marie recalled the events of the evening of February 25, when she'd seen Marcia in Mrs. Howard's driveway with two individuals.

Under hypnosis, Marie Maxwell described the two individuals in great detail. A summary of the session indicated that she said she first thought "Marcia was selling cookies to Mrs. Howard, but the person was too tall and dark complected, and he was wearing pants." Marie described the taller male having a "round face and dark complexion." He had brown fluffy hair combed back and covering his ears, with long sideburns. He wore a blue shirt, dark gray pants with cuffs, and a long dark green coat. She said the man gave a general sloppy appearance. His shoes were "beat up." Mrs. Maxwell described the other male as a "little boy" with brown shaggy hair. He was wearing a short jacket, and possibly glasses.

From the beginning of the investigation, police had considered the likelihood that March Egerton was the smaller male whom Marie had seen in the Howard driveway. Officials questioned March after Marcia disappeared and interviewed him later in the presence of his father. The ten-year-old had provided no new information. Given Marie's description under hypnosis, investigators felt the possibility was even greater that Marcia's friend, the boy who had sold cookies with her earlier in the afternoon, was also with her in Mrs. Howard's driveway, talking with a larger person. But Marie Maxwell knew March, and she had not identified him as the smaller figure, though she'd also said she hadn't gotten a good view of his face.

The taller man, as described by Marie Maxwell, was the subject of a new composite sketch. Police told reporters they planned to show the sketch to neighbors and church members before releasing it to the public. Hopes that had plummeted the week before rose again with the new information. On March 21, the *Banner* reported that Metro Intelligence sergeant Sherman Nickens, the Trimbles' old friend, was still "convinced the person who abducted the girl lives in the Trimble neighborhood." Meanwhile, the Youth Guidance task force circulated four thousand flyers with Marcia's photo and description to law enforcement agencies throughout the country, in case a kidnapper had taken her far from Nashville.

The composite drawing was finally distributed to the news media on March 26. Along with the drawing was a detailed description of the man: a slender white male between eighteen and twenty-five years old, five feet seven inches to five feet nine inches tall, with a dark complexion and dark brown hair, thick and wavy. He was described as wearing a light blue shirt, gray pants with cuffs, and a long green army coat. A description of the boy who accompanied him was also given: white male, five feet to five feet two inches tall, straight brown hair reaching to the collar, wearing glasses, a blue jean jacket, and dark pants. The release of the sketch to the public brought a deluge of new tips. The roller-coaster investigation was back on track.

Six days before Easter, a *Banner* headline read, "Mrs. Trimble Expects Easter Miracle—Marcia's Return." Virginia Trimble told reporters she was "excited." She said, "It's a miracle time of year, and I feel my daughter will be home by Easter, that God will perform a miracle."

Police were hopeful, too. A possible break in the case had occurred as Easter approached. Information surfaced about a religious sect that was known to "take very devout Christian children without their parents' knowledge, or permission, and carry them to unknown destinations for mysterious religious instruction," according to the *Banner*. The new composite sketch resembled a man thought to be a leader of the religious sect. His photo appeared in an old Nashville newspaper. Police knew his identity. Mrs. Trimble had once visited his church. She said she had a "strong feeling" about this man.

Meanwhile, another psychic contacted police. Twenty-one-year-old Rev. R. D. Finzer II of St. John's Metaphysical Episcopal Church in Titusville, Florida, persuaded police to check out an abandoned mill. He had an impression of a girl in the bottom of a shaft. Although he had never been to Nashville, he knew details that police confirmed as accurate. He described the scene the evening Marcia vanished.

"The guy who swiped the girl lives in her neighborhood," Finzer said. He gave a description: dark hair, pockmarks on a long face, a cleft chin, track marks on his arms.

More than one hundred tips came in the week before Easter.

Good Friday was Marcia's tenth birthday. Virginia Trimble told reporters the family would observe the day by fasting and praying.

"The Trimble household seems to be waiting expectantly," reporter Frances Meeker wrote in the *Banner*.

"It is a time of miracles," Virginia reiterated to the press. "And who knows what may happen?"

7
March 30, 1975

Easter, a holy day of great significance for Christians, is widely celebrated in Nashville. Like Easters before, Sunday, March 30, 1975, began with sunrise services throughout the city. The morning was cool, not uncommon for Easter in Nashville, not reaching above 46 degrees. Children dressed in new outfits chattered about Easter egg hunts as church choirs sang the "Hallelujah Chorus." But this year, in many pulpits, prayers were offered up for Marcia Trimble, the little girl who had now been missing for thirty-three days, and for her family, who waited for her.

Charles, Virginia, and Chuck Trimble attended services at the Lord's Chapel, accompanied by Judy Bawcum from Youth Guidance. Virginia had become the spokesperson for the Trimble family, facing the TV cameras while her husband stood in the background. Sometimes he looked unbearably sad, sometimes just distracted. The previous week, when Virginia spoke with reporters, she made a statement that would come back to haunt her: "I feel my daughter will be home by Easter."

*   *   *

The Thorpe family, John and Marie and their children, Louise and John Jr., lived on Estes Road. The Thorpes had a houseful of weekend guests for Easter: Marie's sisters and their families—Harry and Peggy Moffett and their two children from Memphis; John Ed and Jackie Fuller and their four children from Bristol. On Sunday morning the Thorpes and their houseguests, including teenage neighbor Ann Edson, who had stayed overnight, attended the 9:00 A.M. service at Westminster Presbyterian Church on West End Avenue. Louise, John Jr., and Ann sang in the choir. The Thorpes and their guests returned home after the early service, visited for a few minutes, and had coffee. Then John Thorpe took the children back to church so they could sing at the later service.

Harry Moffett had arranged to buy an outboard motor from his brother-in-law, John. About the time church bells were ringing for the eleven o'clock services across the city, Harry went to a garage at the rear of the Thorpes' property, where John had said he was storing the motor. The structure, more of a shed than a garage, had no doors on it. It was used simply for storage. Harry went inside and looked over the clutter— old bicycles, flowerpots, gas cans, boxes, a garbage can, a boat paddle, bags of mulch, and the like. He saw the outboard motor, perched on an old toilet seat. He also saw three tires, one on the right wall and two others on the rear wall. John had told him he could have an old tire to use for transporting the motor. Harry first checked out the tire on the right wall. It looked too new for him to take. He maneuvered through the junk, heading toward the rear wall, to see about the other tires.

He was facing the left corner of the garage. Watching his step, he saw what he first thought was a doll's face.

But he knew in one heart-stopping moment that it was not a doll.

The body of a little girl lay faceup in the corner, with her right arm across her blue and white checked blouse.

With three families in the Thorpe house, the weekend had been one long flurry of activity. Harry considered what to do. He decided to get John Ed, his other brother-in-law, away from all the chatter and commotion. He called to John Ed and asked, "Can you help me with something in the garage?" He tried to appear calm because he didn't want to alarm the women and children. He was hoping against hope that he was wrong, that what he'd seen was not the little girl he'd heard was missing from the neighborhood.

John Ed crossed the yard with Harry. He later noted that Harry was "very pale." When they reached the garage, Harry said, "I think I've found a body. Back there."

The men made their way through the clutter. Harry indicated a toy swimming pool turned upside down, obscuring part of the body. He said, "Please tell me that's not that girl's body over there in the corner."

John Ed said, "I think it's a doll."

Her blond hair was tangled in a basketball goal. Harry pointed out dark-colored marks around her mouth and neck. A few inches of skin were exposed between the blouse and blue jeans. John Ed took a long-handled broom from the wall and used the handle to touch her arm, to see if it was real. He had hoped it would feel like a wooden doll, but it didn't.

The men did not have to say anything more to each other. They left the garage and returned to the house. John Ed called 911.

The youth choir had just finished their performance when Ann Edson's father Gilbert located John Thorpe. "Come out here!"

Gilbert said, pale and agitated. On the church steps he delivered the news: "They think they found Marcia in your garage."

Marie Thorpe had called the Edsons, and Gilbert had come to the garage. Marcia "looked like a little china doll," he said. He then left to get John Thorpe.

Police cars were everywhere when John and the children arrived home. The Thorpes, saddened and shocked by the death of the neighbor child, could not fathom that she'd been discovered *in their shed*. How could this be? Police had made several searches of the storage shed. Sixteen-year-old Louise had recently been in the outbuilding looking for a sunlamp. Only two days earlier, on Good Friday, Marie herself had rummaged in the garage, picking up flowerpots, taking out chairs to put on the patio for the guests she expected.

Was it possible that Marcia's body had been in the storage shed the entire thirty-three days? How had the police missed it?

These questions would be asked over and over in the coming months and years.

A few minutes after the 911 call from the Thorpes' house, Major Currey was notified. He was in the congregation at Glencliff Presbyterian Church. "It was the worst feeling you can have," Major Currey said, remembering the moment he heard Marcia was dead.

The Trimbles, accompanied by Judy Bawcum from Youth Guidance, were just leaving the service at the Lord's Chapel. Bawcum got word from Major Currey: *Bring the family back home.* Chief Casey called the pastor, Rev. Billy Moore, and told him of the latest development. He asked Rev. Moore to follow the Trimbles home.

Sergeant Nickens and Chief Casey were waiting in front of the house. Their faces said everything as Charles, Virginia, and Chuck walked from the car.

Nickens told them, "I have some news."

Virginia asked if they could go inside.

Other police and Youth Guidance officers were standing around in the living room as the family took seats on the couch. Virginia looked at the blue carpet. It was brand new, bought with money donated by their church to replace the carpet worn ragged by the foot traffic while their house was used as a command post.

Anita Lowrance of Youth Guidance sat down beside Virginia and held her hand.

"We found Marcia, and she's dead," Nickens said.

No one in the living room would ever forget that moment. After Marcia's parents and brother shared tearful embraces, Virginia gained her composure and offered up a prayer that the Lord would help them "bear the loss" of their child. She prayed, "God, please don't let me forget her face."

The search was over. Now Marcia's family had to find the strength to get through the days ahead, the days of mourning and healing. They could not have imagined that days would turn into weeks, months, and years. But on this day, March 30, 1975, they had to think about burying their little girl.

The missing person's case, which had been classified a kidnapping, was now a case for Homicide. As anticipated, Lieutenant Tom Cathey took charge of the investigation.

CID—the Criminal Investigation Division, which handled robbery, sex abuse, and homicide—received the call at 11:12 that morning. Lieutenant Cathey was informed that the body of a child had been found in a shed on Estes Road. Lieutenant Cathey and Detective Tommy Jacobs immediately went to the location, where Patrol Officer Perkins, Sergeant Johnson, and Lieutenant Dickens were already at the scene. Lieutenant Cathey ordered Detective Jacobs to secure the garage with rope because there were no doors. He made a call and was advised that Dr. Petrone was standing by, awaiting instructions. Dr. Michael Petrone was a medical doctor, not a forensic pathologist, but he acted as the county medical examiner for Nashville-Davidson County. The state medical examiner's office was located in Memphis.

Lieutenant Cathey wanted planks placed on the dirt floor of the garage to preserve the evidence. Detective Jacobs was able to get planks from neighbors, and Lieutenant Cathey walked on them, approaching the body.

Less than two hundred yards from the Trimbles' front door, Lieutenant Cathey conducted his examination. All Homicide detectives were deputy coroners, and the short, wiry lieutenant was known among his colleagues as a stickler for details. Youth Guidance officer Carol Lawrence took notes and measurements because Lieutenant Cathey wore rubber gloves, while Officer Ray Allen from ID—the Identification Division, responsible for crime scene investigation—took photographs of the victim and of the entire garage and all its contents. The ID unit's mobile van was on the scene.

Marcia's body was lying on top of a bag of fertilizer and a woven basket. Partially covering her legs were an old sheet, a bedspread, and a canvas shower curtain. Her clothes were intact and her boots were zipped up. In her right hand was a small piece of cord. She was wearing violet-colored nail polish that had begun to chip. On top of her body was a green glass jar, and her cookie carton and six boxes of cookies were scattered between her and the wall, though the envelope that had once contained cookie money was empty.

Lieutenant Cathey, assisted by Sergeant Vaughn from ID, moved the body to a table, onto a cloth provided by the funeral home that had been called to come to the scene. Lieutenant Cathey removed Marcia's clothing and made a closer examination. He noted that her windpipe appeared to be crushed, and there was a small laceration on her forehead. Her clothes were placed in evidence bags, while her body was placed in a crash bag and was taken away in a hearse from the funeral parlor. Lieutenant Cathey went with it to the funeral home, where Dr. Petrone did a preliminary exam. Following Dr. Petrone's exam, Marcia Trimble's body was flown to Memphis on Governor Ray Blanton's Learjet for an autopsy by the state medical examiner, Dr. Jerry Francisco.

Charles had asked for details about his daughter's death, but neither he nor Virginia wanted to see the body. They wanted to remember Marcia as she was the last time they saw her, happy, animated, smiling her sunny smile.

Lieutenant Claiborne was left in charge of removing any other evidence at the scene. Detective Jacobs returned to CID to take statements from the witnesses. Late in the afternoon Harry Moffett, John Ed Fuller, Gilbert Edson, and the Thorpes all went to CID and gave their statements. Police ran polygraph tests on John Thorpe and his son, as a matter of elimination.

By now, Marcia Trimble's discovery was known throughout Nashville. The city was in shock. Marcia's family was heartbroken. The grief-stricken neighbors were asking how this could've happened in their own neighborhood, a safe place.

Easter 1975 was a day of shock and sorrow in Nashville. Years later, a statement by police captain Mickey Miller would come to define the Marcia Trimble murder: "In that moment, Nashville lost its innocence. Our city has never been, and never will be, the same again. Every man, woman and child knew that if something that horrific could happen to that little girl, it could happen to anyone."

8

No Unsolved Crimes

Bright sunlight washed over the grassy hill in Mt. Olivet Cemetery. Historic Mt. Olivet, in southeast Nashville, served as the final resting place for 1,500 Confederate soldiers, several Tennessee governors and members of Congress, and famous Tennesseans such as Adelicia Acklen, whose antebellum mansion was a Nashville landmark, the focal point of Belmont College. And now on the balmy first day of April, 1975, a grave was prepared for Marcia Trimble, the child Nashville would remember as the Girl Scout who went across the street to deliver cookies, and never returned.

Pink and yellow roses covered the small light pink casket. The group of family members and friends gathered at the cemetery was more intimate than the several hundred people who earlier in the afternoon attended the funeral at the Lord's Chapel, on the corner of Granny White Pike and Old Hickory Boulevard. The service was punctuated by uplifting songs, "Hallelujah" and "I've Been Redeemed," and reading of the Scriptures in which Jesus said, "Let the children come to me, do not hinder them; for to such belongs the kingdom of God." Frank Sutherland wrote in the *Tennessean*, "Sorrow did not overwhelm the congregation" and Charles and Virginia's "fundamental beliefs in religion" pervaded the service.

Many children—Marcia's cousins and friends from school, church, and the neighborhood—sat in the packed church and now stood in the crowd that encircled Marcia's grave. They would not forget. They would grow up remembering, still asking why.

Police officers and investigators who had played such a vital role in the Trimbles' lives since February 25 maintained a low profile on this spring day, for a few hours. Reporters allowed the family their privacy.

The previous afternoon Virginia and Charles had faced the cameras in front of their house, looking out on the yard that was all but destroyed during the search. The street was remarkably quiet, reminiscent of the day Marcia went out to deliver cookies.

The weeks of operating on adrenaline, the shock of Sunday's discovery, the ache of unspeakable loss—all of it had taken a mighty toll on both parents, as could be seen in their faces. Still, Virginia managed a brave smile. She said, "I believe Marcia is living with Jesus." Her belief that Marcia was in heaven was the source of her strength, she told reporters. Charles thanked the officials and volunteers who had searched tirelessly for Marcia, and the thousands of people from all over the country who had sent letters of encouragement, many of them children.

Tuesday, April 1, marked five weeks since Marcia had disappeared, weeks of waiting. After the grave was filled in and flowers covered the small mound of dirt, Charles and Virginia spent a few minutes alone at the graveside, their arms around each other, and then they departed, too. The burial ritual had its own finality, but Marcia's family was just beginning a different kind of waiting.

* * *

The Nashville Police Department was located in the Metropolitan Safety Building at 110 Public Square. The long, stark white building stretched along James Robertson Parkway, facing the Metro Courthouse, with the Metro jail located behind it. An alley separated the Safety Building and the jail, so police could drive between the two when delivering a prisoner. Near the corner of 2nd Avenue, the entrance was a six-columned portico, a classical touch to the otherwise utilitarian building. The police would relocate in 1982 to a new Criminal Justice Center across 2nd Avenue, but in 1975 the overcrowded Safety Building was the headquarters of the Nashville Police Department, a force of around nine hundred members. Desks were crammed into every possible space. Even closets had been converted to makeshift offices. On a normal day, the Nashville Police Department was a beehive of activity, but nothing had been normal since Marcia Trimble disappeared.

Inside the walls of the department, the pressure was mounting. Nashville had recorded seventeen homicides in January, February, and March, and now police were in a precarious position on the highly publicized Trimble case. After a thirty-three-day search unlike anything Nashville had ever witnessed, the discovery of Marcia's body less than two hundred yards from her home was a slap in the face for the police department. No one who had followed the case as it developed could doubt the gargantuan effort put forth by authorities to find the child or the body, but Nashvillians could not help but wonder, Had police simply bungled the case? The credibility of the police seemed to hinge on answers to the questions, How and when did Marcia Trimble die? How long had her body been in the garage?

The first report came from Chief Joe Casey, based on the preliminary autopsy conducted by Metro Nashville's medical examiner, Dr. Michael Petrone, a few hours after the body was found. Dr. Petrone's examination, performed at Roesch Patton Dorris and Charlton Funeral Home, indicated that Marcia had been dead ten to fifteen days, Chief Casey told reporters. Manual strangulation was the most likely cause of death.

Reporter Bruce Honick wrote in a *Banner* article: "If the girl had been dead just 10 or 15 days, police said they believe she could have been killed somewhere else and then carried to the garage by her assailant, which would explain why she was not found in the garage before Sunday."

But Dr. Petrone was not a forensic pathologist. The state medical examiner, Dr. Jerry Francisco, examined the body Sunday evening after it was flown to Memphis on Governor Blanton's Learjet. Lead detective Lieutenant Tom Cathey, who accompanied Marcia's body to Memphis, was back in Memphis Monday with dental charts, information on scars and moles, and charts of weather conditions from February 25 to March 30. Dr. Francisco released the body late Monday afternoon, and Lieutenant Cathey returned with it to Nashville on the governor's plane. Francisco gave his preliminary findings that afternoon. His assessment of cause of death corresponded to Dr. Petrone's conclusion: "Strangulation by hands on the throat." Furthermore, he said no evidence indicated she had been sexually molested. He did not find hair or skin under the victim's fingernails.

But his opinion on time of death conflicted with Dr. Petrone's estimate. Dr. Francisco stated that Marcia died "close to the time of her disappearance." He was quoted in the *Tennessean*: "The state of decomposition of the body was seven to eight days at 70 degrees. . . . Bodies are preserved at 40 degrees Fahrenheit. Between Feb. 25 and Mar. 30 there were only six or seven days when the temperature was at 70 degrees or above."

Dr. Francisco said the autopsy could not show whether the body had been moved after death, but later there would be plenty of discussion about livor mortis, the purplish discoloration due to the settling of blood in the lower portions of a body, which was consistent with the position in which Marcia Trimble was found. The state medical examiner's analysis left police with the astonishing possibility that for thirty-three days, the body had been exactly where it was when it was discovered—in the Thorpes' garage.

The medical examiner would continue to conduct tests, and the final autopsy report would not be ready for three or four weeks.

Meanwhile, police resisted the notion that the body had been in the garage during the entire thirty-three-day period. Forty police trainees from the Police Academy had been brought in on February 28 to search the neighborhood. Three of the recruits said they had searched the garage. They wrote reports of their findings. One recruit had looked inside the outbuilding, which had no doors on it, but did not plow through the junk. Recruit officers E. R. Downs and Larry Felts wrote detailed statements about the items they remembered during their search—bags of fertilizer, a lawn mower, a wrought iron table, and a child's swimming pool—and the placement of each. They submitted sketches that showed the plastic swimming pool located near the back, on the right side of the garage—not the left side, where Harry Moffett saw it partially covering Marcia's body. Officer Downs said there had been a table in the left corner, which he'd sat on.

Homicide detective Tommy Jacobs stated that he searched the garage on February 26. Officer Donny Biggs reported that he and Detective Jacobs had walked down to the outbuilding with John Thorpe the day after Marcia disappeared. Officer Biggs said he'd stood in the center, about five feet inside, and he remembered seeing the plastic swimming pool in the right-hand corner. He did not move anything or look under anything. In his March 31 report, he stated, "It was evident that numerous items had been moved in and out of the garage and items re-arranged since 2-26-75."

Allen Walden, a member of the Civil Defense, said he and other volunteers had searched the outbuilding in the early morning of February 26. He said, "I would be willing to bet my life she wasn't in that garage when we searched it." Walden, an electrician for L&N Railroad, formerly headed the Old Hickory Civil Defense unit and had participated in a number of searches. He had discovered the body of twelve-year-old Kathy Jones in 1969. After a three-day search for the girl, who lived in Woodbine, a working-class area of Nashville, the body had been found in a weeded lot on Thompson Lane, near the Roller Drome skating rink where she had gone skating. Her white boot skates, a gift from her aunt, lay near her feet. She had been sexually assaulted. Her hands were bound behind her, her clothing stuffed in her mouth. She was cut on the neck and abdomen. The Kathy Jones case had been on the minds of many officials and private citizens when Marcia Trimble disappeared.

Walden said he and the other volunteers who entered the Thorpe garage had used large-beam flashlights, and his son had moved some old tires. According to Walden, he'd also moved the swimming pool, which was leaning against the rear right side, opposite the corner where Marcia was found, and looked behind it.

Bob Seals, a neighbor and friend of the Trimbles, told FBI agent Knudsen that he'd searched the garage with a flashlight the night Marcia disappeared. He did not recall seeing the swimming pool, but he stated that he walked over to the left wall and stood within six to eight feet of where the body was later found.

Another neighbor, John Macey Sr., said he and Jeffrey Womack had also searched the garage with a flashlight that night. He said they stayed about two minutes.

The Thorpes also simply could not believe that Marcia had been found in their garage. John Thorpe said he had been in there after Marcia disappeared to store some things. On Good

Friday, Marie Thorpe had gone in to bring out chairs for the weekend guests who were arriving from Memphis and Bristol. Marie told Detective Jacobs that she and Louise went inside one day to retrieve yard tools. Another day, Marie, her daughter, and her mother-in-law were in and out of the garage all day, looking for various items. Her mother-in-law confirmed her statement. John Jr. also stated that he, too, had gone far enough inside to retrieve the lawn mower.

Even Sheriff Fate Thomas said he'd searched the garage, and "she wasn't there!"

Chief Joe Casey was hard-pressed to explain how so many searchers, both police and volunteers, could have overlooked a body. Even the highly trained German shepherds brought from Philadelphia to track Marcia had come within thirty feet of the garage yet failed to locate a scent. "A dog will go right to a dead body," Casey said. The Thorpes also had a German shepherd, and the neighborhood was full of dogs that could have accessed the open garage. Casey did not address the issue that was mentioned in a related news story the same day, probing the effects of "people stomping around" during the search. The hundreds of searchers in the area had the best intentions, but there were too many footprints in the mud, too many scents.

Shaking his head, the chief admitted it was a "mystery" to him. But he added, "We are going to solve this case."

Early Monday morning, after Easter, Detective Lieutenant Jim Wise had flown to the FBI Laboratory in Washington, D.C., with the physical evidence from the crime scene—five cardboard boxes, forty-one pieces of evidence, including items from the garage and Marcia's clothing, samples from the soles of her boots, and soil samples from the garage floor to determine whether she walked in herself or was carried. Police expected it would take at least a week to get the FBI's findings.

In the meantime, investigators continued trying to identify the two individuals whom Marie Maxwell had seen with Marcia in Mrs. Howard's driveway. "I think the solution lies right in the neighborhood," Lieutenant Cathey said on Sunday, shortly after the body was discovered. On Monday, police began a new round of interviewing residents of the neighborhood. Police talked to Virginia about the list of people who'd ordered cookies from Marcia. Later in the week, they began contacting people on the list.

Questioning of six young people began at the Youth Guidance headquarters on Monday. The next day, the day of Marcia's funeral, the *Banner* reported that police were questioning fifteen to twenty young people from the neighborhood. Later, Lieutenant Cathey said the investigation was concentrating on thirteen- to eighteen-year-olds in a quarter-mile radius of the Trimbles' home. By the end of the week, more than one hundred neighbors had been interviewed, many of whom had been interviewed at least once before, and Lieutenant Cathey said there were "several people we want to double back on."

On the day of the funeral, Officer John Hutchinson reported that Marie Maxwell saw a young man in the congregation who "looked like our latest composite drawing." Marie told Officer Hutchinson she was "almost positive he was the man she observed in [the] Howard driveway on 2-25-75." Hutchinson, along with Officers Rick Lankford and Ron Davis from Youth Guidance, approached the man as he left the church and took him to police headquarters for questioning. The man, identified as Guillermo Alexander Mesa, told police he knew he looked like the composite drawing, and he did own a long trench coat. Officer Hutchinson reported, "Subject was very cooperative in our investigation and agreed to a polygraph examination."

The press and media had not slowed down in their reporting of the Trimble case since that Easter Sunday. Lieutenant Cathey was quoted nearly every day. On April 5 he told reporters that investigators were "leaning toward the belief that Marcia's body was placed in the garage shortly before it was found." On April 6, a *Tennessean* headline asked, "Body Stored in Refrigerator?" Cathey said Dr. Francisco had ruled the body was in "very good condition relative to decomposition." Investigators were asking neighbors, "Do you own a refrigerator not in use?" If the body had been stored until shortly before Easter Sunday and then placed in the garage, not only would Dr. Francisco be able to explain the lack of decomposition over a thirty-three-day period, but police could answer the crucial question of how searchers could've missed finding the body.

Chief Casey tried to do some damage control. Larry Brinton wrote in the *Banner* that the chief said, "I'm convinced in my own mind that Marcia wasn't in the garage prior to a day or two before the body was found." He reiterated the argument that the tracking dogs and dogs of the neighborhood had not located the body, and he put forth another point for consideration: "I'm told Marcia's dogs would follow her anywhere she went. . . . The dogs were with Marcia when she disappeared and if she was taken directly to the Thorpe garage and killed there, the dogs would have waited there beside her body."

Early April was a confusing and frustrating time for the Nashville Police Department. The "turf wars," evident during the search for Marcia Trimble, continued. Lieutenant Cathey put a positive spin on the investigation when he spoke with reporters. He said police were "skeptical of a few young people" in the neighborhood but had eliminated "a number" of others. Reporters had access to a police map that showed investigators were "centering their probe on eight houses on both sides of Estes Road and also two homes near the Trimble residence." Cathey spoke about "a dozen or more names" on a list to reinterview. Yet Sergeant Nickens, now deeply involved in the case, was blunt in his comment: "As far as I'm concerned, we have no suspects at the present time."

While a number of police and volunteers who had participated in the search continued to insist they had looked in the
Thorpes' garage, many citizens raised serious questions about
the credibility of the police. The FBI requested more soil samples at the end of the first week. The ID unit went back to the
crime scene to take more samples. Lieutenant Cathey said he
expected the results from the FBI and the medical examiner's
final autopsy report to provide the "necessary clues to solve
the murder." He was overly optimistic.

In the absence of any new facts in the case, a new crop of
rumors sprouted for the public to pass on and embellish,
many of them related to Virginia Trimble. Though Lieutenant Cathey insisted that there was "absolutely no truth" to the
rumors that police were questioning the Trimbles, reports by
Detective Jacobs and Officer Bawcum of interviews with Virginia and Charles on April 7 and April 8 indicated that police
were interested in their activities on the weekend before Marcia's body was found.

The night of Good Friday, Charles Trimble had ridden
around with Officers Judy Bawcum and Shirley Davis for
about two hours, from 6:30 to 8:30. At 10:00 or 10:30 P.M.
he left home and went to Nero's to drink until 1:30 or 2:00 in
the morning. He'd helped two of the waitresses lock up. Virginia was home all night. Her sister, Mary Allen, and Mary's
daughter Rhonda spent the night with Virginia. Another friend
stayed until about 11:00 P.M.

On Saturday night both Charles and Virginia were at home.
A couple of friends were at the house helping to trim doors
where the new carpet was being laid to replace the one that
had been ruined during the time the house was used as a command post.

The public's attitude toward Virginia, in particular, had
taken a nasty turn. Virginia was having lunch with a friend

when a local radio station broadcast that she had confessed to killing Marcia. Charles was at work when he heard the same report over the airwaves. He rushed home, not knowing Virginia was out with her friend. Matt Pulle wrote in his 2001 article in the *Nashville Scene* that when Charles didn't find Virginia at home, "he worried himself sick." Calls came to the Trimble home, bellowing at Virginia. One caller warned that Virginia would be getting a bomb in her mailbox.

When Virginia came in from teaching kindergarten, she used to like sitting on her back porch and listening to Teddy Bart's talk-radio show on WSM-650 AM. Now callers wanted to talk about *her*, blast her, accuse her of killing Marcia. Bart always defended her.

The unfounded, bizarre rumors were so rampant that the rumor mongering itself became news. The *Tennessean* ran an article on April 7 entitled "Few Facts Fuel Rumors in Slaying." Reporter Alan Carmichael wrote that "a thousand times a day" someone would ask, "Have you heard the latest about the Marcia Trimble case?" Dr. Mayer Zald, Vanderbilt professor and chairman of the Department of Sociology and Anthropology, provided a lengthy commentary on the nature of rumors and why people spread them.

On the same day, when police seemed to have nothing to offer as progress except more interviews with people in the Trimbles' neighborhood, Dr. Francisco called Lieutenant Cathey to report the results of some of his tests. He said Marcia had eaten a small green pear two to three hours before her death. Francisco also related that male sperm were present in the vagina, but there were no tears in the vagina or rectum. He stated that it was possible that the subject ejaculated without penetrating the vagina.

Most startling was his revised estimation of time of death.

He now believed the time of death was between March 20 and March 27.

The *Banner* headlines on April 10 read, "Killer Kept Marcia Alive." Larry Brinton wrote, "Young Marcia Trimble apparently was kept alive by her abductor until a week or 10 days before she was found strangled to death, Metro police learned today."

This new development almost certainly meant the murderer was not a stranger. Brinton's article continued, "The latest disclosure raises strong possibilities the Julia Green Elementary School fourth-grader . . . was held captive in her own neighborhood until she was slain."

"We still believe the answer is in the neighborhood," Lieutenant Cathey said in an April 11 *Tennessean* article. "Until we eliminate everyone there, we are still concentrating our efforts in the area."

The same article explained that Dr. Francisco "based his newest estimate entirely on the hourly temperature outside in the general area" during the time Marcia was missing. The average daily temperature ranged from 30 on March 2 to 28 on March 28 with a high of 79 on March 23 and a low of 21 on March 4. The article reported, "Francisco said the revised estimate is also provisional as was his first, and can change again as more information, either from investigators or from his continuing tests, becomes available."

His estimate would change again.

Adjacent to Green Hills, where the Copeland-Dorcas neighborhood was located, Hillsboro Village lay in walking distance of Belmont College and Vanderbilt University. In February and March, a string of crimes had occurred in the Hillsboro-Belmont-Vanderbilt area—rapes, attempted assaults, even a murder.

A review of the Marcia Trimble homicide investigation, prepared by Captain Mickey Miller and Lieutenant Tommy Jacobs in 1990–1991, stated, "It should be pointed out that there were no unsolved crimes of this nature around the time or area that Marcia was raped and killed. There was no indication of a multiple rapist loose on the community."

They were wrong.

The string of crimes by a rapist/killer began just twenty-three days before Marcia disappeared.

PART 2

A String of Crimes

9

February 2, 1975

Nashville has been known as the "Athens of the South" since the late 1800s, a period when institutions of higher learning were flourishing all over the city. Vanderbilt University was founded in the spring of 1873 when Commodore Cornelius Vanderbilt made a gift of $1 million to establish a new university. Built on seventy-five acres of land in the heart of Nashville, Vanderbilt enrolled 307 students in its first year. By 1975, the enrollment was over 7,000, and the institution had earned a reputation as one of the outstanding universities in the nation.

The year 1975 was an exciting time at Vanderbilt. Having celebrated its one hundredth birthday just two years earlier, the university was continuing to increase in size and prestige. In 1979, Vanderbilt would merge with Peabody College, making the university the largest private employer in the region, and the second-largest private employer in Tennessee.

The year 1975 was also an exciting time for nineteen-year-old Sarah Des Prez. A native of New York, Sarah had moved to Nashville with her family when she was nine years old. Her father was Dr. Roger Des Prez, a professor of medicine at Vanderbilt University School of Medicine and married to Patricia Waterfield. Sarah's mother, Dr. Patience Bannister, lived in Alexandria, Virginia. Sarah had three sisters, Patricia, Julia, and Eleanor, and two brothers, Edward and Walter. The Des Prez family home was located on Estes Road, not far from Copeland Drive. After graduation from Hillsboro High, Sarah went to college in Florida for her freshman year, but returned to Nashville to be closer to her family. By 1975, she was a sophomore at Vanderbilt. Bright, pretty, and spirited, Sarah—or Sally, as her family and friends called her—enjoyed classical music and had a reputation as an accomplished pianist.

The early weeks of 1975 were a busy time for Sarah. Prior to Christmas break, she had taken a run-down third-story apartment on 20th Avenue South at Graylynn Apartments, a converted single-family home that now housed seventeen small apartments. *Modest* would be an overstatement for Sarah's cramped one-bedroom apartment, but she was glad to have the place. It was only a block from campus, much closer than her previous apartment had been, and the $90-a-week rent was within her limited student budget. Her friends commented that her secondhand furniture, all mismatched pieces that could have come from someone's attic, matched the tiny apartment. But Sarah wasn't concerned with the décor. She was on the go with a life of classes, studying, work, and an occasional date. She took a job as a night clerk at nearby Mims Hall, a girls' dormitory.

Sarah had also added something special to her life—a black and brown German shepherd puppy that she named Tex. Tex cheered all the neighbors as much as Sarah. Her schedule as night clerk at the dormitory, combined with her social life, made her worry about Tex. She wasn't at home much. But her neighbor Lynn Fussell offered to keep Tex at night while Sarah worked, and it was a good arrangement for all three.

Whenever the puppy stayed over with Lynn, Sarah would pick him up between 6:00 and 7:00 in the morning.

Sarah slept late on Saturday, February 1, 1975. She went to the grocery store in the early afternoon and ran some other errands. She had a date that night, and Lynn had agreed to keep Tex. Sarah's date was with Trammell Hudson, a senior at Vanderbilt. Trammell, a member of Sigma Alpha Epsilon (SAE), was a bright young man who fit the image of a typical preppy Vanderbilt frat boy. It was their first date, and they were going to a movie. Sarah picked out a white blouse with green embroidery that the Nashville *Banner* would later describe as an "embroidered western shirt."

On Saturday evening Trammell picked Sarah up and they went to the mall to see *Murder on the Orient Express*. Sarah ate popcorn and Milk Duds at the movie. Afterward, they went to Mississippi Whiskers, a nightspot on Elliston Place near the Vanderbilt campus and popular with Vandy students. Sarah and Trammell talked and drank a few beers, and then Trammell suggested they drop by his fraternity house, which was having a band that night. They arrived at the SAE house at around 11:40 to find the party in full swing. People were crammed in every room and the band was blasting away.

Trammell and Sarah began dancing. Between dances they gulped mixed drinks. The dance floor was so crowded that it was difficult to move. People wiped sweat from their faces; the temperature in the room was stifling. Between the heat and the drinks, Sarah began to feel queasy. She told Trammell she wanted to go get some air. After a while on the porch, Sarah became ill and vomited. Trammell could tell she was embarrassed. He reminded her that the only thing she had eaten was some popcorn and Milk Duds. She should have had more to eat before they started drinking.

They agreed that he would take her home.

They arrived back at Sarah's apartment around 1:40 A.M. Trammell walked her to the front door of the building.

"Can you make it?" he asked. He had a feeling she didn't really want him to walk her up to her third-floor apartment.

She smiled and said, "I can make it."

Trammell watched Sarah walk up the steps, carrying her black raincoat.

By 11:00 Sunday morning, Sarah's puppy, Tex, was hungry. Lynn Fussell and her brother Ron, who was visiting that night, were both students at the University of Tennessee, Nashville. They realized they didn't have any food for Tex, so Lynn decided to go into Sarah's apartment for dog food. She had a key, and took the dog with her. As she approached the door, she noticed Sarah's raincoat hanging over the banister. Lynn unlocked the door and walked into the small kitchen while Tex scampered into the bedroom. From the kitchen, Lynn could see Sarah lying on the bed in her bedroom, sheets in disarray. Lynn figured Sarah had had a late night and wouldn't want to be bothered. She found the dog food and started to leave. When she called for Tex, the dog came out of the bedroom slinking and whining. Lynn paused, wondering why Tex was acting like that, but she didn't stick around. She ordered Tex out, locked the door, and returned to her apartment with the dog food.

About 3:30 Sunday afternoon, Tex was hungry again. Lynn returned to Sarah's apartment to get more dog food. Assuming Sarah was still asleep, Lynn didn't even look in the bedroom. By 9:00 Sunday night, Sarah had not come to get Tex. Lynn considered waking her, since Sarah was due at her job at the dormitory at 11:00 P.M., but she didn't.

* * *

It was a cold, rainy night. Sometime after 11:00 P.M., Dr. Roger Des Prez received a phone call from the dorm clerk at Mims Hall.

"We're trying to find Sarah," the girl said. "She was supposed to work tonight, but she hasn't shown up."

This was not like Sarah. The doctor wondered what could be wrong, to make his daughter miss her work and not call in. He decided to go to her apartment. His son, Roger, went with him. Dr. Des Prez unlocked the door, using the key Sarah had given him. He and Roger entered the apartment.

Sarah was lying on her bed in a tangle of bed linens, wearing only her blouse. Her face was bruised. She had no pulse. Dr. Des Prez tried to get her breathing again, but she was dead. He told his son to call the police.

The first officer to arrive was Thales Finchum, who described Sarah's father as "devastated." Detective Morris McKenzie from Homicide was called to the scene. He quickly determined that it was not a natural death. The next morning, when the day shift arrived at police headquarters, Detective Diane Vaughn was also summoned to the crime scene and assigned the case.

In the initial investigation, police found that no one in the other seventeen units of the apartment building had seen or heard anything unusual. An examination revealed that the victim had had sexual relations prior to the homicide. Finally, police determined that Sarah's murderer did not force his way into the third-floor apartment.

The police were left with two possibilities: Either Sarah knew her killer, or the killer was waiting for her in the dark walkway outside her apartment.

The rape and murder of coed Sarah Des Prez sent shock waves throughout the Vanderbilt University campus. The fact that the victim's father was a noted Vanderbilt physician brought the tragedy even closer to home. Administration sent memos to the students, placing them on alert. Female students were nervous, walking to class in pairs. Vanderbilt University security intensified their coverage, but securing the campus was a tough assignment. The university covered 650 acres in an urban setting. It was located near two major thoroughfares, near downtown, and on the edge of a high-crime area. In fact, the area between Belmont College and Vanderbilt had been referred to on numerous occasions as "the rape capital of Tennessee."

About ten days after the Des Prez murder, in the early morning hours of February 12, Vanderbilt University security officer Williams drove his police car around the campus. He and other members of the Vanderbilt police force had been briefed on the details of the Des Prez murder. Although the murder technically took place off campus, it was still extremely close to Vanderbilt property. The question circulating around the university was whether the crime was a random incident or part of a larger pattern. Rumors at the security office were that Metro Police had no witnesses.

Now that spring was in the air, temperatures at night were mild and it was common to see students roaming around campus at all hours of the night. Although Monday had been warm with the temperature reaching 60 degrees, the night was still cool, in the mid-40s. No one was out on the Vanderbilt campus on that Tuesday night.

As Officer Williams drove down West End, with the campus on his right, he decided to turn into the last dormitory parking lot before West End intersected with 21st Avenue South. There was no sign of activity. The officer pulled his cruiser to a halt in the lot. Nothing seemed unusual or out of place in the parking lot. The girls' dorm was dark and quiet. Williams continued his rounds by driving behind the dorm on the narrow service lane. At the back of the dorm, as he was turning the car around, he caught a glimpse of movement between a window and one of the dormitory's Dumpsters. Williams flipped on his spotlight and pointed it at a dark figure. He automatically flipped the switch in his car that turned on his emergency light bar and grabbed his radio, sending a message that he had discovered an intruder on the campus.

After advising the dispatcher of his location, Williams got out of his vehicle and walked toward the person. Vanderbilt police were trained that when approaching someone on campus, they were to first determine whether the individual was a student or someone who had no business on campus. The person stood motionless in the edge of the bright spotlight as Williams approached. The emergency lights throbbed, casting an eerie glow against the wall of the dormitory. Officer Williams looked up at a tall black male with a hard face. The man was wearing a long dark tweed overcoat. There was no reason to ask a question about student identification.

"You're under arrest," Williams said in a strong, clear voice.

The intruder raised his hands in the air.

The Vanderbilt campus was approximately five miles from Copeland Drive.

10

February 16, 1975

Two miles southwest of downtown Nashville, Belmont College sat on seventy-five acres of the antebellum estate once owned by Joseph and Adelicia Acklen. The Acklens, one of Tennessee's wealthiest couples in the 1800s, built their ornate twenty-thousand-square-foot villa on one of the highest hills in Nashville. They called the estate Belle Monte, Italian for "beautiful mountain." Over the years, a quadrangle of academic buildings and dormitories was constructed on the front lawn of the mansion. Gardens, gazebos, and statues of Belmont's historic past dotted the elegant grounds.

The original Belmont College for Women was established in 1890, offering education for young ladies from elementary school through junior college, but the institution gained its prestige when it merged with Ward Seminary in 1913 to become the highly esteemed Ward-Belmont School for Women. In 1951, supported by the Tennessee Baptist Convention, the school became known as Belmont College, with a mission to offer Christian education to both sexes. The name would change again in 1991 to Belmont University, and the institution would eventually conclude its relationship with the Tennessee Baptist Convention.

Belmont was often perceived as a "protected" environment, especially for young women, with housemothers, curfews, and requirements to sign out when leaving the campus, but in the era of the late 1960s and early 1970s it was difficult for the small, genteel community to remain entirely insulated. The college was within walking distance of three vibrant areas: Hillsboro Village, Vanderbilt University, and Music Row. Belmont itself was transforming as new construction began to accommodate a growing student population. One of the buildings constructed at the onset of Belmont's expansion was Wright Hall. The dormitory, built to house about two hundred females, was located near the gymnasium, at the other end of the campus from the "sheltered" quadrangle.

In February 1975, Audrey Judy Porter, known as Judy, was a twenty-three-year-old senior at Belmont. She lived in room 112 at the end of the first floor of Wright Hall, above the ground floor, which contained a recreational room.

On Saturday night, February 15, Judy Porter stayed up late. She'd had a busy day and wanted to relax. Her roommate was gone for the weekend. Judy listened to some records and then fell asleep at approximately 3:30 A.M.

Several days earlier, Judy Porter had had a troubling experience. Her niece was visiting her in her dorm room one evening, and they were standing at the window. Black males, mingling in the parking lot, were staring at Judy and her niece. One of them called out, "Get away from that window, you white bitch!" Judy was surprised and frightened. No one had ever spoken to her in that tone, or used those words.

The incident added to the uneasiness that had filtered through the campus following the news of the Des Prez murder just two weeks earlier. Sarah Des Prez's apartment was located between Vanderbilt University and Belmont. A number of female students complained about the Belmont administration's lax role in providing security. One young woman was quoted as saying, "The administration is more concerned with girls getting out than intruders breaking into the dormitories."

On February 16, at about 4:30 A.M., Judy awoke, startled and smothered by someone's gloved hand on her mouth. A man was kneeling over her with a knife, holding the blade to the back of her neck. In the pre-dawn light, she could make out a few details. He wore work gloves. She could see that he was black.

He whispered, emphasizing each word, "If you make one move or scream or holler, I will kill you."

Wide-awake, confused, and frightened, Judy could not believe this was happening to her in the illusory safety of her own room.

The man continued to hold his hand over her mouth. "I came in here to get some pussy," he said. "I want pussy, you understand that?"

Powerless, Judy surrendered to him as he forced her legs open and assaulted her. During the attack, he hissed, "You white bitch! You white bitch!" When he finished, he sat on the side of the bed and pulled Judy's head down, forcing her to perform oral sex. Gagging and coughing, she fought against her reflex to vomit. But the intruder was not finished with her. He threw her back onto the bed and raped her again.

After the second time, he let Judy put on her panties. He asked her how much money she had. She told him she had a $1 bill and some change. He reacted with fury by grabbing her throat. She thought he was going to choke her. He repeatedly demanded that she not look at him and threatened to kill her if she did.

"I have a knife and I'll run it right through you," he said. Judy believed him. She tried to appear calm and assure her assailant that he didn't have to worry; she couldn't identify him. It wasn't light yet, and her glasses were on the chair by the bed. "I'm blind as a bat. I couldn't see you if I wanted to," she said. She was trying to connect with the perpetrator on some human level, but it didn't work. When she spoke to him, he became infuriated and instructed her to be quiet. His voice was low, hushed, almost a whisper, but vicious. He accused Judy of lying when she said she didn't have any more money.

The rapist took his time. He conducted a methodical search through her clothes in the closet. In frustration, he growled, "You white bitch, you know I could kill you right now! I want money!"

"I want to live," Judy told him. "I swear to you on everything that is holy that I wouldn't lie to you and if I had one thousand dollars, I would give it to you." As she spoke, she realized she might have something of value. "Oh! I know where some money is. On my desk, I have about four hundred pennies."

"I want paper money!" he yelled. Then he asked suddenly, "Do you have a car?"

"Yes. You can have it."

The rapist paced around the room cursing to himself. "You have a big wad of money hidden in the room!" he said. "If I find money, I will kill you."

He ordered Judy back onto the bed and put a blanket over her head. Then he turned the light on and told her, "If you try to look at me, I'll kill you." She prayed a silent prayer that he would leave. She could hear him slamming drawers as he rummaged through them. The noise stopped as abruptly as it had started. In an overly exaggerated attempted bluff, he acted like he'd caught her in a lie. "You white bitch, I found money! You said you didn't have any!" His rage escalated even more as he said "white bitch" over and over, reminding Judy that he had a knife and could kill her.

Suddenly, then, his manner changed, his voice cold and detached. He said simply, "I want some more of your hot white ass." He turned off the light and brutally assaulted Judy again. She had no power against this deranged man. All she could do was submit. And pray.

"Do you want to live?" he snarled.

"More than ever," Judy said. She was degraded and weary, but she meant it.

"Who do you believe in?" he badgered.

"God," she whispered.

He kept on. "Who is your Lord?"

"God."

His speech accelerated. "I'm gonna ask you one more time, bitch, and you better tell me right because if you don't, I'm gonna kill you. Who is your Lord?"

Defeated, not knowing what she was supposed to say, she blurted out the only answer she thought he could want: "You!"

"All right, white bitch." The man made her say over and over that he was her Lord and Savior. Judy could tell he found sick enjoyment from making her wonder if she would live or die.

He got off of her, finally. She panicked. What horrible thing would he do next? She started pleading with him not to kill her. He put the blanket over her head again and turned the light back on. He asked her about a certain ring, which she later described; she knew he'd found her Linde Star ring. He also asked her about the ring she was wearing. He took all the rings and then turned the light out again. Under the blanket, Judy was trembling violently. The intruder told her to calm down, that he wouldn't kill her but he needed her word that she wouldn't tell anybody.

She promised. He made her swear to God. Judy asked him if he'd swear to God that he would not come back and he said he would. He opened the door, and she thought he was leaving. Then he closed it. "I'll have to kill you if you tell anybody," he said. He told her not to call the cops. "They are all a bunch of dumb asses! You'll look like a whore that was raped by a black man." He said if he found out she had told, he would come back and kill her. Then he ordered her, "Put all this stuff back up just like nothing ever happened. You're gonna find some things missing because I'm taking some things with me."

The rapist closed the door. There was no sound from the hallway—which meant he would escape undetected.

In deep shock, Judy trembled as she listened through the door. She glanced at her clock by the bed. It was 5:30 A.M. That monster had been in her room only an hour but it had felt like an eternity. After a few minutes, Judy stumbled out into the hall. She saw her friend Carmen standing in the hallway.

The girl frowned, searching Judy's face for answers. "I heard noises coming from your room," she said.

In a burst of emotion, Judy Porter collapsed into the safety of her friend's arms.

Wright Hall on the Belmont College campus was less than five miles from Copeland Drive.

11

February 23, 1975

A rainy Saturday night turned into a dreary Sunday morning. Charlotte Shatzen had spent that night taking care of her boyfriend, Russ Hill, who was sick with some kind of bug. Charlotte and her friend, Janet Fort, stayed at Russ's house until the early morning hours. At about 5:00 A.M., Janet gave Charlotte a ride home.

Petite and pretty Charlotte Shatzen, twenty-four years old, was between jobs at the time. Like Sarah Des Prez, she lived in an old house that had been converted into small apartments. Her apartment was on Fairfax Avenue, just three doors down from 21st Avenue. Both the Vanderbilt and Belmont campuses were visible from the intersection of 21st Avenue and Fairfax. This was Hillsboro Village, an area of shops, studios, the popular Pancake Pantry, and a mix of single-family dwellings and student apartments. It was a neighborhood in transition. Students and commercial establishments geared to students were moving in as the older residents moved away from their early- to mid-twentieth-century houses.

Charlotte was aware of the reputation of the Hillsboro-Belmont-Vanderbilt district when she leased the tiny efficiency apartment. The area was a dangerous place for single women living alone. She had read the news reports on the Des Prez murder and the Belmont rape case, but she was not some wide-eyed eighteen-year-old freshman.

As Janet turned onto Charlotte's street, she asked, "What time is it?"

Charlotte told her it was 5:30.

"It's still really dark for 5:30 in the morning," Janet said.

They chatted about daylight savings time, which had gone into effect just two hours earlier. It was early in the year for this time change, which normally happened sometime in April, but that year was different because of the energy crisis. Charlotte and Janet talked about how confusing it was.

As they approached Charlotte's apartment, the rain started again. It had rained off and on all night. Charlotte was glad she'd brought an umbrella.

"You don't have to pull into the driveway. Just let me out in front," she said.

"You sure? I don't mind," Janet told her.

"Out front is fine."

Janet stopped the car by the front sidewalk.

"Thanks again for helping with Russ. Let's get together next week," Charlotte called as she got out of the car.

"Sure, call me." Janet waited until Charlotte walked up the sidewalk. Then she turned the car around at an apartment complex parking lot across the street and headed off.

Charlotte climbed the front porch steps. She hadn't thought to leave lights on in her apartment, and there were no other lights on in the house. The house was inky black. In this dark hour before dawn, only the soft patter of the rain pervaded the silence.

Charlotte laid her umbrella down, opened the storm door, and unlocked the door to her apartment. She stepped back and bent down to pick up her umbrella. As she was closing the umbrella, someone grabbed her from behind. A large hand gripped her mouth, and a heavy arm went around her chest. A knife pressed against her back.

"Don't scream. Don't try to turn around. Don't try to run or I'll stab you," the attacker told her.

Charlotte spun around anyway and faced a black male, approximately six feet two inches tall. He was holding a knife. The man struck at Charlotte, slashing her neck three times. She clutched the umbrella, her only defense, and lunged at him. But he was a big man, his face full of rage. He fended off her feeble attack and threw her into the concrete porch column. He grabbed her throat and began choking her.

Charlotte rammed the point of the umbrella into his stomach, causing him to jump back and let go of her. She took advantage of the moment and screamed.

The man seemed shocked by his inability to control her. He looked at the front door, then turned, jumped off the porch, and ran west on Fairfax Avenue. Charlotte continued to scream. Bleeding profusely from the three deep knife wounds on her neck, she staggered inside her apartment, locked the door, and dialed 911.

Charlotte Shatzen's apartment on Fairfax Avenue was less than five miles from Copeland Drive.

12

March 9, 1975

Some two miles west of downtown Nashville, directly across West End from the Vanderbilt University campus, lay Centennial Park, "Nashville's premier urban park."

After the Civil War, the site served as the state fairgrounds. It was later turned into a racetrack. In 1897, the spacious site was the location of the Tennessee Centennial and International Exposition. Appropriately, it was renamed Centennial Park. As a part of the exposition, an authentic re-creation of the original Parthenon in Athens, Greece, was constructed, complete with a forty-two-foot statue of Athena. The Parthenon, Nashville's monument to classical architecture, was the centerpiece of Centennial Park. Adjacent to the Parthenon was Watauga Lake, named for a region in North Carolina that produced many of the pioneers who became Nashville's first settlers.

Twenty-two-year-old Dianna McMillan was a newlywed in March 1975, and life was good. She had married Bobby McMillan three months earlier. They rented an upstairs apartment in an old house on Acklen Park Drive, named after Adelicia Acklen, the mistress of Belmont. The house lay on a hill above Centennial Park. Acklen Park intersected with West End Avenue, three blocks west of the park. Their building was a once attractive home now converted into several units. The McMillans' apartment was small, nothing fancy, but it was their own place. They were happy in their first home.

Bobby worked nights at a temporary job. Dianna was looking for work, and she thought her most recent interview had gone well. But with both of them between jobs, the couple needed the money Bobby was making. They agreed the night job would be a temporary thing. Something would turn up soon, Dianna was sure.

Though she understood that Bobby had to take the night job, Dianna missed him terribly, especially when the old house creaked and moaned. It seemed the creaks and moans only occurred in the darkness of midnight when she was alone.

Dianna had caught bits and pieces of the vicious crime spree that had erupted in February 1975 out on the West End Avenue–21st Avenue area of Nashville. A neighbor filled her in on the details of the murder of Sarah Des Prez. One of Bobby's co-workers knew the family of a girl who lived down the hall from Judy Porter at Belmont.

In addition, the story that consumed Nashville was the abduction of Marcia Trimble. All three local television stations, the radio outlets, and even the wire services provided continual reports. The two daily newspapers assigned teams of reporters to cover the mysterious case from every angle, each trying to out-scoop the other. If you were living in Nashville, it was impossible not to follow the story.

March 8, 1975, was a Saturday, and Bobby's boss had asked him to work that night. At about 2:00 Sunday morning, the phone rang. It was Bobby.

"They're letting me off early," he said. "Can you come pick me up?"

"Sure," Dianna said. "Let me get dressed and I'll be right there."

She slipped on a sweater and jeans, put on her shoes, and ran a brush through her hair. She locked the apartment door behind her and hurried down the stairs. When she opened the large wooden door at the front entrance, the cold night air stung her face. Her breath made crystals on the frosty air.

She dashed down the steps and over to the carport on the side of the house, where their car was parked. The carport was a structure of three walls and a roof, with an open front. Dianna unlocked the car door and climbed behind the wheel. Closing the door, she turned the key in the ignition. Nothing happened. She tried again. Nothing. On the third turn, the motor sputtered, coughed, and died. Maybe it was just cold, like everything else, Dianna thought. But the timing couldn't have been worse.

She was frustrated and freezing and not expecting anyone else to be out at this hour. The stranger was suddenly *there*—like a demon appearing out of the mist. A tall black man walked straight toward her, just a few feet from her car door. He wore a long tweed coat and dark stocking cap. A bandana covered his nose and mouth.

Dianna didn't think; she just opened the door. It was a mistake she would never forget.

"What do you want?" she asked the stranger.

"Get out of the car," he demanded. "I have a gun. Get your purse." She followed his orders. He told her to get into the neighbor's car, also parked under the carport, but when she tried the door, it was locked.

"Don't say nothing, or I'll blow your brains out," the stranger growled. He pushed her out of the carport, gripping her with one arm. Still pressing the cold gun barrel into her flesh, he forced her to walk to the edge of her yard and into the yard across the street.

"Please don't hurt me," Dianna pleaded.

"Shut up or I'll blow your brains out, you white bitch," he said. "Don't look at me, either. Where do you live?" Dianna pointed back at her apartment.

"Is anybody home?" he asked.

"My husband's coming home. He might already be there," she said, trying to frighten the man, but she could see he didn't care.

Just as they were entering the house, the man paused. "I'm cocking the gun," he told her. Dianna heard the metallic click.

He directed her upstairs to her apartment, to her bedroom.

"Give me money!" the man ordered.

"I don't have any," she said. Trembling, she opened her purse and shook out all the contents on the table by the bed. There was only about eighty cents.

"Take off your clothes and close your eyes," the man barked.

She knew she had no choice. Fighting tears and nausea, Dianna began to remove her clothes.

"Now lay down on the bed."

Dianna McMillan had never imagined a nightmare like this. She had never felt anything like the terror that coursed through her body. What could she do? Praying that Bobby would miraculously come rushing in and save her, she clenched her eyes and lay down on the bed. The stranger unzipped his pants and forced his penis into her mouth. Then he raped her, calling her "white bitch" over and over. If he would just get finished and leave—but no, he took his time with her.

When he finished violating Dianna, he made her get up and help him search the apartment for more money. She found two silver dollars in a jar and gave them to him. He brandished the pistol, searching the kitchen and living room. Surely he would leave, Dianna was thinking, when she heard the click of the front door being unlocked. Bobby had found another way home. "That's my husband!" she said, but the rapist showed no fear. He ran into the living room. Dianna knew Bobby had no chance against a gun. She rushed to the top of the stairs and called out to her husband, "Be careful! Take it slow!"

Bobby McMillan took his time climbing the stairs, puzzling over what Dianna was saying. Suddenly, the rapist ran out from the living room and pointed the gun at Bobby, demanding, "Get in the bedroom!"

In the bedroom, holding the couple at gunpoint, the intruder demanded Bobby's wallet. He shuffled through it and found $20. "Lay on the bed, face down," he hissed. The McMillans obeyed. They heard a ripping sound from the wall and then a clang as the rapist slammed the phone into the floor. Then the terrified couple heard the man scramble down the stairs and escape out of the apartment.

Bobby McMillan ran to the neighbor's apartment and called the police.

The McMillans' apartment on Acklen Park Drive was less than five miles from Copeland Drive.

13

March 12, 1975

It was pouring rain.

Judy Ladd, a special education teacher at Buena Vista Elementary, settled on the couch in front of the TV. At twenty-six, she had been teaching in Metro Schools for four years. Some would say it takes a certain type of person to teach special ed—determined, resourceful, gutsy. Judy fit the bill. Her job also took tremendous energy, and Judy finished each day exhausted. On March 12, 1975, still dressed in the pants and sweater she'd worn to school, Judy watched TV as night fell over the Bransford House Apartments, a modern apartment complex in Berry Hill, one of seven satellite cities of Nashville. Once a tree-lined neighborhood of 1940s cottages, the area began a period of rapid change when Nashville's first mall, One Hundred Oaks, opened in 1968 at the corner of Powell Avenue and Thompson Lane. By 1975, many of the cottages in Berry Hill had been converted to commercial establishments, housing eclectic retail shops and recording studios. The "city" of Berry Hill was contained in one square mile.

Judy shared the couch with B. B., her four-year-old Chihuahua, black with brown markings. She had turned on the light in her living room. Her apartment, number 13, was located three steps down from the sidewalk. The sidewalk and parking lot didn't offer much of a view, so Judy had closed her curtains.

But she loved the sound of the rain. On this Wednesday at the end of winter, she had opened the apartment's big front door. The storm door, half glass, half screen, was not locked. The lock hadn't worked for a while. The cool rain-scented air that drifted through the screen smelled like spring.

It was about 8:20 P.M. when all at once, B. B. sprinted off the couch and headed to the door, barking furiously. Judy wasn't too alarmed. B. B. was a protective little dog. Any strange noise would make him react. But she went to the door to take a look.

About twelve feet away, a shadowy figure caught her attention. A man with his shoulders hunched, collar up, and hands in his pockets stood near the stairs, just out of the rain. He was wearing a long, dark overcoat. Since he was facing the parking lot, Judy thought he must be waiting for the rain to let up a little so he could run to his car. She went back to her couch.

But B. B. was still in a frenzy. His barking grew more insistent as he dashed from door to couch and back, trying to get Judy to take him seriously. Though Judy was not by nature suspicious, she wondered why B. B. was so agitated. Again she went to the door. The dark figure still had his back to her, but he was two or three feet closer than he'd been a few minutes earlier.

Judy slammed the solid wood door and locked it. No doubt about it; the danger B. B. sensed was real. She started to call the police, and then she remembered there was a gun in the bedroom. Her boyfriend Jerry, a policeman, had left it there. As B. B. continued his fierce barking, Judy raced to the bedroom and grabbed the .22 pistol.

She went to the window and pulled back the curtain just enough to see out—and to show the man she had a gun. The pistol was not loaded, but she held it up, in plain view. He would see she was not defenseless. She wasn't used to handling firearms. The long barrel smacked against the glass. The man was still out there, and he had moved closer, no more than six feet from her door.

A large, dark figure in the gray night, the man was now not only looking at her, but wearing a stocking cap and a bandana over his face, the kind bandits in old westerns wore. Judy could see enough around the eye area to tell he was a black man.

She dropped the curtain and ran to the phone to call Metro Police. She reported the masked man at her door and said, "Please radio my boyfriend!" Jerry was on duty. He would know what to do.

The dispatcher took her address and said, "That's Berry Hill. You need to call the Berry Hill police." Frustrated, Judy fumbled to look up the number. By the time she reached the Berry Hill police, B. B. had settled down. The man had gone away. She called Metro Police again and eventually was able to reach Jerry.

The Berry Hill Police Department was located on Thompson Lane, just a couple of miles from the apartments. Officers Herman Jett and Tom Lunn responded within minutes. As they came onto the Bransford House property, before they ever reached Judy's apartment, they passed the laundry room and saw a man trying to break in. He fit Judy's description—a tall black man with a stocking cap, wearing a full-length tweed overcoat. They arrested him and transported him to the custody of Metro Police.

The six-feet-two-inches-tall suspect was double-dressed. Underneath his black top and light-colored pants was an outfit of reverse colors, and police found a blue and white bandana.

He carried a long knife and a gun, a .22 pistol like the one Judy had—but his was loaded.

A check of police records indicated that the man had several outstanding warrants for failure to appear in court. It was also noted in the arrest report that the suspect "is presently on parole from a Tennessee State prison on a sex charge."

Judy later learned that the man had gone to a neighbor's door first. The neighbor had met him with a shotgun.

"He didn't hurt anyone else after that night," Judy Ladd later said. "All because of my dog."

Bransford House Apartments were just over five miles from Copeland Drive.

14

The Detective from Alpine

Within a couple of hours after the discovery of Sarah Des Prez's body on February 2, Lieutenant Tom Cathey, head of the Metropolitan Police Department Homicide Division, had taken charge of the crime scene. He spoke with each officer who was initially at the scene, including Detective Morris McKenzie. Lieutenant Cathey was interviewed by the media. He ordered Des Prez's bedclothes, coat, and hair samples to be immediately sent to the FBI Crime Laboratory. He assigned three more investigators to the case: veteran detectives Bill Robeck and Barry Touchstone, and a relatively unknown twenty-eight-year-old detective from Overton County named Diane Vaughn.

Overton County, Tennessee, is approximately 110 miles northeast of Nashville, is a region of unparalleled natural beauty, and sits in the rugged Cumberland Mountains adjacent to Fentress County. Pristine Dale Hollow Lake lies on the county's northern border. Diane Vaughn was from Alpine, a small village east of Livingston, the county seat. Despite being barely five feet four inches tall, Diane was a standout basketball player in high school for Livingston Academy. She was always considered a tomboy. Growing up, she was known as an outstanding marksman, nicknamed Annie Oakley. She kept her hair cut short and did not wear makeup. After graduation from high school in 1965, Diane enrolled at Tennessee Technological University in Cookeville, Tennessee, only thirty miles from Livingston. Although Tennessee Tech did not receive media coverage like other state institutions such as Middle Tennessee State University and the University of Tennessee, people in the know considered it a premier academic university in the state of Tennessee.

Diane Vaughn enjoyed her time at Tech, but her heart had always been set on one career: law enforcement. At the end of her sophomore year, she announced to her family and friends she was applying to become a Nashville police officer.

Diane made an excellent impression in her interviews with the police department. Speaking with a slight Upper Cumberland accent, she was down-to-earth, obviously sincere and genuine, and well qualified to become a Nashville police officer. Her problem was gender. In 1967, women who desired to go into law enforcement were viewed suspiciously, not treated seriously. The police personnel officer told Diane she would be put on a waiting list. She accepted the news and got busy. She had a plan and was going to stick to it, but she had to wait. In the meantime, her friends helped her to find a job at South Central Bell.

Finally, in 1970, Diane received the letter she had been waiting for. She was hired as a police officer for the Nashville Metropolitan Police Department.

On the surface, the Nashville Police Department looked the part of a professional law enforcement agency, but appearances were deceiving. As with many institutions, a peek beneath the surface revealed a very different reality.

The "good ol' boy" culture that defined the department in

1970 made police work a difficult career choice for women. Cowboy boots and Stetson hats ruled. Female officers were referred to as the "pussy patrol." Women working in the police department were considered by the "cowboys" to be either lesbians or whores. It was not unusual for female clerks to find dildos in their desk drawers. When some of the women left in the evening, their bosses would ask them for a "good night kiss."

Diane Vaughn accepted the culture and ignored the insults. She was doing what she'd always wanted; she was living her dream.

But there were other hurdles as well. Nashville policewomen were not allowed to be frontline officers at that time, not given any type of high-profile assignments, not allowed to be alone in squad cars. Often they were used as babysitters for female suspects and other times as decoys when conducting surveillance. They assisted the "true" detectives or officers. They were expected to wear skirts and high heels and carry a purse. The purse was for their handgun. Women were given the choice of Youth Guidance or Vice cases. Occasionally they could take the lead in Sex Crimes unless the male detectives wanted the case. Generally, female detectives had to prove themselves before being trusted, unless they had a political connection to get promoted or moved into a desired assignment.

Diane Vaughn chose to work Vice. She did anything to build her experience, volunteering for dangerous midnight shifts and working the tough cases that no one else was interested in. The cases involved everything from prostitution stings to serial rapists.

Early in her career, she was working the midnight shift on the desk at the front door of police headquarters on James Robertson Parkway. She heard gunfire outside, and the next minute a police officer burst through the door followed by a man brandishing a pistol. The man fired at the officer, who fell to the floor. Officer Vaughn shot the assailant; then she held the wounded officer in her arms until medical personnel arrived.

She was eventually promoted to detective, which included a 5 percent raise and clothing allowance. Women in the department could now wear slacks and carry their weapon on them. Still, there were only a handful of female detectives. Eventually she was assigned to work homicides in addition to rapes. As years passed, Diane Vaughn continued to work the difficult cases. She was outstanding on the police shooting range. Vaughn spoke with a raspy voice; she smoked and drank coffee constantly. Male fellow officers were not threatened by her. Although they never imagined her capable of an upper-level position in the department, she had earned a grudging respect from the good ol' boys.

She was working as a Homicide detective on vicious rapes and murders when she received a call from her boss, Lieutenant Cathey. It was Monday, February 3, 1975. Diane Vaughn was assigned to the Sarah Des Prez murder. She was ready.

15

On the Trail

Like other female detectives in 1975, Detective Diane Vaughn dressed in a plain dark shirt, navy slacks, and simple black shoes. She wore her hair short and never bothered with makeup. There was nothing fancy or flashy about Diane Vaughn. The waitresses, cabdrivers, and street people knew her by word of mouth. She didn't wear a badge or any indication that she was a detective. The outline of a holster was just barely visible under her jacket.

From early Monday morning, Detective Vaughn worked on the Des Prez case almost nonstop, trying to locate any possible lead or suspect. As a part of her assignment, her boss, Lieutenant Tom Cathey, had transferred her from midnights to the day shift. So she worked days in her official capacity, but her best work came at night, in the long, dark, early hours after midnight. This was the time she could focus on her cases. She wasn't getting much sleep.

After her Monday meeting with Lieutenant Cathey, she drove to Vanderbilt University and interviewed David Wood, the dean of Admissions and Records. Vanderbilt provided her a copy of Sarah Des Prez's records and gave her the address of the victim's ex-roommate, Ann Ramsey. After the meeting at the Admissions office, she went to Mims Hall where Sarah Des Prez had worked. She interviewed Yvonne Batey, a resident assistant for the dorm. Yvonne told her that Sarah was very open with people about her life and was punctual for work, that Sarah enjoyed talking for hours with the residents in the dorm.

Later, Vaughn met with Lisa Burris, another Mims Hall resident, who said that Sarah was not dating anyone regularly. Vaughn continued to interview coeds from Mims Hall and learned the identities of other men Sarah had dated. None of the coeds showed any indication that Sarah's dates could have been threatening. Vaughn interviewed Clark Williams, the immediate supervisor of the dorm, and he identified several Vanderbilt male students who'd come over to the dorm while Sarah was working.

Another friend of Sarah's repeated the same information, that Sarah was open to people and not as cautious as she should have been. All the coeds confirmed that Trammell Hudson, Sarah's date on the night she was murdered, was a nice guy and never appeared to be strange or threatening. Vaughn took meticulous notes. None of the information she'd gathered at Mims Hall raised any red flags, but who knew when some random detail might become useful?

Late that Monday afternoon, Vaughn tracked down Ann Ramsey, who was Sarah's ex-roommate and closest friend. Vaughn drove to Oak Hills, not far from Green Hills, and interviewed Ann at her parents' home. Ann also identified a number of Vanderbilt students who had dated Sarah. She discussed her last conversation with Sarah, about her plans to go out with Trammell Hudson. She confirmed that her friend was not seeing anyone regularly. As far as she knew, Sarah was not having sexual relations with anyone recently.

Ann, who was familiar with the victim's apartment, also said that the door did not lock properly. She said Sarah never really knew if it was locked or not. "I warned her to be more careful because of the neighborhood," Ann said, "but Sarah was sort of scatter-brained, and didn't really listen."

On Tuesday, February 4, Vaughn received a call from Dr. Roger Des Prez, Sarah's father, about a lead. Someone had called the doctor and told him that a man named Bennett had murdered his daughter. Vaughn assured Dr. Des Prez that she would follow up. She found the address of Bennett's parents and drove out there with another detective. They learned that Bennett was unemployed and lived somewhere on Acklen Avenue. He owned a blue Volkswagen. Vaughn left the parents' home and drove back looking for a blue VW. They found the automobile in an alley, parked by a house on Acklen. They called for a uniformed officer and then went to the house, where they met Bennett's roommate, who gave Vaughn permission to search the house. After the search yielded nothing, Vaughn went to several local restaurants where Bennett had worked, all in the Vanderbilt–West End area: Ireland's, Exit In, and Friday's. About 1:00 the following morning, Bennett finally showed up at the downtown police headquarters and was interviewed. His sister would later confirm that he'd stayed home on the night Sarah Des Prez was murdered.

Trammell Hudson had voluntarily gone to police headquarters and given a statement. On Tuesday, February 4, Vaughn contacted Vanderbilt officials and gave them the names of all people mentioned in Trammell's statement. The Vanderbilt security department arranged for her to interview those people. Officer McNeill assisted in the interviews. The students all said that Saturday night was normal. Nothing unusual happened. One of them remembered seeing Trammell and Sarah at the SAE party. Another student saw the couple at the movie theater at One Hundred Oaks Mall.

Vaughn met with Detective Barry Touchstone, also working the case. She learned that Charles Mintlow rented one of the apartments in the building where Des Prez lived. Mintlow, a black male, was a graduate of MTSU with a major in music. He told the detectives that Des Prez sometimes came down and ate popcorn in his apartment with him and other friends.

Diane Vaughn related the details of her interviews, filling the pages of her reports with neat, tight printing.

Vaughn started off the day Wednesday perusing a list of men with a history of sex crimes. The next two days, she concentrated on investigating known sex offenders on the streets of Nashville. On Thursday, February 6, she interviewed John Woods, who'd been recently charged with assault with intent to commit murder. The victim was a young white female. Woods freely discussed his whereabouts on Saturday night and Sunday morning, February 2. He had been with his two sisters at a birthday party on Gallatin Pike. Police later confirmed Woods's alibi.

On Friday, February 7, Vaughn interviewed a number of people in the neighborhood of Sarah Des Prez's apartment building. The interviews were time-consuming but necessary—the nature of her work. None of the neighbors gave her any clues. Most did not know Sarah Des Prez. Students tended to come and go in the apartments. They didn't put down roots in the neighborhood.

That afternoon, Diane Vaughn and another detective picked up Trammell Hudson and drove him around the Vanderbilt campus. They discussed Sarah Des Prez, and Trammell talked about their date. Vaughn found Trammell to be open, honest, and ready to answer any questions. He said Sarah had been able to walk when he took her home and was in control of her movements. She didn't have any scratches or bruises on her face; he would have noticed them.

Diane Vaughn continued to follow leads, hoping for a break in the case. She interviewed a Peabody College student who claimed she'd heard a man at the Village Pub state that he was wanted for the murder of Sarah Des Prez. The man was checked out and another lead proved false.

On Friday, February 7, Detective Vaughn interviewed twenty-year-old Benjamin Blanton, an old friend of Sarah's. An officer working the Des Prez case had called Benjamin on Monday, February 3, and asked him to come downtown and give a statement, but he'd never come to the station.

It was obvious to Diane Vaughn that Benjamin Blanton was nervous. He admitted knowing Sarah Des Prez since high school but denied ever having sex with her. He admitted he had seen her ten or twelve times in the last month. He said he drank beer with her on Friday night. Vaughn asked him point-blank if he liked girls. He said yes. Vaughn noticed Benjamin had scratches on his forearms. He claimed he had received them while walking in the woods.

Benjamin Blanton also admitted he had visited Sarah's neighbor, Lynn Fussell, and Lynn's brother Ron, on the night of Sarah's murder. They had watched movies on TV, and he was able to provide specific titles and the exact times they aired. Benjamin also said that at midnight Saturday night, he and the Fussells went to his parents' house and got a bottle of wine. When they returned, Lynn and Benjamin went into Sarah's apartment to borrow a corkscrew. At that time, Sarah had not returned from her date.

When Benjamin Blanton finished his statement, Vaughn asked him to take a polygraph test. He refused. She left him with the feeling she had more questions now than answers.

* * *

There was tremendous pressure on the Metropolitan Police Department to quickly locate a suspect in the Des Prez case. The murder of the daughter of a prominent Vanderbilt physician was rare in Nashville.

On Monday, February 10, Lieutenant Cathey held a meeting of the detectives working the case. Diane Vaughn dreaded these meetings. She didn't wear slick suits or flashy jewelry like the cowboys. She wasn't one of the guys. But she accepted that fact. The thing that really bothered her was what actually occurred—or didn't occur—in these meetings. This particular meeting went as she expected. Lieutenant Cathey explained how much pressure the department was receiving from the public and Vanderbilt University to solve the terrible crime. Then Cathey went around the room asking each detective to report on his investigation. There was a typical mumbling and "I'm waiting on an informant's phone call." Diane Vaughn reported on her interviews and the persons she had eliminated as suspects. Unlike the men, she gave an organized, detailed account of her progress. She got the attention of Cathey and the other detectives when she told them Benjamin Blanton had been with Sarah Des Prez on the Friday night before her murder and he had refused to take a polygraph. After the meeting ended, as Vaughn walked down the hallway to her desk, she realized she had not learned anything new about the investigation. Each detective was determined to be the hero, and the cowboys just weren't going to share anything with Diane Vaughn.

On Wednesday, February 12, Lieutenant Cathey called Detective Vaughn to his office. Cathey said he had received a call from Captain Daily of the Jackson Police Department. He said Daily had located a possible suspect in the Des Prez murder. Cathey told Vaughn to make contact with Daily and follow up on the suspect. She called and left a message for Daily to call her back. She continued to check out her informants and track down any and all leads. On Friday, she finally received a telephone call from Captain Daily of the Jackson Police Department advising her that she could interview the informant on February 17.

Vaughn went home that Friday night with the Des Prez murder still on her mind. She sat in her apartment and reviewed the file again and again. The other detectives were confident the murderer was a former boyfriend or neighbor. There was no evidence of forcible entry. The back door in the kitchen that led to the fire escape was locked. But there was something about this case that did not point to boyfriends or neighbors. In her mind, she played out the event. She saw the student alone, climbing the steps to her apartment. In the darkness, she sensed something sinister was waiting for Sarah.

The sharp ring of the phone startled Diane Vaughn awake. She normally woke early, but this was Sunday morning, her day off, and she had decided to linger in bed a little longer. She looked at her alarm clock. It was 8:00 A.M. on February 16. She reached for the phone.

A male officer was on the line and introduced himself. "I'm working a forcible rape where the assailant used a knife," he said. "We're with the victim at Baptist Hospital."

"Where did the rape take place?" asked Vaughn.

"Belmont College, Wright Hall. It was actually inside the victim's dorm room. We've dusted for prints. The victim gave a good description and wasn't hurt," the officer said.

Vaughn remained professional, overlooking the suggestion that a victim raped at knifepoint was not hurt. She asked, "Is the victim going to be able to give a statement?"

"Yes, we're going to take her to CID shortly."

"Tell her I'm on my way. I'll meet you downtown," Vaughn said.

She fixed a pot of coffee, drank a glass of orange juice, and jumped in the shower. The shock of the cold water brought her into focus. Detectives were not paid overtime. This was just part of the job. She was scheduled to go to Jackson, Tennessee, early Monday morning to interview an informant in the Des Prez case. Now this. She finished her first cup of coffee as she dressed. She poured another cup, put her holster on, grabbed her badge and wallet, and walked out of her apartment, ready for her next task.

Diane Vaughn walked into the conference room at 10:30 A.M. and introduced herself to Judy Porter, the Belmont student victim. Vaughn asked Porter to tell her a little about herself. The girl appeared exhausted, as if she'd been awake for a week. Vaughn saw that her eyes were red and swollen from hours of crying, which was natural after such a horrendous ordeal—though with some rape victims, it was the other extreme: blank faces, hollow eyes. Traumatizing rape could affect victims in a number of ways.

Diane Vaughn explained to Judy Porter that she would be taking her statement and that she understood this was very personal, but it was important to get as many details as possible. A male officer had been waiting with Judy. Vaughn asked him to leave the room. She turned on the tape recorder.

Judy began by describing how she had stayed up late Saturday night into Sunday morning and listened to some records as she went to sleep, which was probably around 3:30 A.M.

Judy told how she awoke, with someone standing over her, holding a weapon on the back of her neck. She described in detail how the man forced her to have oral sex and then raped her repeatedly. The transcript of her description would take up several pages.

She said the rapist instructed her several times not to look at him, threatened to "run his knife right through her," and demanded money. Vaughn raised her eyebrows in response to those details. Judy told him she didn't have any money. The rapist said he'd kill her if he found any money in the room. He put a blanket over her head, turned on the light, and began to canvass the entire dorm room. She could hear him tearing through the drawers closest to the bed and closet, becoming increasingly angry as the search revealed no money. When he found no money, he grabbed her and raped her again. Vaughn was careful to maintain a neutral expression, not to show any reaction to the details that had to be so hard for the young woman to recall.

Judy Porter went on, telling how the man began speaking faster, telling her he was going to kill her. He made her say he was her Lord. After he was through with her, he repeated his search of the room. The rapist told her that if she told the police, he would come back and kill her. He took her ring and several other items and left.

When she finished giving her account, Vaughn sat in silence for a brief moment. "Can you think of anything else?" she asked, with kindness in her voice. She knew that the girl had been very thorough. She had talked for a long time. Judy lowered her head as she recalled the brutal nightmare again. "He said over and over, 'Do as I say, white bitch, and you won't get hurt.'"

Vaughn asked Judy Porter for another description, and she gave the same details she had given the officer: tall, black, male. Vaughn thanked her for her time and told her she wanted to meet her at her dorm room in the next day or two.

When she finished talking to Judy Porter, Vaughn went back to her desk. She found a note saying that both the *Nashville Banner* and the *Tennessean* had been calling, which indicated that she was the lead detective on the case. Reporters didn't call rookies. Because it was Sunday, her office was quiet. Recalling the interview, Vaughn was struck by Judy Porter's statement. She had been doing this job for a while and had gained experience on a number of rape cases. This was different. She hadn't put her finger on it yet, but it was different.

Vaughn called the reporters back and made a short statement. She told the press that the man had been in the victim's room for at least forty-five minutes, maybe longer. "A guy has to be pretty brazen to break into a dormitory and stay that long," she said.

Monday morning, February 17, the *Tennessean* reported the news of the crime at Belmont. The article concluded, "Earlier this month a Vanderbilt University freshman, Sarah Des Prez, was found dead of asphyxiation in her 20th Avenue South apartment. Police suspect she died as a result of strangulation and say she had been sexually assaulted. No arrests have been made in the Des Prez case."

The *Tennessean* had linked the two crimes. So had Diane Vaughn.

16

Putting the Pieces Together

Wild-goose chase.

On Monday, February 17, a sleepy Diane Vaughn drove up to the Jackson Police Station. She'd been up since first light and had driven two hours to make the 9:00 A.M. meeting with Captain Daily. Cathey had asked her to do this, and she would do it, but she knew she should have been back in Nashville, working the Judy Porter rape and following leads on the Sarah Des Prez murder.

Captain Daily was nice enough. He had arranged for a squad car to take Vaughn to meet with a woman at her home on Leland Drive. The middle-class lady was not the typical stuffy informant. She happened to have overheard a conversation.

After an hour and a half interview, Vaughn thanked the informant and said she'd be in touch with the Jackson Police Department. It turned out the woman had just overheard someone running his mouth, a man who had left his wife in Nashville and moved to Jackson to live with another man. He had been treated for a mental condition, and his comments, even if taken for truth, had nothing to do with implicating him in the crime. Vaughn thanked the Jackson Police and informant and headed back to Nashville.

By 2:45 that afternoon, Detective Diane Vaughn was in Wright Hall interviewing Belmont coeds about their knowledge of the Saturday night and early Sunday morning that Judy Porter was raped. She received a call from ID officers, advising that they had two fingerprints from one palm print at Porter's dorm.

At 7:00 that Monday evening, Vaughn received a phone call from Juanita Wardin, dean of women at Belmont. There had been reports of obscene phone calls coming in, and officials at Belmont wanted to know if they were connected to the rape.

On Tuesday, February 18, at 9:00 A.M., Vaughn was back at Wright Hall, this time speaking with Judy Porter herself. She asked Judy to draw sketches of the ring and other jewelry that had been stolen. Vaughn took the sketches to a colleague who worked the pawnshops, and he assured her he'd check them daily and get back to her.

She drove to Belmont again and at 12:30 P.M. provided Judy Porter with some photographs of potential suspects. Judy said she could not positively identify anyone in the photos as her attacker. When that interview was complete, Vaughn received a phone call from the ID officers advising her that one of the prints from Judy's dorm room had been processed and turned out to be a good print. Vaughn had previously given the ID officers a description of the suspect and told them to run a printout of possible suspects through the National Crime Information Center computer. She was informed that the computer had selected 153 possible suspects from the description given. Of these 153 possibilities, 10 were in the immediate area when the rape occurred. Vaughn checked those 10 with

Central Records that afternoon; none of them had a previous sex offense record.

On Thursday, February 20, Vaughn called Scott Pogue with the security office at South Central Bell and advised him that obscene phone calls were being made to the coed dormitories at Belmont. He agreed to set up a tracer system. Vaughn called Dean Wardin at Belmont to tell her the telephone company would begin tracing phone calls. Vaughn took Judy Porter to an administration office at Belmont and had her listen to traced calls. Judy did not match any voice with that of the attacker.

Detective Diane Vaughn was back at her desk at the police station early Monday morning, February 24. She was still adjusting to not working nights and not sleeping well. By this time, she and the other detectives had interviewed more than 150 individuals in the Des Prez case. She noticed, on the corner of her desk, a note attached to a Metropolitan Police Department report. The note said, "For your information, thought you might be interested in this."

Vaughn had befriended a number of patrol officers over the years. They respected her and knew that she would never blow smoke or try to take advantage of them. She had street credibility with the frontline officers.

She picked up the police report, complaint number 75-29259, and saw that the victim's name was Charlotte M. Shatzen. The victim lived on Fairfax Avenue. An attempted rape had occurred in the wee hours of early Sunday morning, February 23. What caught Vaughn's eye was the item on the left side of the form, near the top of the section, in the space for "Trademark of Suspect." The notation read, "Don't scream, or I'll stab you." Vaughn continued reading. The man had not been able to complete the assault; the victim fought him off with an umbrella. Shatzen described him as a black male, approximately six feet two inches tall.

Vaughn put the copy of the Shatzen report into her Judy Porter case file.

Tuesday, February 25, had been another long day—a nice springlike day, though, unseasonably warm. Detective Vaughn turned on one of the local TV channels for the ten o'clock news. The announcer was reporting that a young Girl Scout in Green Hills was missing, and the police department's Youth Guidance Division was heading up the investigation. Over the next couple of weeks, the search for Marcia Trimble drew national attention. Although Homicide was not in charge, Lieutenant Cathey had advised his detectives to be on call and follow up with their informants to see if any of them had information relating to the missing child. Meanwhile, Vaughn continued working her regular rape files as well as Des Prez and Porter, both major cases. She was so busy that she missed the Homicide detectives meeting—something unusual for her.

Sunday morning, March 9, on Diane Vaughn's day off, she turned on the news and heard another report on the expanding search for little Marcia Trimble. She had personally followed up a couple of leads, but nothing had turned up. Lieutenant Cathey had not shared any information about the case with her. His excuse was that since it was still a missing person's case, Homicide was not involved.

As she ate a piece of toast, the phone rang. It was Detective Robeck, asking, "Vaughn, did I get you up?"

She told him no.

"I've got something you might be interested in. Forcible rape." There was a pause. "We oughta have a report by the time you get down to CID, but it happened over at Acklen Park off West End."

Robeck proceeded to give the details. Despite her experience and reputation, Vaughn was stunned. Robeck said that the victim, Dianna McMillan, was getting her car to go pick up her husband from work at about 2:00 A.M. when a black male approached the car. The man had a pistol and ordered the victim out of her car and back into the apartment. He told her he'd kill her if she didn't do what he said. He raped her and then searched the entire house looking for money. He did this even though the woman told him that her husband was on his way home from work. When her husband did arrive, the assailant pulled a pistol again and ordered them both on the bed, searched for more money, and finally left.

Vaughn showered, dressed, and drove down to CID. As she drove, she thought about the location of the most recent rape. Acklen Park was not far from Sarah Des Prez's apartment or Judy Porter's dormitory at Belmont College.

The report was waiting on her desk. On the top left part of the report under "Trademark of Suspect Action or Conversation," the following sentence was typed: "Do as I tell you, you white bitch, and you won't get hurt."

Vaughn read it over and over. It was the same language that the assailant had used with Judy Porter. The latest victim, Dianna McMillan, described the rapist as a black male over six feet tall. Once again, Vaughn started going through her list of possible sex offender suspects who were on the streets of Nashville.

Over the next few days, Diane Vaughn relentlessly worked the Porter, Des Prez, and McMillan cases, in addition to helping on the Marcia Trimble case. On Saturday, March 15, Detective Ralph Langston called Vaughn and said he had some news. Thirty minutes later, Langston was sitting by Vaughn's desk. Langston, a weight lifter, was a formidable-looking man whose muscles appeared as though they were about to burst out of his suit. He told Vaughn of an arrest that Berry Hill officers Jett and Lunn had made on March 12: They'd arrested a black male and charged him with "breaking and entering and carrying a weapon for the purpose of going armed." The suspect had been attempting to break into a white female's apartment at the Bransford House Apartments on Berry Road. When the suspect was arrested, he was wearing a long dark tweed overcoat and a blue stocking cap.

Vaughn sat quietly, letting Langston's news sink in. Dianna McMillan said her rapist had been wearing a dark tweed overcoat.

"Ralph, we have work to do," she said.

The suspect arrested in Berry Hill had given police a home address on Jefferson Street, the main thoroughfare in Nashville's predominantly black neighborhood. At 2:00 P.M., Vaughn spoke with the owner of the apartment building at that address, who said the suspect was staying in the apartment with a friend named Evan Bailey. He'd been living there for about three weeks. The suspect's roommate was not there at that time.

The next morning, Sunday, March 16, Vaughn drove to Judy Porter's room at Belmont. She asked Porter to give a complete description of all the articles taken from her room by the rapist. Among those items were a gold wedding band, gold cuff links, a topaz ring, a black leather shaving case with a razor, and a plastic container with a red lid. Vaughn contacted the suspect's roommate, Evan Bailey, who agreed to meet with her first thing Monday morning.

At 8:15 Monday morning, Vaughn met Detective Ralph Langston in the parking lot of the police station to drive over to the apartment building. Vaughn had a "Consent to Search" form for Evan Bailey to sign. On the short drive over to North Nashville and Jefferson Street, Vaughn reminded herself of all the hot leads that had turned into dead ends. "We might not find anything," she said, as much to herself as to Detective Langston.

As he drove, Langston nodded.

They met Evan Bailey outside the apartment on Jefferson Street. A small black man, Evan agreed without hesitation to sign anything they wanted. He opened the door and they walked into a musty one-room apartment with a closet. Wallpaper peeling off the walls, a naked lightbulb hanging from the kitchen ceiling—the place was rough. It didn't look like anyone actually lived there. Vaughn noticed that the kitchen sink was full of dishes that had been left for some time.

Evan Bailey pointed to a room on the left side of the kitchen. "That's his things," he said.

The furniture consisted of a small cot, a scratched-up dresser, and a side table. The detectives walked over to the table. Langston picked up a black Gillette razor case and held it up to Vaughn. He continued over to the closet and pulled out a radio antenna and plastic battery container. At the table, Vaughn picked up a plastic container with a red lid. She opened it to find a gold wedding band, topaz ring, gold cuff links with the initials A. J. P., and the rest of the items stolen from Judy Porter. The detectives gave each other a look that said, *Got him!*

Evan jumped in. "He ain't paid any rent and he's been here for three weeks. He said he's gonna leave. All those things you're finding are his, not mine."

The detectives assured Evan that they understood. They thanked him for his cooperation.

By noon, Vaughn was back at the CID office. She met the suspect, Jerome Sydney Barrett, a twenty-six-year-old, six-feet-two-inches-tall black male from Memphis. Barrett admitted he had been in prison for carnal knowledge of a female. He said he was divorced. Vaughn advised him of his rights. Barrett began talking. He said he needed help and wanted to confess to the rape of a young white girl at Belmont College. Barrett said he was a messenger sent by the Nation of Islam, and he was ordered to do the thing he did to the girl.

The police laid out the various articles taken from Barrett's apartment that Judy Porter had described and sketched for

Vaughn. Barrett pointed to the articles and identified them. He even told the police where in the dorm room each item came from. Barrett stated that he would walk around the college campuses and when he saw an open window, he'd go in. He said he had first seen the Belmont girl in the hallway of the school. Though he confessed freely to the rape of Judy Porter, he denied assaulting the woman on Acklen Park Drive.

The police took Barrett into a separate room and called the victim. Judy Porter arrived at the police station within an hour. She identified the articles spread out on Lieutenant Cathey's desk—rings, a razor, cuff links, and a plastic container that had contained pennies—as hers. Officers Jett and Lunn of the Berry Hill Police arrived and also identified Barrett as the person they'd arrested trying to break into the Bransford House Apartments. They also identified the pistol as being the one they took from Barrett at the time of the arrest.

It was a busy day for Vaughn and Langston, with the cases all coming together. Thirty minutes later, Dianna and Bobby McMillan came in. Bobby immediately identified the long dark tweed coat as the one worn by the assailant. He also identified the blue stocking cap. Dianna identified the coat, a blue bandana, and a pair of gloves. Both identified the pistol as being the same pistol used in the assault.

Vaughn asked the McMillans to step into a room and look at a lineup. At this point, Barrett refused to answer any further questions and the police called his attorney at the public defender's office.

At 1:45 P.M. on Monday, March 17, Detective Diane Vaughn arrested Jerome Sydney Barrett for the rape and armed robbery of Dianna McMillan. She then arrested him for the rape and robbery of Judy Porter.

Four days later, on Friday, March 21, police placed Barrett in a lineup. Vaughn brought in Charlotte Shatzen, the victim of the assault that had occurred on February 23. Shatzen identified Barrett out of the lineup. Thirty minutes later, Diane Vaughn also arrested Barrett for the assault on Charlotte Shatzen.

But the puzzle was not complete. The Sarah Des Prez case remained unsolved. The district attorney filed a motion with the Davidson County Criminal Court. The motion, based upon an affidavit by Detective Diane Vaughn, asked that the State be allowed to collect hair samples from Jerome Sydney Barrett and that the samples be sent to the FBI Laboratory in Washington, D.C. The results of the test were to be used in the Des Prez case.

Thursday, March 26, at 2:00 P.M., Judge Allen R. Cornelius Jr. of the Criminal Court of Nashville-Davidson County signed an order granting the State of Tennessee's motion to obtain samples of Jerome Barrett's hair.

The quiet, professional detective from Alpine had done a remarkable job. Surely the cowboys would give her a chance to solve the Des Prez case.

PART 3

Prime Suspect

17

The Boys in the Neighborhood

Copeland Drive was looking more like spring with each April day. Like every other year, spring of 1975 brought blossoming redbuds and dogwoods. Plantings of tulips and impatiens bloomed in the manicured yards. The new green of shrubs and trees shimmered in the gauzy sunlight.

But this spring was unlike any other year for the families who lived in the neighborhood. Inside their tidy houses, residents pondered the horrible, incomprehensible thing that had happened here—the murder of a child. And police believed that one of their own was the murderer.

The newspapers carried daily briefings by Lieutenant Tom Cathey. His quotes were variations on a single theme: "We still believe the answer is in the neighborhood." Police were waiting for the FBI's analyses, waiting for Dr. Francisco's final autopsy, re-interviewing residents in the area.

The full effects of the murder and the investigation on the families on and around Copeland Drive—especially the children—would not be realized for years, even decades, but the continuing interviews with residents indicated that this neighborhood was traumatized. One father reported his child was afraid to sleep in his own room; the boy was sleeping at the foot of his parents' bed in a sleeping bag. In another household, the parents would not allow their daughter to go upstairs by herself. Another girl, afraid to be home alone, would carry her fears well into adulthood. Children were not out and about on their bikes or roaming freely within the Copeland-Dorcas loop as they had done before February 25. The skies were blue, the spring breezes balmy, but a cloud of anxiety hung over the once idyllic neighborhood.

Dr. Jerry Francisco was in Chattanooga on April 12, 1975, at the annual meeting of the Tennessee Medical Association, where he was slated to receive the TMA's Distinguished Service Award. Dr. Francisco had been chosen for the award in January, before the Marcia Trimble murder, but as the result of his participation in the case, the state medical examiner had received statewide prominence. Questions abounded about the Trimble case. Dr. Francisco said, "My objective findings show the girl could have been killed between March 20 and March 27, but I cannot say this definitely was the time and our assessment may change from time to time." All the necessary tests had not been completed. Francisco said, "There are many questions yet to be answered."

The medical examiner's revised estimate had made the Nashville news two days earlier, on April 10. As police, the media, and the public considered the implications of this new information, more of Dr. Francisco's findings leaked out. On April 16, *Tennessean* headlines read, "Sperm Traces Found on Marcia's Body?" Lieutenant Cathey refused to comment when asked about the presence of sperm. Reporter George Watson Jr., who quoted "sources" as saying that sex was now considered a motive in the murder, wrote that Cathey and other investigators had "become more secretive about the police investigation." Police had originally indicated that they believed robbery was the motive, because the money from Marcia's cookie sales was missing from the envelope found at the crime scene. Asked about motive, Lieutenant Cathey said, "I feel there has been enough speculation as far as the case is concerned; therefore, I decline to comment."

Several investigators expressed doubts about Dr. Francisco's work on the case, saying they didn't "place much stock" in his findings. The medical examiner had earlier stated there was no evidence of sexual molestation. How long could sperm remain on a dead body? One investigator cited a Harvard medical professor who gave a window of time as three or four hours after death.

By the time the afternoon *Banner* hit Nashville streets, following that morning's *Tennessean* scoop, Lieutenant Cathey had confirmed that Dr. Francisco had found "traces of human sperm on the girl's body" but did not find evidence of "penetration."

Cathey got in his jab, saying that information leaked in recent days had hindered work on the case, but he emphasized that police were not changing course.

The focus remained the boys in the neighborhood.

Ten-year-old March Egerton, who helped Marcia deliver Girl Scout cookies the afternoon before her disappearance, was a target of police suspicion from the beginning. Investigators believed he was the smaller of the two individuals whom Marie Maxwell saw with Marcia at about 5:30 P.M. in Mrs. Howard's driveway, and as time went on, they became convinced he was withholding important information.

Police first spoke with him the night Marcia disappeared. March told authorities that he had been out with Marcia from about 4:30 to 5:00, delivering cookies. Later he and Chuck were "shooting baskets" when the grandmother arrived. Marcia came outside and put four boxes of cookies in her grandmother's car, then went back in and came out with her "big cookie box," March told police. She said she'd be back to play HORSE and then walked across the Rolfes' yard toward Mrs. Maxwell's. That was the last time he saw her.

March's mother, Ann Egerton, was questioned by the FBI the next day. On the previous evening at about 5:15, she had left home in her blue Volkswagen to pick up her older son, Brooks, at the Hillsboro YMCA and get some dinner from McDonald's. She saw March playing basketball with Chuck Trimble at that time, and she called her son over to the car to ask what he wanted from McDonald's. Mrs. Egerton returned home between 5:30 and 5:45. March was still playing ball with Chuck. At 6:00 or shortly thereafter, March came home. Mrs. Egerton said about 6:30 he went out, telling her he was going to "run up his appetite." He ran down to the street and back. She did not know why.

When asked where he was after he played HORSE with Chuck, March said he went "somewhere." Asked why he went out at 6:30, he said he "was looking for something" and he thought he saw "Chuck or somebody from his house" outside.

At 8:30—about the time the search for Marcia was gearing up—March said he thought he saw a shadow from his window.

Later that night, Faye Seals pulled into the Egertons' driveway, asking to borrow a flashlight for the search. She told investigators she saw March sitting at the picture window, staring at the Trimble house.

Suspicious behavior for a ten-year-old boy whose friend had simply vanished.

Officers Shirley Davis and Judy Bawcum interviewed March Egerton nearly two weeks later, on March 9. His father, author John Egerton, was present the evening the officers came to their home. March remembered that Chuck told Marcia he'd seen the Maxwell car pull in the driveway; that was when she went inside for her cookie box.

Then came the shocking discovery of Marcia's body on Easter. The day after the funeral, John Egerton spoke with police and told them how upsetting Marcia's death had been for his son. Three days later, on April 5, Officer Arlene Moore and Sergeant Doug Dennis were back at the Egerton house.

Now March was not sure of the time he went out to deliver cookies with Marcia. He was not sure what time his mother left to pick up his brother, but he remembered that while he was playing basketball with Chuck, she'd called him over to the car and asked what he wanted for dinner. Officer Moore's report said, "The best March can remember, Chuck said, 'There is Mrs. Maxwell, she just came home.'" He thought Marie Maxwell came home, and Marcia came out with her cookie box and crossed the street, before his mother left, but he could not be sure.

The officers interviewed March's older brother Brooks Egerton as well. Brooks stated that he did not see Marcia at all that day. He said it was about 5:35 when he and his mother arrived home, and he started playing basketball in his own driveway with Jody Macey, John Thorpe Jr., and Overton Thompson.

Sometime later, John Egerton informed police that he had retained counsel and they would not be allowed to talk to March again. It would be fifteen years before they'd get another chance.

Just two houses up from Mrs. Howard, the Egertons were at a higher elevation than the Trimbles and the Maxwells. Their driveway was visible from the yards down the street. Virginia Trimble had been able to see the boys playing basketball at the Egerton residence, but like so many other neighbors who were outside on the springlike afternoon of February 25, the boys had not seen Marcia in Mrs. Howard's driveway. They had no information about who she might have met there.

One of the boys who played basketball with Brooks Egerton, Overton Thompson, said he arrived at the Egertons' house at about 5:30, before Brooks and his mother returned home. Jody Macey and John Thorpe Jr. were already there. Brooks came home shortly thereafter, and the boys played basketball until 6:10 or 6:15. Overton remembered seeing Chuck Trimble riding his minibike in the Trimbles' front yard. Overton also said he had an old army coat that belonged to his father, similar to the one in the composite drawing, but he wasn't wearing it that day.

Statements from the four boys gave the same general chronology. Jody Macey, the first to arrive at the Egertons' house, said it was about 5:20 when he got there and began to shoot baskets. He saw Mrs. Egerton drive down Copeland and turn on Dorcas. John Thorpe Jr. arrived about five minutes later, and in another five minutes, Overton drove up. The boys told police they had not seen Marcia that day.

Nothing linked any of them to the crime, but they were still subject to repeated interviews both before and after Marcia's body was discovered. Lieutenant Cathey had implied that police were closing in on someone in the neighborhood. By April 17, the *Banner* headlines were more explicit: "Marcia's Killer Believed a Teen."

For a couple of hours Thursday morning, April 17, Dr. Francisco was in Nashville. At police headquarters, he looked at photographs of Marcia's body taken at the crime scene and pictures taken at the morgue. He spoke with two FBI agents in regard to the evidence police had sent to the FBI Lab, including soil samples. Then he visited the Thorpe garage, where he took temperature readings inside and out, in order to determine how the temperature inside the dark garage compared to the outside. His newest estimate, putting Marcia's death at between March 20 and March 27, was based on the hourly temperatures outside in the general area during the time Marcia was missing. The readings obtained on his visit to the garage showed that the inside was somewhat cooler than the outside. An April 19 *Tennessean* article predicted that Dr. Francisco would make yet another revised estimate on the time of Marcia's death. He did.

On April 29, Dr. Francisco released his final autopsy report on Marcia Trimble. The report stated, "The time of death is at or about the time of her disappearance. The time of death is probably within a few hours of 1730 on February 25, 1975." The medical examiner had based his latest—and now official—estimate on several conditions present in Marcia's body: a fragment of pear in her stomach, consistent with a statement by Virginia Trimble that there was always fruit in the house; livor mortis, consistent with the position of the body when it was found; the general cleanliness of the clothes, suggesting she had not survived long after she disappeared; and the state of early decomposition due to the cold temperatures during the thirty-three-day period she was missing. Dr. Francisco came to the last conclusion after discovering the differences between the "environmental temperature recorded at the weather bureau and the environmental temperature present in this garage."

Police were back to the question of how so many who searched the Thorpe garage could've missed the body. But the final estimate of time of death left the door open to pursue the theory that the killer was one of the boys in the neighborhood. The teen who had aroused police suspicions the night Marcia disappeared remained at the top of the suspect list.

Investigators believed Jeffrey Womack was the taller of the two individuals Mrs. Maxwell saw with Marcia in Mrs. Howard's driveway. They believed he was Marcia's killer.

* * *

About a mile from Copeland Drive, on Lindawood Drive, another basketball game had been in progress on the afternoon of February 25, 1975. The four boys involved in the game were not immediately questioned by police; Lindawood Drive was in an adjacent neighborhood, not the main focus of investigators. But the boys were drawn into the investigation when Jeffrey Womack said he'd been playing basketball with one of them that afternoon.

After Detective Jacobs, Sergeant Jackson, and Sergeant Nickens questioned Jeffrey the night Marcia Trimble disappeared, Thomas and Christine Womack retained attorney John Hollins to represent their son. Jeffrey passed a private polygraph test as well as a second lie detector test administered at police headquarters. He was not questioned again until the case became a homicide. Sergeant Doug Dennis and Officer Arlene Moore visited the Womack home a few days after Marcia's funeral and wrote in their report, "Jeffrey and his mother and brother Jonathan were very receptive. They showed interest and concern in finding the murderer. They appeared honest in their answers."

Three weeks went by as police questioned other boys in the neighborhood. Meanwhile, many interviews with residents were directed toward gathering information about Jeffrey Womack. Amy Norvell, who worked with Jeffrey at Peggy Morgan's day care and had gone with him to McDonald's on February 25, was questioned first on February 26 and again on March 19. FBI agents conducted both interviews, focusing primarily on Womack's whereabouts the afternoon Marcia disappeared. By the time Amy was re-interviewed in April, she'd had a falling-out with Peggy and was no longer working in the day care—and she had plenty to tell. According to Amy, thirty-two-year-old Peggy Morgan and fifteen-year-old Jeffrey Womack were having an affair.

Police had noted that Peggy was oddly protective of Jeffrey when she appeared with his mother at the Trimbles' house the night he was first questioned. When she was interviewed on March 18, she said she could "vouch for every minute of Jeffrey's time" on the afternoon Marcia disappeared. She recalled the afternoon for Officers Davis and Bawcum. At 3:00 P.M. she ran the Overbrook "hook-up"—the term Nashvillians used for carpooling children to and from school—before returning home at about 3:25. She said that Jeffrey, who was at her house while she was gone, left with Amy to go to McDonald's at about 5:15, and they'd returned at 5:45 or 5:50. In this interview she did not mention that Jeffrey went to his house around 4:30 and was gone forty to forty-five minutes.

Sergeant Dennis and Officer Moore questioned Peggy again on April 2, and she passed a polygraph on April 9. But as police learned more about her and Jeffrey, they were convinced she could provide additional information vital to the case. Maybe Jeffrey had even confessed to her.

During the April 9 interview, Peggy stated that the night before Marcia's body was found, the dogs in the neighborhood were all "going crazy." Police followed up with other neighbors who said the same thing. Some investigators believed that the reason for the dogs' barking was that perhaps the killer had brought the body to the garage the night before Easter. That theory would continue to float around among those who had serious doubts about Marcia's body having been in the Thorpe garage for the entire thirty-three days despite the medical examiner's conclusive autopsy report that Marcia was killed shortly after she disappeared.

On April 29, Detective John Hutchinson and Officer Arlene Moore went to Peggy Morgan's home to speak with her again. Jeffrey opened the door. Peggy was out picking up children from school, he said. He invited them inside to wait. They had not counted on this opportunity, but in the few minutes before Peggy arrived, Jeffrey made a statement that conflicted with the timetable investigators had put together on him for the afternoon Marcia disappeared. From 4:00 until about 5:10 that day, he said, he'd been playing basketball in his backyard with a friend named Doug Green.

Two days later, Officer Moore and Detective Bill Robeck conducted an interview with Doug Green that turned up the information about the basketball game in a neighborhood located a mile away from Copeland Drive. Doug stated that he'd gone to a friend's house on Lindawood at about 4:00 on February 25, and the two of them then went to another friend's house on the same street. They began playing basketball.

Jeffrey Womack was not with them at all that afternoon.

Doug Green later stated that Jeffrey asked him if he didn't remember they had played basketball that day. Doug said no. Jeffrey told him the cops were "trying to can him" and asked Doug to just tell police he didn't remember. But Doug *did* remember the basketball game and the boys who were part of it. He could not give Jeffrey an alibi for the 4:00–5:10 window of time.

Now police were even more focused on Womack. It appeared he had lied about being with Doug Green; it was likely they could poke holes in other parts of his story.

The Marcia Trimble murder investigation was one of the most puzzling cases Nashville Police had ever encountered, and it was a case the public would not let go. The media needed something new to report every day.

The lack of communication among the "cowboys" involved in the case also hampered the process. An April 19 *Banner* article reported that the FBI was upset with Nashville Police. Lieutenant Tom Cathey continued to say police were waiting for results from the FBI Lab. Special Agent Ted Gunderson, in charge of the Memphis division of the FBI (which included Nashville), stated that results had been furnished on several dates, on all tests except the soil samples. Gunderson also said that the FBI had spent two thousand man-hours on the case.

Around the courthouse and city hall, others expressed concern about the direction of the investigation. On April 22, a *Tennessean* report indicated Tom Shriver, district attorney, had complained that investigators were not communicating with his office about the Trimble case. He named Lieutenant Cathey, specifically. The article went on to say, "A great deal of effort has been exerted to break the case. Nothing has succeeded. One reason may be that a lack of cooperation and an absence of communication have existed among some investigators."

Another issue, besides friction between the various authorities, was the sheer magnitude of the investigation, which kept producing more questions than answers.

On April 5, Detective Tommy Jacobs noted, "We found that Marcia was not as introverted as we were led to believe by her parents. Marcia had participated in child games that involved pulling down of pants by both girls and boys."

He went on to report that "her brother—Chuck—and March Egerton and most of the neighborhood kids participated in these games." The information came initially from Marcia's twelve-year-old cousin, Rhonda Allen. Rhonda took a polygraph on April 6. Sergeant Hackett, who administered the lie detector test, said she was truthful.

On April 24, Officer Moore and Sergeant Dennis picked Rhonda up from Washington Junior High School, with her mother's permission, and Rhonda gave more details of the "sex games." March had a porno book that he got out of a garbage can, she said, and they would look at the pictures and try to do what they saw. Asked if anyone was rough in this game, she said no. It was mostly touching "privates" against each other. They played these games in the clubhouse behind the Trimbles' house, in Marcia's room, in the tree house behind the Egertons' house, and in the woods.

The police recruits who joined the search for Marcia on February 28 had found a book outside the Thorpes' garage that fit the description of the "porno book" Rhonda described. About the size of a *TV Guide*, it had pictures of seminude women and cartoons, and it showed various "sex positions," according to the recruits. They took it on the bus back to the Police Academy, looked at it, and threw it away.

Rhonda gave names of others involved in the "sex games," as police referred to the experimentation activities. One of the other children interviewed called the game "Touch and Dare." Another child police questioned said that they frequently played in the woods, that once they'd found a pack of cigarettes, and they all smoked. Repeated questioning by police resulted in children implicating other children. The childhood indiscretions shocked parents and made them suspicious of their children's friends, and the friends' families.

The residents on and around Copeland Drive would never get over Marcia Trimble's death. Throughout the laborious and emotional weeks of the search, neighbors rallied in support of the Trimble family, working with the authorities in hopes of finding Marcia. After her body was discovered, the families continued to cooperate with police in hopes that her killer would be found. Now parents' attitudes began to change as they witnessed their children being viewed as suspects and subjected to relentless interviews. Now the atmosphere of anxiety was charged with anger, too—anger toward police for the investigation that created even more upheaval in their neighborhood.

Two years after Marcia's murder, *Nashville!* magazine published an article by Jacque Srouji entitled "Who Killed Marcia Trimble and Other Unsolved Murders." Srouji reported, "A special government investigator called in on the case when it first opened immediately detected a heavy presence of drugs in the general area. Drugs like cocaine and heroin." Srouji referred to a story Marcia had written, a few days before she disappeared, about a little girl finding a treasure in a "metal box" in the woods. A report by Officer Arlene Moore gave further details. The girl in Marcia's story saw some men burying the treasure, and after they left, she dug it up and put it under her bed. She saw the men looking in the window at her, so she put it in her closet. Later, she discovered it was gone. She was afraid to tell her parents because she didn't think they would believe her.

Srouji posed the theory that Marcia could have seen a drug dealer burying something in the woods behind the Maxwells' house. If such an activity had taken place, was it not possible a drug dealer was back on the afternoon that Marcia walked in the edge of the wooded area toward the Thorpes' house?

By the end of April, police had received the official results of evidence submitted to the medical examiner and FBI. Dr. Francisco's report put time of death at about the time Marcia disappeared. The report from the FBI Serology Unit indicated no blood or semen on her panties, no blood on her jeans, but semen *was* identified on the jeans, and both semen and blood were found on her blouse. The lab could not get a blood group (A, B, AB, or O) from the samples. In a *Banner* interview, Dr. Francisco said that theoretically, if the semen had been properly preserved and was in sufficient quantity, analysis of the semen could "determine the blood grouping the man falls under." Homicide sergeant Hackett explained that semen analysis was a very complicated test.

The FBI Soil Lab also reported a match between the samples from the soles of Marcia's boots and samples from the floor of the garage, indicating that Marcia could have walked around in the shed. Nothing in the lab reports pointed to a particular suspect, though police believed the Soil Lab results supported the idea that Marcia knew her killer. She was not carried or dragged into the outbuilding.

At this point, police had expected to be ready to make an arrest; Lieutenant Cathey implied as much in his briefings with reporters. Charles and Virginia Trimble had remained in close contact with investigators. When they appeared at police headquarters to be briefed by detectives, hopes rose that an arrest was forthcoming. But it didn't happen. Chief Joe Casey admitted there was "no new information" in the investigation. With the media and the public exerting intense pressure to solve the case, police had little to offer but their original theory: The killer was a teenage boy from the neighborhood.

18

A Case Against Jeffrey Womack

Dogged investigators pursued the Marcia Trimble case relentlessly—obsessively, some would say. Phone calls continued to flood the police department. Calls from McMinnville, Pulaski, Woodbury, Waverly, Memphis, and as far away as New York and Canada brought new potential leads. Police were compelled to check out each story. The tips would continue for the next two years.

Chief Joe Casey, looking somber, met with *Banner* reporters on April 29, 1975, to comment on the case. He said, "I don't know how close we are to solving it, because we don't have one prime suspect."

Chief Casey's statement was true from an official standpoint. But detectives leading the Trimble investigation had nevertheless considered Jeffrey Womack a suspect since the night he'd appeared at the Trimbles' house with "FUCK YOU" written on his shoes. FBI agent Richard Knudsen wrote in a Teletype the next day, "Metro PD has developed as possible suspect Jeffrey Womack." They just didn't have sufficient evidence to make an arrest.

The interview with Amy Norvell on the morning of April 29, conducted by Detective Hutchinson and Officer Moore, offered insight into the strange relationship between Peggy Morgan and Jeffrey Womack. Amy said Jeffrey had confided in her about his affair with Peggy, and she had seen Peggy and Jeffrey lying on the couch together and, at other times, holding hands. Jeffrey's mother Christine Womack knew about the affair, according to Amy, but she couldn't stop her son and just gave up. Amy also stated that Jeffrey had kissed one of the nine-year-old girls who came to Peggy's house; the girl's mother had taken her out of the day care. Amy also told police that on February 25, Peggy gave *her*, not Jeffrey, the money to pay for hamburgers at McDonald's.

The investigators had lucked into a conversation with Jeffrey Womack when they went to Peggy Morgan's house later on Tuesday, April 29. It was on this occasion that he said he'd played basketball with Doug Green the afternoon Marcia disappeared, a story that proved untrue. When Peggy arrived with children from school on that April afternoon, Detective Hutchinson and Officer Moore asked her to come to CID for questioning. She did, and Sergeant Nickens and Sergeant R. C. Jackson were present for the interview.

Peggy said she'd picked Jeffrey up at school on February 25 and took him to her house. He watched the *Mickey Mouse Show* and then left at about 4:30 or 4:40 to go home, taking her three-year-old son Wallace with him. Peggy said he was gone about thirty minutes, returning to her house at about 5:10.

While he was gone, Wallace came out of the house by himself. Jeffrey's mother, who was across the street at Anita Collins's house getting her hair fixed, saw Wallace and took him inside the Collins's house with her until she was finished. Then she gave him some raisins and sent him home to Peggy's. Jeffrey arrived at Peggy's house soon after that.

Hutchinson and Moore commented on Jeffrey's careless-
ness in letting a three-year-old go outside by himself. They
reported that Peggy was "defensive of Jeffrey." She further
stated that when she and Amy went bowling at 6:00 that
evening, they left Jeffrey at her house with nine children:
Peggy's three, Amy's two, and four other children in the day
care.

Peggy denied that she and Jeffrey were having a sexual
relationship. She said she knew he had told Doug Green and
Amy Norvell that he'd slept with her, but she attributed his
statement to "acting like any normal young man wanting to
top what the other boys said they did." Investigators reported,
"She did not seem too upset about Jeffrey saying this." She
said Jeffrey and his brother Jonathan had both spent the night
at her house before. They ran a paper route for a while, and
she helped them.

When asked about the nine-year-old girl whose mother
had pulled her out of the day care because she said Jeffrey
kissed her, Peggy defended Jeffrey. She said the little girl "had
chased after him."

Peggy had already been interviewed twice, besides the
time she passed a polygraph on April 9. Hutchinson and
Moore asked her if she would take another polygraph, and she
said she would.

The next day, the investigators questioned Christine Womack. She said she saw Marcia sitting in front of her house
at about 4:45 on the afternoon of February 25. Christine left
Anita Collins's house at about 5:00 and went home. Jeffrey
was there. He left soon after that to return to Peggy Morgan's.
She stated that she didn't give Jeffrey an allowance; in fact, he
paid her $5 a week for board and bought his own clothes. Both
Christine and Peggy knew about the condoms Jeffrey had in
his pocket. He had told both of them he'd bought the condoms
to sell at school, conflicting with the statement he initially
gave to police, that he'd bought the condoms for a concert at

the Municipal Auditorium. Police were left to wonder if either statement was true.

If Jeffrey left home a few minutes after 5:00—as his mother stated—and arrived at Peggy's by 5:10—as Peggy stated—and left for McDonald's at 5:15—as Amy stated, he had no window of time to meet Marcia in Mrs. Howard's driveway and lure her to the Thorpes' garage. But somehow, investigators believed, he did just that.

Authorities interviewed Marie Maxwell repeatedly during the spring—and over the months and years to come. She would one day testify that she was interviewed approximately twenty times, and subjected to several sessions of hypnosis as she tried to recall details about the three people she saw in Mrs. Howard's driveway. Marie was the last person known to have seen Marcia alive, if, indeed, Marcia was one of those individuals. Police were convinced Marie Maxwell saw Marcia's killer. Her estimate that she arrived home at about 5:30 coincided with the statement given by Sally Ray, who got off the bus at Hobbs and Copeland at 5:20 or 5:25. As she walked down Copeland to her house on Dorcas, a seven- to ten-minute walk, she saw Marie Maxwell, and Marie saw her.

In one of her statements, Marie said that about seven weeks after Marcia disappeared, Jeffrey Womack, Peggy Morgan, and some of the children from Peggy's day care came to her door, collecting money for a charity. Marie told police she had a "gut feeling" Jeffrey was the taller person in Mrs. Howard's driveway. She had not known what Jeffrey Womack looked like before that day. They made eye contact, and she thought he knew what she was thinking. The papers had reported that she was a witness. Marie was afraid, but she wondered why he would come to her house if he knew she could recognize him.

Marie Maxwell's description, under hypnosis, led to the composite drawing that police circulated prior to the discovery of Marcia's body. Now that she had also pointed a finger at Jeffrey Womack, police felt closer to proving that he was in Mrs. Howard's driveway with Marcia, adding fuel to the theory that Marcia went to the Thorpes' garage with him, where he killed her. The timeline didn't work yet, and the fifteen-year-old had passed two polygraphs, but as spring slid into a languid Nashville summer, investigators were even more locked in on Jeffrey Womack as their prime suspect.

The Thorpes emptied the garage and made plans to tear it down. Maybe razing the structure would remove some of the horrible memories that haunted their family and the other neighborhood families. Detective Jacobs met with Mrs. Thorpe to be sure police needed no further evidence from the garage and to give the go-ahead for the demolition.

As she was cleaning out the garage in May, Mrs. Thorpe found a pair of prescription sunglasses and gave them to police. The sunglasses became something of a mystery. At last, nearly six weeks later, the owner came forward. Virginia Trimble said the sunglasses were hers. The Trimbles had been vacationing in Florida in June during the time police tried to find the owner of the sunglasses. It was not the vacation they had been planning before Marcia's death, but it was a distraction from the investigation, a much-needed break. The Trimbles and police had maintained almost daily contact since February 25.

Detective Diane Vaughn, now assigned to the Trimble investigation, talked to Mrs. Trimble about the sunglasses. Her explanation was that some weeks after Marcia's body was found, Mrs. Trimble asked Sergeant Dennis and Officer Moore to take her to the Thorpes' garage, and she had accidentally left her sunglasses behind. The explanation satisfied police, but like so many of the details in this baffling case, the sunglasses would come up again.

* * *

Each month found investigators with fewer new leads to track. Calls still came in, and police checked out men who had made incriminating statements or who looked like the composite drawing, but without any new information of value. Some of the subjects implicated were men with mental disabilities. People called saying they'd had visions from the Lord about certain individuals. Some of the members of the Lord's Chapel cast suspicion on each other. Police set up surveillance on one man from the neighborhood, but his clandestine activities turned out to be directed at meeting a young woman who was not his wife. The fact that her parents were the man's neighbors proved to have no bearing on the murder case.

The media's coverage of the investigation fell off, and without the case in the headlines each day, dinnertime conversations turned to topics other than Marcia Trimble. But the murder and the mystery surrounding the murder were never too far from the minds of Nashvillians, as fall brought a nip in the air, relief from the humid summer.

Lieutenant Cathey, commander of the Homicide Division, had under his supervision fifteen Homicide detectives and ten Armed Robbery detectives, with two sergeants for Homicide and two sergeants for Armed Robbery. Detective Tommy Jacobs was his lead detective on the Trimble case. Jacobs had earned distinction on the force in 1971 when he was in plain clothes, investigating a series of rape and molestation cases in the Green Hills area. During that case, he was shot three times—in the shoulder, spine, and face—and left for dead. Unable to speak, he wrote information for Tom Cathey—at that time a sergeant—that led to the capture of his assailant. In 1973, Jacobs and Detective Sherman Nickens were the first Metro Homicide detectives on the scene when Grand Ole Opry performer "Stringbean" Akeman and his wife were murdered. Lieutenant Cathey was commander of the Homicide section by that time. His detectives' work led to the arrest and conviction of two of Stringbean's cousins, who committed the murders trying to find money in the Akemans' house.

Detective Jacobs was one of the first detectives on the scene at the Trimble house the night Marcia was reported missing. Along with Detective Sergeant Jackson and Sergeant Nickens, he questioned Jeffrey Womack that first night. Jacobs and Jackson from Homicide stayed with the search and then remained on the case when it became a homicide. Detective Jacobs worked under Lieutenant Cathey's supervision until Cathey was transferred from Homicide in February 1976, a year after Marcia first disappeared, when the case seemed to be going nowhere. Sergeant Nickens stepped into Cathey's position.

The winter of 1975–1976 was a barren time for detectives working the Trimble murder. Calls continued to come in, but no leads brought investigators closer to solving the case. It was no secret that Nashville Police had lost credibility with the public. Detective Jacobs, still lead detective, worked with Sergeant Jackson and Detective Mike Erwin to reorganize and review the Trimble file and to sort and inventory all the Trimble evidence from the Metro Police property room.

Sergeant Jackson spoke with Dr. Francisco in Memphis. The state medical examiner agreed to review his files. On March 11, 1976, Detective Jacobs and Sergeant Jackson met the medical examiner at the Nashville airport. Dr. Francisco stood by his autopsy report, reiterating that Marcia had died shortly after she disappeared, that she'd died in the garage and remained there for the entire thirty-three days. He explained that the reason Marcia's dogs didn't find the body was that her scent changed after she died.

Detective Jacobs continued to focus on Jeffrey Womack. In March 1976, a year after the murder, Jacobs outlined his theory of the case. He began with his opinion that Marcia "knew the killer" and followed by saying that she "went to garage voluntarily, was killed Feb. 25 (5:30 p.m.-6:00 p.m.), had a sex act in the garage." The list continued with "killer is male, killer not adult, killer was neighborhood kid, no car involved."

He listed twelve suspects, most of them boys from the neighborhood. Jeffrey Womack was number one.

By spring of 1976 Copeland Drive, with its new green manicured yards, was not visibly different, but investigators knew the damage the neighborhood had suffered. Virginia Trimble, still willing to cooperate in any way, was hypnotized again in the hope that she would recall something that would help find Marcia's killer. Investigators re-interviewed several neighbors, including Marie Thorpe. Looking at photos of the corner where Marcia's body was discovered, Mrs. Thorpe said she was "positive" Marcia could not have been there the whole time.

On March 24, Detective Erwin and Sergeant Jackson followed Jeffrey Womack to Copeland Drive. After Jeffrey pulled into his driveway, Detective Erwin introduced himself and said, "I'm sorry for any treatment by the police that you've felt was unfair."

It was a good way to start. It diffused the tension. Jeffrey was willing to talk.

"Can you tell me about the penny wrappers you had in your pocket, that night at the Trimble house when you talked to police?" Erwin asked.

"I roll pennies and cash them in," Jeffrey said. "I take them to the Scooter Market."

"You had a five-dollar bill, too," Erwin said.

"Yeah. Peggy Morgan gave it to me," Jeffrey said.

Detective Erwin asked about the child Jeffrey was supposed to be watching that afternoon, three-year-old Wallace.

"He was wearing a red cowboy suit," Jeffrey said. "Yeah, he got out of Peggy's house, and I had to catch him."

Detective Erwin concluded in his report, "Jeffrey either lies when there is no apparent motive or he actually did have penny wrappers (as did Marcia when she was killed) as Sergeant Jackson remembers."

During the initial investigation, a woman from the neighborhood had come forward to tell police that Jeffrey Womack had sexually abused her little boy. In April 1976, police reinterviewed her and her son. The child, who was about Marcia's age, told investigators about two incidents that took place when he was around six years old, in 1972 or 1973. The boy said he'd been in the woods with Jeffrey, and Jeffrey said he'd "hurt him" if he told anyone what happened. The boy kept the secret until Marcia disappeared. At that time, he was afraid, and he told his mother what he recalled Jeffrey had done.

In spite of accusations against Jeffrey, he was never charged by the police with sexual abuse. However, police continued to gather information they believed presented him as a good candidate for the murder, and Jeffrey himself made statements at Hillsboro High School that added support to the case against him.

In the fall of 1976, DA Tom Shriver contacted investigators. He had information that sounded like an admission of guilt. Detective Erwin was one of the investigators who followed up. He talked to a boy named David who referred to a conversation he'd overheard in gym class. According to David, Jeffrey told another boy he had "fucked" Marcia and then was embarrassed because of her age, so he suffocated her.

Another boy named Eric stated that he'd overheard Jeffrey talking in gym class to someone who asked, "Why did you kill her?"

Eric said Jeffrey answered, "Oh, you know how it is."

A third boy also stated that in gym class he heard Jeffrey say, "Yeah, I did it."

Investigators spoke to another young man named Billy who had worked with Womack at the Afterthought Restaurant. Billy had moved to Pensacola, Florida, with his family. He told Jacobs and Erwin that he overheard Jeffrey talking to a dishwasher at the Afterthought. The dishwasher asked him if he'd killed Marcia, and Jeffrey replied, "Of course I did." Billy said Jeffrey admitted to the murder on several other occasions, but he couldn't remember exactly when.

Detective Jacobs later told a reporter, "What are we supposed to do? Ignore a confession?"

The investigators also re-interviewed Peggy Morgan, Amy Norvell, and Marie Maxwell in the fall of 1976. Officer Arlene Moore spoke with Marie Maxwell. This time Marie was less descriptive of the two individuals she had seen in Mrs. Howard's driveway. The taller person was facing her, she said. According to the officer's report, "It was more like a silhouette and she never looked at the face of the taller person."

19

The Jolly Ox

Among the faux-English steak houses that flourished in Nashville in the 1970s, the Jolly Ox, located on Cleghorn, behind the Green Hills mall, was a favorite. With its dark wood and stone exterior, the restaurant featured a dimly lit interior, Tudor beams, bricks with thick, jagged, mortar joints, and stained glass windows. The Jolly Ox was known for its steak and lobster tails, and its lounge was a popular watering hole. It was also known for its music. In any lounge in Nashville, from the upscale hotels to the dives on Lower Broadway, it was possible to hear incredible music by up-and-coming artists. Some who made it in the music business, such as Marshall Chapman, started out at the Jolly Ox as a waitress/entertainer. In her book *Goodbye, Little Rock and Roller*, Chapman wrote that the Jolly Ox was a kind of "songwriter heaven." It was not unusual to find Nashville songwriters such as Waylon Jennings, Jessi Colter, and Harlan Howard sitting in on a set. Sometimes, one of them would take the stage and sing with the band.

In December 1976, Jeffrey Womack was working in the kitchen at the Jolly Ox. As they had done for nearly two years, investigators continued to keep tabs on Jeffrey's movements, and they decided to send in an undercover officer to pose as a co-worker.

Terry McElroy was a rugged, street-smart thirty-year-old detective who had been on the police force since 1969. A cop who could project a tough-guy image, McElroy was placed on special assignment as a dishwasher at the Jolly Ox, hoping to gain Jeffrey Womack's confidence. He told the other employees he was an ex-con from Alabama.

The first day McElroy saw Jeffrey at work, the seventeen-year-old was wearing a long green army field jacket with a hood. McElroy struck up a conversation. Jeffrey became friendly when he heard McElroy say he was just out of prison.

Over the next few days, the two chatted several times.

"Why were you in prison?" Jeffrey wanted to know.

"I killed a guy in a fight," McElroy said.

Jeffrey had more questions. *What happened? Why'd you kill him? How'd you do it?*

McElroy spun his story.

The kitchen manager, Chris Richards, and Jeffrey were buddies. They went out together after work, partied and drank beer, and during the next few weeks, McElroy joined them. They usually took Jeffrey's or Richards's car and drove around in the south part of Davidson County and Williamson County.

McElroy reported, "The subject was known to me after a few days to be a heavy drinker and user of narcotics (grass and speed)." Jeffrey complained about his parents who "could not or would not attempt to control his actions," according to McElroy, meaning the parents couldn't make him go to school or keep him from smoking grass.

According to McElroy, some of the employees who had worked with Jeffrey for a while said that one day he was so stoned, he stuck his hand in a pot of boiling water. They had to lock him in the office so he wouldn't keep hurting himself.

McElroy told reporter Matt Pulle in 2001 that Jeffrey and Chris Richards "were always a little leery of me," maybe because of the age gap. Teenage Jeffrey wasn't into sharing confidences with a thirty-year-old.

McElroy talked to Detective Tommy Jacobs, and the detectives came up with a plan. One evening Detective Jacobs walked into the Jolly Ox lounge, where someone was belting out a Top 40 tune. As the detective strolled into the lounge, McElroy noted that Jeffrey "became very upset and nervous."

"You know who that guy is? He's a homicide detective," Jeffrey said.

McElroy pretended he didn't believe it.

Jeffrey insisted, "I know who he is. He tried to pin a murder rap on me for a little girl in my neighborhood that was killed. My lawyer made a fool of them all."

Things were going in the right direction, McElroy thought, when Chris Richards came in with two employees. The five of them moved to the back of the lounge.

Jeffrey was still fixated on Detective Jacobs. He pointed out the detective to the others and told them Jacobs had been watching him.

"Why?" the employees wanted to know.

Richards said, "The police are harassing Jeffrey because they found a girl dead in his neighborhood."

Jeffrey took up the story of Marcia's death. "They found her in a garage, wrapped up in a tarp."

McElroy reported that the conversation that night was the only time Marcia Trimble's murder was ever discussed while he was on the assignment. But he thought about the word "tarp." He had never heard it used in regard to the crime scene.

Further checking by Detective Jacobs revealed that one of the objects recovered near Marcia Trimble's body was a shower curtain with metal eyelets. Upon closer inspection, he saw that it had been used as a drop cloth. In the weeks that followed, the FBI assisted in testing the paint scrapings, comparing them with the samples police had collected from homes in the Trimbles' neighborhood. The paint scrapings from the shower curtain matched paint samples from Peggy Morgan's home. Jeffrey Womack worked in Peggy's day care and spent lots of time at her house, so he could have had access to the "tarp." However, the paint also matched other homes in the neighborhood. It had been used by a contractor who'd painted several of the houses.

Detective Terry McElroy finished his undercover assignment on January 2, 1977. In his report, he stated, "It is my opinion after being on assignment and closely associated with Jeffrey Womack that he should be considered a prime suspect in this case," and he listed five reasons. The first was Jeffrey's attitude toward the female employees. Second was his "heavy use of drugs and liquor." The third reason was "his unstable mental condition regarding his attitude, life, and wanting to stay 'high' all the time." McElroy listed as his fourth reason that Jeffrey had become "paranoid and nervous at the appearance of Detective Jacobs," and finally, he listed Jeffrey's mention of the "tarp."

McElroy concluded his report by stating his general opinion of Jeffrey Womack, that he was "below average intelligence" and "has no desire to better himself." He pointed to the fact that Jeffrey was not attending school and "the only thing he lives for is to get high." McElroy believed Jeffrey might have told Chris Richards "the facts in the murder of Marcia," but his undercover assignment failed to get the proof of Jeffrey's guilt that police had hoped to obtain.

20

Case Cleared by Arrest

For four and a half years, investigators built their case against Jeffrey Womack. It was not a case constructed brick by brick; it was put together pebble by pebble. Jeffrey Womack had passed polygraphs, and he'd left no physical evidence at the scene. But all the time the public had accused police of making no progress on the case, investigators had been collecting a mountain of circumstantial evidence. In the summer of 1979, police felt that they were ready to make an arrest.

The district attorney's office was ready, due in large part to the efforts of ADA Pat Apel. Apel was a bright young prosecutor, a graduate of Princeton University and Vanderbilt Law School, who had spent three years in the U.S. Army Legal Corps before joining Metro Nashville's legal department in the fall of 1976. In April 1977, he went to work for DA Tom Shriver. The Trimble case fell into his lap in March 1979, and in the short time frame between March and August, he and his team sorted through boxes of evidence and stacks of files, working hard to push the case toward a conclusion. A case like this could make a young prosecutor's career—or break it.

Jeffrey Womack, even knowing he was a suspect, had made statements that were coming back to bite him. Besides his comments to other students at Hillsboro High School, he had told Chris Richards from the Jolly Ox that he killed Marcia. While working as a dishwasher at another restaurant, the Afterthought, he had also told two people that he killed Marcia. According to one of the witnesses, Jeffrey said he'd meant to trick Marcia out of her cookie money so he could buy marijuana and stated he had beaten the polygraph. The witness believed Jeffrey was serious. The other witness thought Jeffrey was making a "sick joke."

Police had questioned Amy Norvell Watson, who'd worked with Jeffrey at Peggy Morgan's day care, several times over the period of years, and each interview added fuel to their case. She said that when Jeffrey returned from his house at about 5:10 on the afternoon Marcia disappeared, he was "out of breath." Later she said he had come to Peggy's house, sweating, looking like he'd been running. In October 1976, she had told Officer Arlene Moore that Jeffrey was always asking reporter George Watson "if they had found Marcia" in the weeks after Marcia disappeared. Amy, now married to George Watson, said Jeffrey also told George, "You'll never find her alive."

Kimberly Patterson, another part-time worker at Peggy Morgan's day care when Marcia disappeared, said she and her mother went to Peggy's after they heard on the ten o'clock news that Marcia was missing. She saw Jeffrey come out of the Trimble house, crying. Sometime after Marcia was found, he told Kimberly that he had searched the Thorpes' garage that night, and the plastic swimming pool was hanging on the wall.

Kimberly told police that about two weeks before Marcia

disappeared, she and Amy were spending the night with Peggy, and about 2:30 A.M., she heard Peggy screaming. She went to the doorway and saw Jeffrey pinning Peggy to the wall. He was yelling, "I deserve a reason why!" Kimberly woke Amy. She took Peggy into the kitchen while Amy talked to Jeffrey. Peggy kept saying, "I don't understand what he wants. I just don't know." Later, Jeffrey told Kimberly, "She's not cutting me off. She needs it."

Kimberly reported that in March 1979, she was eating at Houston's, where Womack was then employed. She told him, "If they get you, you should make sure Peggy goes down with you." He said, "No, I can't do that to Peggy."

The police's timeline for Jeffrey Womack's activities had proven an impossible obstacle to overcome in showing he had an opportunity to kill Marcia. But in the interview with Kimberly in March 1979, police learned Peggy had two clocks, one that ran ten to fifteen minutes fast, and one that ran ten to fifteen minutes slow.

This was a break for investigators. Finally, they could punch a hole in Peggy's statement about the time Womack arrived at her house. Without an accurate clock, how could she possibly know exactly what time it was?

Sometime before 1979, Peggy Morgan had submitted to a lie detector test by a private polygrapher. She finally admitted that she and Jeffrey were involved in a sexual relationship when he worked for her. She further stated that at least once, he had choked her when they were arguing.

At long last, the case was coming together.

ADA Apel had worked with police, deciding exactly how and when they should make the arrest. The time was set for 2:00 A.M. on Tuesday, August 28. The public wanted police to make an arrest; this one would be a dramatic event. As a further element of the cloak-and-dagger operation, officers woke Juvenile Court judge Richard Jenkins at about 1:00 A.M. to sign the arrest warrant.

But when asked why the arrest was made in the middle of the night, Apel said they were afraid Jeffrey might attempt suicide if he knew he was about to be arrested. Apel also told reporters, "We started trying to locate him Monday morning but we didn't make real good visual contact until about 12:30 a.m. Tuesday. Earlier, on Monday night, detective Tommy Jacobs spotted him but lost him a short time later."

Jeffrey Womack, who turned twenty on August 27, 1979, the day before the arrest, was staying with his brother at the Parkside Apartments, not far from the Vanderbilt campus. Though Apel and police intended to surprise their suspect, when four police cars arrived at the apartment building, the seven arresting officers were the ones surprised. Jeffrey was waiting for them.

John Hollins, who, along with Ed Yarbrough, represented Jeffrey Womack, later said, "We had a mole in the police department. We knew what they were doing as soon as they were doing it." Matt Pulle, in his 2001 article for the *Nashville Scene*, wrote, "In one of the case's many intriguing subplots, a source in the police department, convinced that authorities were unfairly targeting the young suspect, took it upon herself to leak their case to the suspect's lawyers."

Jeffrey met the police at the door. He was barefoot, wearing cutoff jeans and a T-shirt from Spats, a popular restaurant in the Vanderbilt area. His dark hair was nearly shoulder length, and he had a mustache. He cooperated with the arresting officers, even told them he'd been expecting them. One of the officers replied, "This is your day of reckoning."

Jeffrey was handcuffed and placed under arrest. Officer Arlene Moore, one of the first officers to arrive at the Trimble home the night Marcia disappeared, read the suspect his rights. Police did not give him time to put on his shoes and socks. He was transported to Juvenile Court because he had been fifteen years old when the murder occurred, and it was yet to be decided whether he would be tried as an adult. He was held in detention until his bond hearing.

Several hours after the arrest, Jeffrey Womack appeared before Judge Jenkins and was charged with first-degree murder. Judge Jenkins set him free on $25,000 bond.

Office Moore prepared her report of the night's activities. Across the page, she wrote, "Case Cleared by Arrest."

21

The Battle in the Courts

The whole city was once again caught up in the Trimble case, much like it had been in 1975. Headlines announced Jeffrey Womack's arrest. News stories proclaimed that he had been charged with Marcia Trimble's murder. Throughout Nashville, the debate was on: Had police finally gotten it right? Would Marcia's killer be brought to justice at last? Or was Jeffrey Womack simply the best suspect police had? Jeffrey's attorney, John Hollins, said, "They went out and tried to hotbox him and get a confession out of him. The public wanted an arrest, and that's what they gave them."

Investigators still would not say definitively whether Marcia's body had been in the Thorpes' garage during the entire thirty-three days. Police insisted that the outbuilding had been searched thoroughly after Marcia's disappearance, by officials and volunteers alike, and the body was not there at the time. Yet if they were clinging to the theory that her body was brought to the garage only a few days prior to its discovery, how could Jeffrey Womack be the killer? He was a teenager, without a car, living with his parents. Where would he have kept the body, prior to moving it? How could he have transported the body from another location to the Thorpes' garage?

Jeffrey Womack's parents and close friends maintained his innocence, and even members of the police force had their doubts. Captain Noble Brymer had administered lie detector tests to Jeffrey Womack. As early as February 28, 1975, just three days after Marcia disappeared, Detective Tommy Jacobs wrote in a report, "Captain Brymer ran Womack on the polygraph and definitely eliminated him as a suspect." In June 1976, police again asked Jeffrey to take a polygraph test. One investigator said that Jeffrey showed "some emotional response" to some of the questions, but not enough to indicate he was lying. According to John Hollins, after the second test, Captain Brymer told Jeffrey Womack's attorney, "John, that boy is telling the truth." In addition to the two lie detector tests administered by Captain Brymer, Jeffrey took three private polygraphs, including one on August 30, 1979, two days after his arrest; all indicated he was truthful when he denied having killed Marcia.

Nevertheless, Sergeant Doug Dennis, one of the arresting officers, was confident they had nabbed the right person. "There was no doubt in my mind the suspect is guilty," he said. His opinion was shared by other investigators who had tracked Jeffrey Womack for four years.

Matt Pulle wrote in his article for the *Scene* that the manner in which Jeffrey Womack's arrest was handled "embodied everything right and wrong about its investigation." Investigators on the case were dedicated to bringing Marcia's killer to justice, and they had worked tirelessly to that end. But had they lost their objectivity? Some suggested the ordeal had become too personal, or, as Pulle put it, that police were "at times unable to handle the case in a professional way."

Even Virginia Trimble was ambivalent about the arrest. The *Tennessean* quoted her as saying, "That boy is not guilty until a jury decides that he is. And I think this community owes it to him to consider him innocent until a jury changes that."

The police department and district attorney's office received harsh criticism for their tactics. John Jay Hooker, a colorful political figure who later became publisher of the *Banner*, had been a Vanderbilt Law School classmate of DA Tom Shriver. Hooker wrote an editorial declaring his disapproval of the arrest "in the middle of night like the Gestapo." Shriver read the editorial and contacted Hooker.

"I think you're right," Shriver said.

On September 10, 1979, shortly after Jeffrey Womack's arrest, ADA Pat Apel resigned from his position, ostensibly after conflicting with Shriver on the Womack matter. For a while, the resignation of the prosecutor overshadowed the case itself. The *Tennessean* reported that Apel's resignation was a response to reports that Shriver was bringing in a former aide, State Inspector General John Rodgers, to take over the Trimble case. By October, Apel had a new job as deputy Metro legal director. Along with DA Shriver, ADA Victor (Torry) Johnson assumed responsibility for the case that once again held Nashville in its grip.

Juvenile Court judge Richard Jenkins set October 9, 1979, for the hearing to determine whether Jeffrey Womack should be tried as an adult. But what should have been a straightforward transfer hearing took on huge proportions, with attacks and legal maneuverings by both sides. Throughout the fall, with angry quotes from Hollins and Shriver and courtroom tensions dominating the news, the focus seemed to shift from the young man at the center of the controversy—and especially from the nine-year-old girl who was at the heart of everything. The legal battle took on a life of its own.

Jeffrey Womack's attorneys filed the predicted motion to dismiss the day after the arrest. Judge Jenkins took the motion under advisement. The reasons Hollins and Yarbrough gave that the murder charges should be dropped were: (1) Womack had already been cleared by polygraph examinations by the police; (2) police had engaged in "persistent and harassing" tactics without cause; (3) the delay in charging Womack violated his rights under the Constitution; (4) the evidence police were bringing against him was available in 1975; and (5) the unwarranted delay had resulted in severe prejudice against Womack. Hollins minced no words in his brief: "The defendant's case should not be prejudiced by the failure of law enforcement officers to properly do their work."

While Shriver cited "new evidence" in the decision to charge Jeffrey Womack with murder, the defense team argued that no new evidence had been uncovered in the four and a half years police had pursued their client.

In a September 18 hearing, Judge Jenkins denied the motion for dismissal. He also denied the defense's discovery motion requesting that the prosecution show them all evidence against Jeffrey Womack, as well as evidence against three other suspects the police investigated in 1975. The judge's ruling was based on the fact that the requests were premature, not appropriate for the transfer hearing.

Jeffrey Womack's lawyers, losers in the first round, came back with more steam. As the date of the transfer hearing grew nearer, the defense's list of eight subpoenaed witnesses included three that the prosecution opposed. Jeffrey's attorneys wanted to question Dr. Jerry Francisco, state medical examiner, who performed the Trimble autopsy and gave conflicting opinions about the time of death. They subpoenaed Sergeant Sherman Nickens, who had taken over as head of Homicide after Lieutenant Cathey left, and requested that he bring them all the evidence in the Trimble case. ADA Johnson called it "an attempt to get discovery through the back door."

But the subpoena that created the most strife was the one

issued to Detective Diane Vaughn. Defense attorneys wanted Vaughn to testify about the sunglasses Marie Thorpe had found at the garage as she was emptying the structure for demolition, sunglasses belonging to Virginia Trimble. Virginia had told Diane Vaughn she'd finally had the courage to go to the garage with Sergeant Dennis and Officer Moore, eight or ten weeks after Marcia's body was discovered there, and she'd left the glasses in the garage at that time.

Shriver lashed out at Hollins, who was his classmate in Vanderbilt Law School and was once his top assistant. He called it a "cheap shot to cast suspicion on Mrs. Trimble" and charged that the defense did it for publicity purposes. Hollins shot back that he was surprised by Shriver's response and that the statements "reflected unfavorably upon the high office of public responsibility and trust that Tom Shriver holds."

On October 3, in yet another hearing in Juvenile Court, Judge Jenkins quashed the subpoenas for Francisco, Nickens, and Vaughn, saying that the three were "adverse witnesses." But the next day, in Davidson County Circuit Court, Judge Harry Lester reversed Jenkins's ruling, allowing the three subpoenas. The matter was still not settled. ADA Johnson asked Judge Lester for permission to appeal his ruling. Lester stated he was "really not impressed" by the request, but he guessed it was "only fair" to grant it.

On October 5, just four days before the scheduled transfer hearing, Judge Jenkins postponed the hearing until early December. The issue of the subpoenas had to first be decided in the Tennessee Court of Appeals.

In arguments back and forth, attorneys and judges continued to point out that the transfer hearing was not a "full-blown trial." But as fall hurtled toward winter, with all the legal skirmishes leading up to the December hearing, it was easy to forget that the purpose of the hearing was to decide whether Womack would be tried as an adult, not whether he was guilty or innocent.

* * *

During the few weeks in the fall when the newspapers were not reporting courtroom activities, reporters sought out several potential witnesses who had given statements to police. Jeffrey's high school classmate who had worked with him at the Afterthought now lived in Pensacola, Florida. He repeated to Bill Hance from the *Banner* that he thought Jeffrey was making a "sick joke" by saying he killed Marcia. Another former classmate, now living in California, said that Jeffrey laughed after he said he raped and murdered Marcia. "He was kind of kidding about it but I believe he was telling the truth," the young man said. Hughes Dedmon, who reportedly heard Jeffrey's statement in physical education class, was subpoenaed to testify in the Juvenile Court hearing in December.

Chris Richards, the restaurant manager from the Jolly Ox, told *Tennessean* reporters about an incident that happened one night when the two were out drinking beer, shortly after Jeffrey had been given a polygraph.

"How'd you do?" Chris asked, and Jeffrey said he passed, that there were "no errors."

Then Chris asked, "Did you kill that little girl?"

He told reporters that Jeffrey said, "Yes I did." But then Jeffrey slapped Chris on the arm and said, "You know I'm only kidding."

Sometime in late 1976, Sergeant R. C. Jackson and Detective Tommy Jacobs asked Chris Richards to give a statement, and he related the entire conversation to them. They gave him the statement to sign, and Chris admitted he didn't read it carefully. He told reporters that he'd recently read the statement, and he noticed the "only kidding" part was omitted.

Chris Richards said that on another occasion, police convinced him to wear a taping device to get information from Jeffrey about how he'd passed the polygraph. Jeffrey answered, "It's simple. I told the truth." Once again, Chris asked him if he killed Marcia, and Jeffrey said, "No, Chris, you know I couldn't do anything like that."

ADA John Zimmerman represented the State in the Court of Appeals on November 29. Zimmerman challenged the subpoenas for Francisco, Nickens, and Vaughn, arguing that the preliminary hearing should not be used as a "fishing expedition." But the panel of judges, Henry F. Todd, Frank Drowota III, and Sam Lewis, upheld Judge Lester's ruling, allowing the defense to subpoena the three witnesses. The Court also held that defense attorneys could ask investigators about other suspects besides Jeffrey Womack.

But the matter was not settled yet. The following day, State attorneys went to the highest court in the state and asked the judges to review the Court of Appeals decision.

Jeffrey Womack's attorneys continued their winning streak. The Tennessee Supreme Court refused to stay the Court of Appeals ruling but also refused to review their decision. Judge Jenkins scheduled December 4–6 for the preliminary hearing in Juvenile Court to decide at last whether Jeffrey Womack should be tried as an adult.

Jeffrey Womack wore a dark blue suit and his hair was groomed as he entered Judge Jenkins's courtroom with his lawyers. News photographers snapped pictures of Jeffrey, and of Charles and Virginia Trimble, as they arrived at Juvenile Court. Front-page headlines of the local papers announced the event. The hearing was not a trial, but it captured Nashville's attention just as every development in the Trimble case had.

In the national news, Iran's Ayatollah Khomeini threatened death sentences for fifty American hostages being held at the American Embassy in Tehran. But Nashville's attention was tuned to Jeffrey Womack's hearing. The nearly five years since Marcia Trimble's death had done nothing to diminish the city's appetite for details about the case.

Virginia Trimble testified for an hour, remaining composed as she recounted the evening her daughter disappeared. She said Marcia told her, "Watch for Jeffrey, because he's going to bring my money for my cookies."

Virginia said she didn't know anything about the "sex play" that was going on in the neighborhood until her son, Chuck, told her, sometime after Marcia's death. She clarified that the sex experimentation was "not intercourse." She said Jeffrey Womack was not mentioned as someone who participated in the activities with Marcia, Chuck, and some of the other neighborhood children. Virginia Trimble also told about the man who had exposed himself to Marcia and the other little girls about several weeks before Marcia's death.

Lieutenant Cathey, who'd led the initial homicide investigation, testified about the location and condition of the body. He said police took fingerprints; none of the fingerprints found on the scene belonged to Jeffrey Womack. But he stated that when Chuck talked with police about the "Touch and Dare" games, he named Jeffrey as a participant.

Hughes Dedmon, a student at MTSU and former Hillsboro High School classmate of Jeffrey's, said he had heard Jeffrey admit that he'd killed Marcia. He testified that "Jeff said he had done it and had had sex with her." But under cross-examination, when Hollins asked Hughes if he could tell whether Jeffrey was "serious or kidding," the young man said, "It could be true or it might not be true."

The tension increased as the hearing went into its second day. DA Tom Shriver, charging that sex and robbery were motives in the murder, used the word "rape" for the first time. He referred to Dr. Francisco's report that said "sperm was present in the vaginal contents." The Trimbles grasped each other's hands. Until then, they'd heard only about the semen on Marcia's clothing. Though the report also said "no vaginal wounds" and Dr. Francisco said he "could not say she was forcibly raped," the issue Shriver raised with his charge was a horrible concept for the Trimbles to grasp. Jeffrey Womack's attorneys hammered at Dr. Francisco about the conflicting reports of time of death that he gave before issuing his final autopsy report. Hollins had made the argument before, related to the time frame the medical examiner gave at one point: March 20–27. What would a teenage boy without a car have done with the child from February 25 to March 20?

Another element of high drama occurred when Sergeant R. C. Jackson testified about his first encounter with Jeffrey Womack, the night Marcia disappeared. He told about the items the suspect had in the pocket of his jacket, including a half roll of pennies similar to the pennies Marcia was supposed to have from her cookie sales. He alleged that Jeffrey failed to remove a condom from his pocket. His statement triggered an outburst from Jeffrey's mother. Weeping, she called out, "Why can't you tell the truth?"

On Thursday afternoon, the participants in the hearing reconvened at an old redbrick building on 2nd Avenue, where boxes upon boxes of files and evidence from the case were stored. Judge Jenkins, on crutches from knee surgery, was pictured in the newspaper looking at a plastic bag that contained some of the physical evidence.

The State's argument centered around Jeffrey Womack's conflicting statements regarding his whereabouts the night Marcia disappeared, the half roll of pennies in his pocket, the fact that he had claimed to have no money to pay for cookies earlier in the afternoon but later had $5 and change in his pocket, and his own statements to classmates and co-workers that he killed Marcia.

The defense made a fierce argument for Jeffrey Womack's innocence. They pointed to other persons who could have killed Marcia and the sexual activities in the neighborhood; they hammered the facts that no witness saw Jeffrey and Marcia together just before she disappeared, his fingerprints were not found at the crime scene, and the composite sketches early in the case didn't look like Jeffrey.

In the end, Judge Jenkins ruled that Jeffrey Womack should be tried as an adult. He was going to Criminal Court.

For the investigators on the case and the district attorney's office, the ruling was good news. But the case that went all the way to the Tennessee Supreme Court was still not over.

Months after Jeffrey Womack's arrest on that hot August night, DA Tom Shriver was on a spelunking expedition with Ed Yarbrough. Though the two were on opposite sides of the fence where Jeffrey Womack was concerned, they were friends, and the tensions of the trial had subsided. According to Matt Pulle's 2001 article in the *Scene*, sometime during the trip, Shriver announced to the defense attorney, "Oh, by the way. My office is going to ask that charges against Womack be dropped."

Shriver and Torry Johnson had taken a long, hard look at the case, interviewing witnesses again, and they were not convinced there was sufficient evidence to present to a grand jury. The defense had exposed some of the holes that were too glaring to ignore. On August 11, 1980, Judge Raymond Leathers approved a motion for dismissal in Davidson County Criminal Court.

Ed Yarbrough told reporters, "There was never enough evidence against the suspect, and today we filed a motion in Criminal Court to have charges permanently expunged from his record." He insisted that at the time of the murder, Jeffrey Womack was falsely accused because of "sloppy police work."

Strong public criticism targeted the district attorney's office when the announcement was made that charges were dropped against Jeffrey Womack. Police continued to intimate that he was guilty, even suggesting he might have been part of a conspiracy that involved other boys from the neighborhood. After the hearing in December 1979, they even obtained another statement from Peggy Morgan, relating to the timeline for Jeffrey's activities on February 25, 1975. Peggy stated that she now believed it was closer to 6:00 when Jeffrey and Amy left for McDonald's. Initially, she'd said it was 5:15. The investigators who had invested five years pursuing Jeffrey did not change their minds about him, even though they had not been able to nail him.

Many believed the police and district attorney's office had simply bungled the case, that Jeffrey was guilty. Others who believed in his innocence criticized investigators for wasting so much time and energy on Jeffrey Womack while Marcia's killer was still out there.

The mystery remained unsolved.

PART 4

Hope

22

The Next Decade

In 1983, Brentwood, a small city outside of Nashville, was experiencing a bubble of prosperity. Between 1970 and 1980 Brentwood's population had nearly tripled, growing from around 3,300 to over 9,400. Many Nashvillians had flocked south, to Brentwood and historic Franklin, to leave the troubled Metropolitan Nashville public schools for Williamson County schools. New developments sprouted in meadows where horses once grazed. New companies in the Nashville area brought an influx of families from other parts of the nation. Much was written about the "quality of life" in Middle Tennessee.

Jeffrey Womack's family had also moved to Franklin in the late 1970s, though their relocation had nothing to do with the school system.

Huff's Food Town had served residents of the Brentwood community since 1949, twenty years before the small city was incorporated. In August of 1983, Jeffrey, then twenty-three, applied for a job as a stocker, checker, and bag boy at Huff's

Food Town, and Mike Huff, the owner-proprietor of the family grocery, hired him. Jeffrey had worked at Big Star and another grocery on 8th Avenue. On his application he listed experience in produce, sack help, and stock. Mr. Huff was satisfied with his work. Within a few weeks, Jeffrey's salary increased from $3.35 to $3.50 an hour.

Another employee at the grocery recognized Jeffrey as the suspect in the Trimble case and told Mr. Huff, who decided he should have a talk with the young man. He asked Jeffrey if his past was going to create any problems. "If it is, I'll have to let you go," Mr. Huff said.

Jeffrey assured his employer that he hadn't killed Marcia Trimble. "I was a cocky kid back then," he said. "I told some people I did it, but I didn't."

Mr. Huff took him at his word, and Jeffrey worked at Huff's for a few months. In November, he left for a job at Delite's Restaurant, also in Brentwood. He had as much experience in restaurants as he'd had in groceries. Besides the Afterthought and Jolly Ox, Jeffrey had also worked at Houston's, a popular spot on West End, near Vanderbilt. At Houston's, he met a girl named Marcia, and they dated for a while, though the girl reported that Jeffrey's lawyers advised him to quit dating her because of her name. She also said that Jeffrey never mentioned whether or not he'd killed Marcia Trimble, but he did admit to an affair with an older lady in the neighborhood in 1975.

During the early 1980s, Jeffrey liked to hang out at Friday's, Tony Roma's, and the Gold Rush, all around Elliston Place, off West End. Jeffrey didn't stick with anything very long, though after a time at Delite's, he landed at Burger King and eventually became an assistant manager. In 1987, while he was working at Burger King in Brentwood, he became involved with a girl named Jennifer, and they had a daughter. Like his previous girlfriend, Jennifer knew about Jeffrey's affair with Peggy Morgan, but she told police that Jeffrey said he did not kill Marcia Trimble.

Although the investigation into the Trimble murder was virtually dormant during the 1980s, Jeffrey Womack was never far off police radar. Chris Richards, who had been Jeffrey's co-worker at the Jolly Ox, told reporters, "He said it seemed like every time he turned around, there was a detective or Metro there, or somebody to do with the law." Friends of the Womacks maintained that the investigation destroyed the family. Jeffrey's father died "prematurely," a friend said, and many who were close to the family believed the stress of the murder investigation played a significant role in his early death.

Marie Maxwell and her family had also moved away from Copeland Drive in 1976. In one of her many interviews with investigators, Marie said that within a matter of days after Marcia disappeared, she and her husband contacted a real estate agent and asked how quickly they could sell their house. The Realtor said they wouldn't be able to get their money's worth for at least a year. A year later, the Maxwells sold the house. "The neighborhood was so jumpy," she said. "Everybody that came through, it was—Citizens Arrest, and Call the Police."

Marie shopped at Huff's for a while. Sometime in the early 1980s, she saw Jeffrey Womack working there. She later told investigators that when she made eye contact with Jeffrey, she pretended not to recognize him, saying she just "half smiled like, 'I don't know who you are.'" But after he checked out her groceries, she began shopping elsewhere. She was "too uncomfortable" to go back to Huff's.

The Maxwells were just one of the many families who had left the neighborhood where the Trimble tragedy occurred. The children who had played with Marcia were growing up, and they continued to carry the burden of her death with them. Already in 1979, when Jeffrey Womack was arrested, more than half of the twenty-two families who lived on Copeland Drive had moved away. The rippling effects of the murder continued into the 1980s.

Charles and Virginia Trimble divorced in 1989, after twenty-seven years of marriage. Virginia told reporters that their "differing manners of coping" with their daughter's murder created a terrible strain on the couple. She also said that Charles was about to inherit a large sum of money, and "he wanted to live a separate lifestyle." Charles was diagnosed with lung and liver cancer, and three days after the divorce was final, he died. Virginia would continue to live on Copeland for another decade, but eventually the Trimble house, where Marcia grew up, where her parents and brother grieved for her, would be torn down, and another house built in its place.

Nashville flourished in the 1980s. Much of the city's new, unprecedented wealth came from the health care industry. Hospital Corporation of America, founded by the Frist family in 1968, was largely responsible for making Nashville a hot spot for health care. In the 1970s, an estimated one hundred millionaires emerged from the music industry, but in the 1980s, Nashville saw its first billionaires, the movers and shakers of the health care industry.

American Airlines opened a major hub at the new Nashville airport in 1985, offering direct flights to London. Governor Lamar Alexander told the *Wall Street Journal*, "Nashville is hot as a firecracker." And not just Nashville. The communities surrounding the metropolitan area were also enjoying growth and prosperity as Nissan came to Smyrna, southeast of the city, and General Motors opened a Saturn plant in Spring Hill, south of Nashville.

The 1980s brought Riverfront Park to downtown Nashville, set along the Cumberland River at 1st Avenue. The historic warehouses of 2nd Avenue became restaurants, clubs, shops, and apartments. New public buildings contributed to the face-lift of downtown Nashville: the Tennessee Perform-

ing Arts Center, the Nashville Convention Center, and a new
Criminal Justice Center. Chief Joe Casey retired in 1989, after
serving as chief for sixteen years. In thirty-eight years on the
force, he had never missed a day of work. He retired with honors,
awards, and respect.

Now and then, tips still came in on the Trimble case, calls
from as far away as Salt Lake City, Utah. But nothing of consequence
had happened in the investigation since the case
against Jeffrey Womack was dropped in 1980.

As the Metro Nashville Police Department looked forward
to the 1990s and the changes that would take them into a new
millennium, the introduction of DNA typing was just beginning
to revolutionize forensic science. The Marcia Trimble
murder investigation had been dormant for a decade—but that
was about to change.

23

Everything Old Is New Again

The Burger King on Richard Jones Road in Green Hills started getting busy and noisy around 4:45 P.M. on August 27, 1990, as moms and kids came in on their way home from swimming pools or day camps or trips to the orthodontist. The teenagers ordering burgers and fries were probably students from Hillsboro High who had stopped first at the library or the mall, both just across the street from the high school.

Jeffrey Womack had worked his way through many of the area's fast-food restaurants, and now he was an assistant manager at Burger King. He was back in Green Hills, less than a mile from where his family used to live on Copeland Drive. August 27, 1990, was Jeffrey Womack's thirty-first birthday. When the police came, it was déjà vu.

Eleven years ago, almost to the day, police had arrested him at his brother's apartment on West End Avenue. They came in the middle of the night, about 2:00 A.M., on August 28. Jeffrey was expecting the arrest that night; this afternoon, he was caught by surprise when the detectives arrived with a search warrant, but their presence was a reminder that he'd always been their prime suspect, even when charges were dropped.

The plainclothes detectives asked for Jeffrey Womack, and he came out of the kitchen.

"Could we go somewhere private?" Captain Mickey Miller asked. With him were Lieutenant Jacobs, Lieutenant Hackett, and Detective Bernard.

Jeffrey led them into a hallway where the restrooms were located.

Captain Miller explained that they needed blood and hair samples from him to use in DNA matching. Jeffrey thought about it for a minute. "I'll have to call my boss first and see if he can get another manager to take over."

Miller told him that was fine. The two went to an office, and Jeffrey made a call to his boss. Then he said, "I'll have to check with Mr. Hollins about this."

"That's fine, too," Miller told him.

"Do you want to wait out in the dining room?" Jeffrey asked.

Miller went out to join the other detectives while Jeffrey called his attorney. Since Jeffrey was cooperating, Detective Bernard and Lieutenant Hackett went back to their cars. Captain Miller waited with Lieutenant Jacobs until Jeffrey called for him. Hollins wanted to talk to him.

Hollins was fuming. "What's going on?" he wanted to know. Miller explained why they were there and what they wanted. Miller wrote in his report, "Mr. Hollins became verbally abusive and I advised him I would only continue our conversation if he would calm down."

"What will you do if we don't consent? Will you leave?" Hollins asked.

"No, I have a search warrant for hair and blood samples," Miller said, "but I'd rather see Jeffrey give the samples voluntarily."

Hollins asked the name of the judge who signed the warrant. He wanted to know who in the district attorney's office knew about this. Miller told him Judge Reuben had signed the warrant and that Torry Johnson and Tom Thurman knew about it—the district attorney and assistant district attorney.

Hollins wanted to talk to Jeffrey again, and Miller left the room. After Jeffrey spoke with his attorney for a few minutes more, he came out and told Captain Miller, "Mr. Hollins needs to talk to you again."

"Jeffrey will consent," Hollins told Miller. The two agreed that Hollins would come to Burger King and drive Jeffrey to General Hospital. Miller said he would wait for a relief manager to take Jeffrey's place.

"I'll be there in ten minutes," Hollins said.

At General Hospital, the doctor took three vials of blood, along with thirty hair samples: head, mustache, chest, left and right arm, left and right leg, and pubic hairs. Lieutenant Hackett initialed the sealed vials in the presence of Detective Bernard, John Hollins, and Jeffrey Womack.

Detective Bernard took possession of the suspect evidence, while Lieutenant Hackett took possession of the victim evidence—Marcia's boots, jeans, blouse, panties, and slides of Marcia's hair—that had to be resubmitted for DNA comparison. The two detectives kept the evidence overnight, and the next day they left Nashville. After spending the night in Manassas, Virginia, they arrived in Washington, D.C., and turned the evidence over to an agent at the FBI Lab.

Chief of police Robert Kirchner Jr., Chief Casey's successor, had named Captain Mickey Miller as commander of the Personal Crimes Division of Criminal Investigation. Miller had grown up in a police family. His father and uncle both had careers as Nashville police officers. A 1974 graduate of Stratford High School in East Nashville, he received a master's degree from Notre Dame and a law degree from the Nashville School of Law.

Homicide, rape, and robbery came under Personal Crimes, and within Homicide there was a unit called the Murder Squad. The unit investigated crimes that went unsolved for some period of time. It was an early version of the Cold Case Unit that would be formed more than a decade later, but the Murder Squad would only review cases when new information surfaced.

Captain Miller reported that in the summer of 1990, he and Lieutenant Tommy Jacobs decided to review the Marcia Trimble case "to see if any new or old investigative avenues could be followed." Lieutenant Jacobs was one of the first detectives on the case in 1975, and he became the lead detective in the homicide investigation. Miller and Jacobs began to familiarize themselves with the files, still in Lieutenant Jacobs's possession. They located the physical evidence in the police property room and the district attorney's property room. They placed all the evidence in six boxes and labeled them—everything from Marcia's clothing, scrapings from her body, and slides containing hair and fiber samples, to soil samples, paint samples, plastic bags of mulch, weed killer, and insecticides, as well as a Girl Scout cookie order form and the envelope that once contained Marcia's cookie money. The evidence also included a basketball hoop and a baseball bat that would not fit in the boxes.

After organizing the physical evidence, Miller and Jacobs turned some of the boxes over to Sergeant Johnny Hunter to see if he could develop any latent prints using technology that had not been available in the 1970s.

In 1990, all the law enforcement magazines were running articles about DNA typing. The science was clear; DNA, short for deoxyribonucleic acid, was the "building block" of a person's genetic makeup, present in blood, bone, tissue, muscles, organs, hair, fingernails, and skin cells, as well as semen, saliva, mucus, perspiration, urine, and feces. DNA profiling was fast becoming a significant forensic tool, giving law enforcement the ability to match perpetrators with their victims.

Police released the news that authorities would be renewing their efforts to resolve the Trimble case using DNA evidence. The story ran on a local television station. Once again, reporters began to follow the developments in the case, reigniting the public's hopes for an arrest in the murder. Marcia Trimble was back in the news.

The first DNA sample obtained was Jeffrey Womack's. Then Miller and Jacobs set about to locate and acquire samples from the other young men—now all twenty-five to thirty years old—who had been boys in the neighborhood in 1975.

March Egerton was at the top of the list of the "boys in the neighborhood." He had delivered cookies with Marcia on the afternoon before she disappeared, and police always believed he was one of the individuals whom Marie Maxwell had seen with Marcia in Mrs. Howard's driveway.

Lieutenant Jacobs contacted March, then twenty-five years old and living in Seattle, Washington. March agreed to speak with Jacobs about the Trimble case. He said he would be in Nashville on September 12, 1990.

In the meantime, March's father, John Egerton, retained attorney Cecil Branstetter on March's behalf. On September 13, when Captain Miller called the Egerton residence to speak with March, John Egerton told him to contact Mr. Branstetter. Miller called the attorney, who said March agreed to meet with police, but he laid down certain conditions: There would be no serious questioning, no blood or hair samples given, and the session had to be recorded. Mr. Branstetter added that police had to promise not to bother the Egertons again.

Captain Miller discussed Branstetter's terms with his superiors and DA Torry Johnson. They decided the demands were unacceptable and proceeded to request a search warrant for hair and blood samples. They made plans to execute the warrant at 8:30 P.M. on September 17.

The Egertons had grown weary with the police. The family had cooperated fully with authorities at the beginning of the investigation, as had other neighbors. Marcia Trimble was March's close friend when he was ten years old, and he had been devastated by her murder. But in 1979, as they were building toward an arrest of Jeffrey Womack, police had wanted March to be hypnotized, believing he might have suppressed certain details about the crime. John Egerton refused to allow police access to his then fourteen-year-old son. He said police had told him there would be no more questioning.

Nevertheless, soon after Womack's arrest, two detectives arrived at the Egertons' house in a squad car and delivered a letter from the district attorney's office demanding that March be available for an interview. John Egerton fumed to the *Tennessean*: "It is a frightening thing for me to see this city's investigative authorities act in such a manner toward law-abiding citizens." He maintained that some of the officials would go to "any lengths to get a conviction in this case, even if innocent people—adults and children—are harmed."

March and his family, now *beyond* weary, were angry at the police intrusion. They insisted that March had told police everything he knew about that awful evening fifteen years ago.

At about 9:20 P.M. on Monday, September 17, 1990, police arrived at the Egertons' home. March was playing Monopoly when police appeared. John Egerton described a frightening scene: "Several carloads of uniformed and plainclothes Metro police officers sped into our driveway, surrounded our house and, with hands on their weapons, closed in on us."

The affidavit that explained why police needed March Egerton's DNA cited the facts that he was selling cookies with her earlier in the afternoon, he was present in the Trimble yard playing basketball with Chuck when Marcia was last seen, and a witness *thought* she saw him with Marcia after the basketball game ended. Police also maintained that March couldn't account for his whereabouts from 5:15 to 6:00. John Egerton called the warrant an "error-filled mish-mash of unsupported assertions and unattributed claims that falsely insinuates that March has withheld evidence."

Over his father's protests, the officers took March away. He was not allowed to call his attorney, and his father was not permitted to go with him. Nevertheless, March went peaceably. He rode to General Hospital with Detective Bernard, Captain Miller, and Lieutenant Jacobs.

On the way to the hospital, Miller and Jacobs took the opportunity to ask some questions. Lieutenant Jacobs reported that March was "somewhat agitated but was willing to discuss the situation." He said he had planned to call the detectives that evening or the next day. He told them he didn't mind the interview, but when he returned to Nashville and talked with his dad, he began to be afraid he was somehow going to be blamed for Marcia's murder.

The detectives said that was *not* the case, but they thought there was a possibility he'd seen something the day of the murder that was so horrible, he had blocked it from his memory.

"I don't believe that happened," March said, "but I can understand why you feel it was a possibility."

March didn't remember much about that day, but when the detectives referred to their notes from his interviews and refreshed his memory, he did recall certain details. The detectives suggested that he might recall other information under hypnosis. March declined to be hypnotized or to be examined by a psychiatrist.

After the doctor took hair and blood samples, Detective Bernard took March home—three hours after police had shown up at his house.

Shortly after the incident, John Egerton's public statement appeared in the *Tennessean*. In it, he stated that though March had never been charged with any crime in connection with the Trimble murder, "the police have often treated him as if he were a suspect—and now, in this latest invasion they have treated all of us as if we were armed and dangerous fugitives from justice." He insisted that his family had "steadfastly supported the law, the Trimble family, our neighborhood and the city, and done everything we could to help solve the crime."

John Thorpe Jr., in whose family garage Marcia had been found, was also asked to give permission for his blood and hair to be taken. On September 6, police had escorted him to General Hospital for the same procedure carried out with Jeffrey Womack, resulting in two vials of blood and thirty hairs for testing. In addition to the samples from Jeffrey, March, and John Jr., police also had a DNA sample from another male who had been eight years old when Marcia Trimble was murdered. Now twenty-three years old, the young man had written a political science paper in 1988 when he was a student at Columbia State Community College. On the back of one of the pages, he had written Marcia's name and address, followed by "Marcia Trimble got what she deserved, the little bitch." Investigators obtained hair and blood samples from the young man. Captain Miller noted that "he could possibly fit the description of one of the two male subjects which may have been seen with Marcia at the time of her disappearance in the Howard driveway."

On September 18, Detective Bernard left for Washington, D.C., headed to the FBI Lab with three more hair and blood samples for DNA analysis.

Captain Miller and Detective Jacobs went back to the beginning, back to 1975. They set about recovering the original slides from the autopsy performed by Dr. Francisco in Memphis. The slides of semen samples, obtained from the vaginal swabs, were located in a file in the basement of the medical examiner's office. In October 1990, the detectives received the slides and sent them to the FBI Lab.

In March 1991, the FBI Lab made their report on the hair and blood samples they had received from Nashville Police—

samples from eight males, at that point, in addition to the original samples found on Marcia's body and clothing. The hairs from the young men were compared with the hair and fibers on Marcia's jeans, and no matches occurred. The report further stated that no DNA profile results could be obtained from the victim's evidence because of degraded or insufficient DNA; "therefore, no comparisons could be made with the known specimens."

Bottom line: No samples submitted from Jeffrey Womack or March Egerton matched anything found on Marcia Trimble.

But the police were not finished with March Egerton. In May 1991, authorities contacted March and asked him to come in for yet another interview. He agreed, but this time he issued a statement of his own, in which he accused the police of "tactics of intimidation." He said, "I have been repeatedly prodded and cajoled by these people to 'remember' things that never happened and to point fingers at people of whom I have no knowledge." The lengthy statement claimed, "A number of the parties involved in this investigation are more interested in making themselves look good than in seeing that justice is served." He insisted that he, as much as anyone, wanted to see a resolution in "this miserable saga."

But the saga was far from being resolved.

The detectives had heard about a private lab, CBR Lab in Boston, that could do a more advanced type of DNA testing called PCR, or polymerase chain reaction. The earlier method of testing, known as RFLP, restriction fragment length polymorphism, required larger amounts of DNA, and the DNA had to be undegraded. But with PCR, the original DNA was copied in a very controlled way, then the copies were copied, those copies were copied, and so on, so even a small amount of DNA would be sufficient. In September 1991, Captain Miller sent the original slides from the autopsy to CBR Lab.

CBR Lab received a number of items from Nashville Police over the next months, including more cuttings from the clothing Marcia was wearing when her body was found. Personnel in the Metro Police Identification Unit conducted an examination using ALS (alternate light source) that caused stains to luminesce. ALS picked up stains in five locations on the jeans. The crime scene investigator made cuttings from the stains. He sent the cuttings, along with a sample from the underwear, one from the left boot, and two from the right boot, to CBR Lab. Other evidence included hair samples from Marcia Trimble, fibers, what appeared to be a piece of fingernail, and slides prepared from vaginal swabs during the autopsy. The lab also had blood and hair samples from Jeffrey Womack and March Egerton.

If investigators anticipated a quick and conclusive resolution because of DNA typing, they were disappointed. According to an estimate by police, 100–150 boys, ages nine to nineteen, lived in close proximity to the Trimbles' neighborhood in 1975. The young men were now scattered everywhere, some impossible to locate. DNA analysis was a tedious and time-consuming process. CBR Lab was able to get a "good conclusive type" from the evidence submitted, but they were unable to obtain a DNA profile.

On December 6, 1991, Lieutenant Jacobs received a call from CBR Lab. The lab had finished most of the requested testing and was able to obtain a reading on the stains on Marcia's jeans. According to Jacobs's report, "Based on the reading and comparing to the victim, Womack, and Egerton, the results suggested that neither Womack or Egerton deposited the stains. There is apparently an unknown third suspect yet to be identified."

Even as they located other possible suspects from 1975 and sent additional samples to be tested, Captain Miller and Lieutenant Jacobs never stopped believing Jeffrey Womack was their man. Nothing had shaken their confidence in his guilt, expressed in the 1990–1991 "Review of Marcia Virginia Trimble Homicide Investigation." In that document, they conceded that there had been "numerous investigative miscues that plagued the investigation." The time element—proving that Jeffrey Womack had a window of opportunity to commit the crime—was always a problem. The "Review" document was written after investigators looked at all the evidence again, re-interviewed witnesses, and were able to construct a new case theory "based on a more accurate account of time sequences on February 25, 1975."

One of their witnesses was Peggy Morgan, who had earlier put up a staunch defense of Jeffrey. FBI agent Knudsen interviewed her in January 1991. In February of the same year, Captain Miller and Lieutenant Jacobs also conducted an interview. By 1991, Peggy had married attorney Robert Doyle and operated a day care called the Lone Oak Day School. At one point in the questioning, Peggy stated that Jeffrey had been "wet and sweaty" when he came to her house the afternoon Marcia disappeared. He had been at his house, and Peggy assumed he had taken a shower.

In this interview she denied having had any sexual contact with Jeffrey Womack, though she said they had sometimes engaged in "horseplay." When investigators told her witnesses saw her and Jeffrey kissing, she dismissed it as nothing more than a "hug and peck." She was worried about charges being brought against Jeffrey because of the bad publicity for her and her day care.

Amy Norvell, now Amy Watson, also spoke with Miller and Jacobs in January 1991. She reiterated her statement from 1976 that Jeffrey was "out of breath and sweating" and added that he also "appeared a little jumpy or edgy" when he came to Peggy's house that afternoon, before he and Amy went to McDonald's for hamburgers.

Both Amy and Peggy had been interviewed several times between 1975 and 1991. Amy "had given varying times on different interviews," Miller and Jacobs wrote. In January 1991, she was asked again about the time sequence. Lieutenant Jacobs went over each detail she had given, asking if she thought it could have been five minutes earlier or if it was possible it happened five minutes later. Toward the end of the interview, Lieutenant Jacobs said, "The best guess right now that you have about actually backing out of the driveway and leaving is about 5:40."

Amy answered, "Right."

Jacobs explained that the time was "very critical" and he wanted to be sure about it. "To your best guesstimate, given the fact that this is 15 years later and I understand that. You left about 5:40, actually backed out the driveway and headed for McDonald's at around 5:40."

"Right," she said.

According to the investigators' report, Amy said Jeffrey returned to Peggy's sometime between 5:25 and 5:30—not 5:15, as she had stated earlier.

Investigators also re-interviewed Sally Ray, who walked from the bus stop at Hobbs and Copeland to her home on Dorcas Court at about the time Marcia disappeared. In March 1975, Mrs. Ray stated that she walked down Copeland between 5:20 and 5:30. She said she always got home in time to hear John Chancellor say, "This is John Chancellor and the news." The news came on at 5:30. Marie Maxwell had seen Sally Ray walking on Copeland. In January 1991, according to the investigators' report, Mrs. Ray said she got off the bus at 5:12 P.M. Her earlier statement had not taken into account how long it could have taken her to walk home and get situated before the news came on.

Also in January 1991, Miller, Jacobs, and other investigators conducted a time study/role play to try to provide a moment-by-moment timetable for certain people in the neighborhood on February 25, 1975. Investigators assumed the roles of key individuals in the neighborhood that afternoon and reenacted the known movements of the subjects. Captain Miller took the role of Marcia Trimble; Lieutenant Jacobs assumed the role of March Egerton. Other investigators played Jeffrey Womack, Chuck Trimble, and Sally Ray. Special Agent Knudsen of the FBI took the role of Marie Maxwell, trying to determine exactly when she arrived at her house and saw Marcia with two other individuals in Mrs. Howard's driveway.

Participants simulated the activities of the individuals and recorded their assigned movements with a stopwatch. Miller and Jacobs concluded from the reenactment that Marie Maxwell arrived home earlier than she'd thought—perhaps as early as 5:15. The time study also had Amy Norvell backing out of the driveway with Jeffrey, heading to McDonald's, at 5:35–5:40.

Special Agent Knudsen of the FBI re-interviewed Marie Maxwell during the same time period. The report of the interview states, "Mrs. Maxwell believes that she pulled in her drive, got out of her vehicle, walked around vehicle and observed Marcia and two suspects at approximately 5:17-5:18 p.m." Marie said in the interview that she always believed the smaller person in Mrs. Howard's driveway was March Egerton, but she never wanted to "point the finger" at him. She also said that "in her heart" she believed Jeffrey Womack was the other person in the drive with March and Marcia.

Marcia's brother Chuck Trimble was interviewed again during January 1991. Lieutenant Jacobs reported that Chuck "has not spoken to March since that day and that March never came to his house again."

The "Review" document prepared by Captain Miller and Lieutenant Jacobs alleged that since "it is now known that Jeffrey Womack did not arrive at Peggy's until 5:30 (approx.) to go with Amy to get burgers," it was possible for him to have enticed Marcia to the Thorpes' garage after he met her in Mrs.

Howard's driveway at 5:15. Investigators of rape cases "tell us that an assault typically takes approximately six minutes," the document said.

The review conducted by Miller and Jacobs in 1990–1991 set forth the theory that Jeffrey Womack was Marcia Trimble's murderer and March Egerton was a witness. But with the failure of DNA to prove their theory, their allegations were just that: a theory.

For all their tireless efforts and good intentions, investigators received strong criticism for choosing to accept certain facts while ignoring others. For example, in their 1990–1991 review of the case, Miller and Jacobs did not mention that Jeffrey Womack had passed five polygraphs administered by police and private examiners, nor did they mention that the DNA testing by the FBI and a private lab both failed to match Womack's hair and blood to the victim's evidence. Also, the detectives wrote in their review that "there was no indication of a multiple rapist loose on the community," yet at the time Marcia was killed, there had actually been several recent rapes and attempted rapes, as well as a rape-murder, at Belmont College, Vanderbilt University, Fairfax Avenue, and Acklen Park Drive, all less than five miles from Copeland Drive.

In 1991 the investigators had access to an FBI criminal investigative analysis of the offender in the Trimble murder. Developed by FBI supervisory special agent Gregory Cooper, in consultation with other members of the National Center for the Analysis of Violent Crime (NCAVC), the "profile" was based largely on materials submitted by the authorities who worked the case. The document described the "offender" as a white male, of average intelligence but an underachiever scholastically, aloof, possibly a loner, sexually inadequate and frustrated while preoccupied with sexual fantasy.

The profilers, drawing from the facts in similar cases, also noted, "If the offender had a criminal record, it would reflect nuisance offenses such as trespassing, loitering, possible voyeuristic activities, and petty shoplifting," and "Age is a difficult factor to predict because we are assessing an emotional level of maturity that may or may not be consistent with the chronological age. Typically, similar crimes of this nature are committed by older offenders."

But investigators focused on the attributes that characterized Jeffrey Womack.

Public criticism of police, resulting from their treatment of March Egerton, did not deter investigators from continuing to obtain blood and hair samples from possible suspects. Most of them gave samples voluntarily, but when they did not, police executed search warrants. Police tested dozens of males and a few females over the next few years. In a package sent to CBR Lab, the private lab in Boston, in June 1992, blood samples from both Chuck Trimble and Virginia Trimble were included along with sixteen others.

Jeffrey Womack's DNA had not matched any of the victim's evidence in tests performed by the FBI Lab or CBR Lab. But in May 1992, when police learned that a writer named Melissa Finch had been in contact with Jeffrey Womack about a book she intended to write, investigators saw another opportunity to catch their prime suspect giving incriminating information. Jeffrey had agreed to an interview. He'd told Ms. Finch that he wanted her to help him write his side of the story. She was supposed to call him on May 16 at 9:00 P.M. to set up the interview. Police reports reflect that Ms. Finch cooperated with police, who furnished her with certain questions they wanted her to ask Jeffrey and made arrangements to monitor the phone conversation.

The male who answered the phone was not Jeffrey. Ms. Finch believed it was Jeffrey's brother Tommy, because she had once worked with Tommy's wife and knew the sound of his voice. Finally, Jeffrey came to the phone and told her to call back on Wednesday. A couple of days later, Captain Miller called Ms. Finch and learned that she had called Jeffrey back that same night. In the second call, Jeffrey told her he would never give her an interview, and hung up.

DNA technology continued to advance, and Nashville Police located a medical diagnostic laboratory, LabCorp in Research Triangle Park, North Carolina, that had the capability of performing even more specific testing than CBR Lab was able to provide. In November 1994, CBR Lab sent eighty-one vials of DNA and slides to LabCorp. LabCorp looked at additional areas of DNA.

No profile had yet been established for the male whose semen was on Marcia's clothing, but CBR Lab had found "mixtures" on the slide samples from the vaginal swabs taken immediately prior to the autopsy, meaning DNA from more than one person. LabCorp testing verified those results, with mixtures on all but one slide. They developed five different profiles, a situation that would cause great confusion for the Nashville Police. Was it possible there had been more than one perpetrator of the crime? Could there have been *several* males involved? Investigators would ultimately come to believe that the autopsy slides had been contaminated during the handling or storing of the slides. "Touch contamination" would account for the multiple profiles, and in 1975, wearing gloves was not standard practice for the people in the medical examiner's office who took swabs and handled slides. But here was another baffling development in the investigation. Were the slides of any use at all? If four of the slides were presumed to be contaminated, how reliable was the single profile from the remaining slide?

In 1995, investigators made a tremendous effort to locate all of the young men who had lived in the Copeland neighborhood on February 25, 1975, now scattered all over the United

States. Letters went out requesting the help of law enforcement officials to contact subjects in Phoenix, Arizona; Riverside, California; Ann Arbor, Michigan; Columbia, Maryland; and Mt. Vernon, Washington. The letters stated, "Our department appreciates your assistance in obtaining blood specimens from the below-listed subject." Along with the letters, police sent packaging for collecting the evidence and instructions for returning it to CID. Some had given blood samples before, but the detectives requested new samples because the technology for DNA analysis was continually advancing.

LabCorp tested fifty-two individuals' DNA, some who had been excluded by previous testing. No matches occurred. Hopes began to founder that DNA analysis could lead to identifying Marcia Trimble's killer. The Trimble case took up more than a dozen four-inch binders on shelves in Captain Miller's office. Most Nashvillians were still eager for any new development in the case, but one letter to the editor called articles on the twenty-year-old murder "sensationalism," pointing out that nothing new had occurred in the case, that it was "just another unsolved murder in a city that counts them by the hundred."

In January 1996, nearly six years after Captain Mickey Miller and Lieutenant Tommy Jacobs had decided to take a new look at the case, Jacobs told reporters that improved DNA testing pointed to involvement by three or four males. He was quoted as saying he believed a sexual encounter involving several neighborhood boys "got out of hand," and when Marcia panicked, they strangled her. However, in Matt Pulle's 2001 *Scene* article, he was quoted as saying, "I would be totally shocked if there was more than one contributor. It's almost inconceivable that you had two, three, or four attackers and nobody talked."

On February 25, 1996, a *Tennessean* article led with "Metro police have made repeated claims of new leads, new evidence and new suspects since 9-year-old Marcia Trimble disappeared from her home in Green Hills 21 years ago today." Captain Miller was quoted as saying the only thing "new" in the case was that DNA testing was advancing. By this time, sixty-six males had given hair and blood samples for DNA testing, without any matches.

Lieutenant Jacobs, who had followed the Trimble case since February 25, 1975, retired from the Nashville Police Department in 1996. Before he did, though, a tip came in that a man wanted to give a deathbed confession to the Marcia Trimble murder. Lieutenant Jacobs and Captain Miller went with a reporter to check out the story. The man told a long, convoluted tale about having raped and killed Marcia when he was blind drunk. His details did not all support the facts in the case, but the detectives sent a nurse to get a blood sample anyway. A police officer took medical forms for him to sign. The man reportedly told the officer, "I got 'em going, don't I?" He got his picture in the paper and a few minutes of notoriety before he died. The Trimble investigation continued.

Jeffrey Womack was still high on Jacobs's list of suspects, but the detective would not see Womack convicted on his watch.

He would not see the case solved on his watch, either.

The public was beginning to doubt the ability of investigators to *ever* solve the case.

24

The Nashville Cold Case Unit

Nashville in the 1990s was a place to get rich. Not necessarily for the locals, but for the "outsiders" who moved in and became millionaires and billionaires.

Phil Bredesen was one of the "outsiders" who seemed to have the Midas touch. Born in New Jersey and raised in New York, he came to Nashville in 1975, the year Marcia Trimble was murdered, and jumped on the for-profit health care bandwagon. He created a health care management company, HealthAmerica Corp., that grew to more than six thousand employees and traded on the New York Stock Exchange. Six years later, he sold the company and went into public service. In 1991, Nashville elected Phil Bredesen mayor.

Bredesen was a Harvard graduate, a smart and energetic businessman, a skillful deal-maker. He swung a deal to bring the Dell computer company to Nashville. He led efforts to bring in two professional sports teams, the National Hockey League's Nashville Predators and the National Football League's Tennessee Titans. The Predators found a home

Missing person's flyer circulated during the massive search for Marcia.

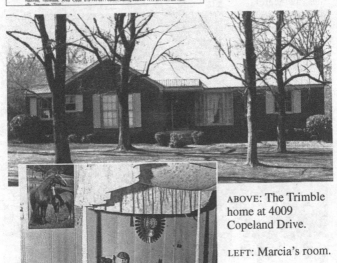

ABOVE: The Trimble home at 4009 Copeland Drive.

LEFT: Marcia's room.

Unless otherwise noted, all photos are courtesy of the Nashville Police Department.

Mrs. Howard's driveway with the Thorpe garage visible in the distance.

Police follow up on Mrs. Maxwell's statement that she saw Marcia and two other persons from her driveway, looking through the hedge to Mrs. Howard's driveway.

Crowds gathered in front of the Trimble house, waiting for news of the missing Girl Scout.

Police fingerprinted Marcia's desk at Julia Green Elementary School.

Police hurried to investigate the writing on the pavement of a church parking lot.

Jeffrey Womack, the fifteen-year-old who lived at 4102 Copeland Drive.

Tracking dogs, Wied and Drux, from Philadelphia, were brought in to search for Marcia. Detective Tommy Jacobs and Major George Currey led the way, with Tom McGinn, the dogs' handler.

Interior of the Thorpe garage showing the back left corner, where Marcia's body was found.

Detective Diane Vaughn was putting the pieces together in 1975 after Jerome Barrett was arrested for raping a Belmont student.

Photo courtesy of Deborah Sullivan

Marcia Trimble's fourth grade class at Julia Green Elementary School, with an empty chair for Marcia.

LEFT: Jerome Barrett's booking photo from when he was arrested in Berry Hill, March 12, 1975.

RIGHT: Jerome Barrett's booking photo after he was served with a grand jury indictment for the murder of Marcia Trimble, June 6, 2008.

The day of the verdict in the Sarah Des Prez murder, Detective Bill Pridemore and Sergeant Pat Postiglione received awards for their work on the Des Prez and Trimble cases. Left to right: Deputy Chief Steve Anderson, Sergeant Pat Postiglione, Detective Bill Pridemore, and Chief Ronal Serpas.

On June 6, 2008, District Attorney Torry Johnson announced Jerome Barrett's indictment for the murder of Marcia Trimble. Left to right: Chief Ronal Serpas, Captain Mickey Miller, DA Torry Johnson at microphone with Deputy DA Tom Thurman behind him, Sergeant Pat Postiglione, and Detective Bill Pridemore.

The prosecution team in the Marcia Trimble trial: Deputy DA Tom Thurman at podium with ADA Rachel Sobrero (left) and ADA Katy Miller (right).

Used with permission by Susan Niland

in a new arena, built on Broadway in the revitalized down-town district. The city built a stadium for the Titans, across the Cumberland River from Fort Nashborough, in sight of the Metro Nashville Police Department. All of this and more during Mayor Bredesen's two four-year terms.

Still, not all Nashvillians were pleased with Nashville's new face. The shift to a major city in the nation brought with it the problems associated with urban environments. Nashville neighborhoods were changing, too, as "new money" sent the real estate market climbing. Million- and multimillion-dollar houses sprouted up everywhere. Upscale suburbs kept taking over pastures on the outskirts of the city. It was a common pattern in some of the traditional neighborhoods: An elderly person moved out or died, and the forty-year-old house sat empty for a few weeks. Then one day, a bulldozer would come in and raze the structure. Trucks would carry off its remains. A few months later, a new McMansion would appear in its place.

Virginia Trimble sold the family house on Copeland in 1998 and moved to a condo. The modest redbrick house was torn down, and a larger upscale house was constructed on the site.

Progress was happening all over Nashville.

A New Yorker and Harvard graduate serving as mayor of Nashville during the 1990s was no more remarkable than some of the changes that occurred in the police department during the same period. The recruit class of 1993 was the most diverse in the department's history. Of the sixty-four recruits, one-third were minorities—African Americans, Hispanics, and Asians. Females accounted for 14 percent of the class. Chief Robert Kirchner implemented a Domestic Violence Division, formed with specially trained domestic violence detectives, with Captain Shirley Davis in command. Davis had worked the Marcia Trimble case in the days of the "old boys' club" when females were just lucky to be police officers. Then in 1996, Emmett H. Turner succeeded Robert Kirchner as chief of police, and Nashville had its first African American chief of police.

Turner had been a Youth Guidance officer in 1975 when Marcia Trimble disappeared. "I worked on the case from the very first night until the body was found," he said. He vowed to keep pressing the Trimble investigation.

February 25, 2000, marked twenty-five years since Marcia Trimble disappeared. Many Nashvillians remembered where they were when they first heard that Marcia was missing, and where they were when they heard her body had been discovered. Veteran *Tennessean* reporter Frank Ritter wrote an article, "Why We Still Wonder: Who Killed Marcia?" He said the case had involved more police man-hours than any other case on file. He compared it to the 1996 murder of JonBenét Ramsey, the six-year-old child found dead in the basement of her home in Boulder, Colorado. Virginia Trimble met the well-respected *Tennessean* reporter when he was working on the article. Their meeting became another life-changing moment—this time in a happy way.

A Metro police detective quoted in the *Nashville Scene* expressed the general feeling of the public when he called the case "the biggest murder mystery in Nashville history." Following the media's coverage of the solemn anniversary, police received a new wave of calls, but the leads did not result in finding Marcia's killer. A decade of DNA testing had not produced Marcia's killer. As Nashville crossed the threshold into the promising twenty-first century, the city was still haunted by the memory of the girl who walked across the street to deliver Girl Scout cookies and never returned.

In February 2002, Davidson County DA Torry Johnson and Police Chief Emmett Turner created Nashville's first Cold Case Unit. The unique team of investigators grew out of the Technical Surveillance Unit, under the command of Detective Terry McElroy. McElroy was the undercover cop who worked with Jeffrey Womack at the Jolly Ox in 1979. Detective Grady Elam, a former member of the Murder Squad, was also in Technical Surveillance. In their spare time, McElroy and Elam reviewed old, unsolved cases. The two were joined by Sergeant Charlie Griffin and Al Gray, an investigator from the district attorney's office. The team was officially named the Cold Case Unit. Detective Bill Pridemore was assigned to the unit later in 2002, followed by Sergeant Patrick Postiglione in 2003. Postiglione assumed charge of the Cold Case Unit as he continued to work the "mystery murders." Though under the control of the police department, the unit was housed in the district attorney's office in the Washington Square building on 2nd Avenue. The multiagency unit worked exclusively with old, unsolved cases—specifically those that had been inactive for five years or more. During 2002 and 2003, the Cold Case Unit cleared nine older homicide cases. The new squad was on a roll.

Bill Pridemore had begun his career in law enforcement after graduating from the Nashville Police Academy in 1976. The Marcia Trimble investigation was a year old, still in the forefront of Nashville's consciousness. Pridemore was familiar with the case but never imagined he might someday work on it.

Although Pridemore graduated from Stratford High School in Nashville, his family had moved to the city from Omaha, Nebraska, when he was in high school, and Pridemore considered himself a huge Nebraska Cornhuskers football fan; as a teenager in Omaha, he'd dreamed of playing for the Cornhuskers. But after his high school graduation, he took some courses at a community college and spent some time working for UPS. He was like a lot of young men, trying to find his place in the world. When he was accepted as a Police Academy recruit, he knew he'd found it.

When Pridemore came out of rookie school in May 1976,

he was assigned to the South Station. His lieutenant was Tom Cathey. Lieutenant Cathey, who initially headed up the Marcia Trimble murder investigation, had been transferred from Homicide in January 1976 when the Trimble case seemed to have hit a wall. Pridemore did his time in Patrol, became a detective in February 1984, and was assigned to Homicide, working what police called "smoking gun murders."

In these cases, there were usually witnesses, and everyone knew who pulled the trigger. The young detective did his job well, and the next year, he was nominated to join the Murder Squad, the unit that investigated "mystery murders," where there was no known suspect. It was an honor to be considered, for the nomination came from the current members of the squad. Solving mystery murders called for keen investigative skills, tracking down leads and clues, following the case to its logical conclusion. The unit unanimously accepted Bill Pridemore, and in late 1985, he started working on the Murder Squad.

As the junior member of the unit, Pridemore was on call at all hours. After the detectives worked the homicide scene, Pridemore would stay with the body until it was finally picked up and taken to the morgue. Spending long hours with corpses became his business. Bizarre, violent deaths became his routine. The week-by-week, month-by-month close encounters with murder took a toll on the detective—not uncommon in his line of work. Visions of the faces of innocent victims came to him at strange hours. Bill Pridemore, known for being both tough and compassionate, wrestled with his own personal hauntings, even as he developed a reputation for solving the toughest cases—cases with no obvious leads.

Pridemore and Sergeant Pat Postiglione began working together on the Murder Squad in 1988, and long before the Cold Case Unit was formed, the detectives were responsible for tracking down some of Nashville's most notorious murderers, such as Paul Reid, whose 1997 killing spree included the murders of seven workers at McDonald's, Captain D's, and Baskin-Robbins fast-food restaurants in two counties. ADA Tom Thurman prosecuted the cases in Davidson County, and in 1999 and 2000, Reid received death sentences. In the years to come, Thurman, Pridemore, and Postiglione would work together on several of Nashville's high-profile cases.

Pridemore and Postiglione were a study in contrasts. Postiglione, who came from Italian and Irish stock, grew up in New York City, in Queens. He'd been in Nashville since 1977 but still spoke with the clip of a New Yorker. Pridemore grew up in the South and Midwest. He had a quick smile and an easy laugh, while Postiglione wore a more serious expression, his dark eyes glinting. Stocky, broad-shouldered Pridemore contrasted with his slender partner. Postiglione, always perfectly groomed, with a thin black mustache, seemed at home in dress clothes—jacket, sharply creased pants, starched shirt, and tie—while the more casual Pridemore gave the impression of enduring a coat and tie until he could change into his comfortable golfing clothes.

But the two made an effective team, forging a relationship as solid as steel—part friendship, but much more. Each trusted the other with his life.

On the heels of the Paul Reid convictions, Pridemore and Postiglione picked up a decade-old case known as the Music Row Murder. A Belmont College student working as an intern on Music Row was shot as he left Evergreen Records one night in 1989. He had discovered an attempt by some independent record promoters to manipulate the playlists of country music radio. Bill Pridemore received the call the night the murder occurred in 1989, and he worked the case with Pat Postiglione. But the case went cold. In 2002, Pridemore's assignment to the Cold Case Unit gave him the opportunity to take another shot at the unsolved case.

Richard D'Antonio, a.k.a. Tony D., was a record promoter on Music Row in 1989. He was living in Las Vegas when Detectives Pridemore and Postiglione cracked the case, proving Tony D. killed Kevin Hughes because he was afraid the promoters were about to be exposed.

By the time D'Antonio was convicted in 2003—another case prosecuted by Tom Thurman—Pridemore and Postiglione were lead investigators on the Janet March case,* a missing person's case turned homicide. Janet March, a young artist, mother, and wife of up-and-coming lawyer Perry March, had disappeared in August 1996. Her husband insisted that she had simply driven away after they argued, and he did not report his wife missing for two weeks. After another week, her car was located with some of her belongings in it, but Janet March was never seen again.

That was a tough one. There was no body. That one would take longer to solve.

As a Cold Case detective, Detective Pridemore learned everything he could about handling old, unsolved cases. He and Postiglione visited the Las Vegas Cold Case Unit to compare how that group worked the long-forgotten files. Pridemore and Postiglione spoke with national experts, anyone who could help them transition into solving cold cases.

Both men learned quickly how much other Cold Case Units relied upon DNA analysis in solving cases. They attended seminars on DNA. They heard the famous Dr. Henry Lee speak on blood, DNA, and how to preserve evidence. The detectives read everything they could get their hands on about DNA as an investigative tool for law enforcement.

Basically, evidence collected from rape kits and crime scenes had to be compared to the suspect's DNA sample.

---

* See *An Unfinished Canvas: A True Story of Love, Family, and Murder in Nashville* by Michael Glasgow and Phyllis Gobbell (Berkley, 2007).

DNA from semen would be "cut" with special enzymes. If the enzymes cut the semen sample and the suspect's blood or saliva sample into the same number of fragments of the same length, the odds of a match would be calculated. DNA analysis could show that the semen sample was not the same as the suspect's, and it could produce a high probability that the sample was from the suspect—for example, only one chance in three hundred million that the semen sample could have come from someone else besides the suspect.

For cold case purposes, in the event there was no suspect, the procedure would be to enter the DNA evidence into the FBI's CODIS, short for Combined DNA Index System, a huge database that conveys information from crimes and criminals throughout the United States. When DNA evidence was collected and stored properly, it could be a valuable forensic tool decades after the crime.

DNA helped Pridemore solve the murder of Tammy Rankin. In 1998, he was called to the crime scene, a crawl space littered with drug paraphernalia and food wrappers. The victim wore dirty purple socks, sneakers with the laces still tied, and pants turned inside out. Police interviewed drug dealers and prostitutes in the area, as well as Tammy's family, and learned that she may have been turning tricks for drugs. She had received psychiatric treatment and didn't always take her meds. Her lifestyle made the investigation more difficult than most, and after a few months the leads dried up.

After the case qualified as a "cold case," Pridemore got another shot at it. He'd had all the evidence from the crime scene collected and bagged, and he was interested in a blue polo shirt with Tammy's blood on it that had been found near the body. He collected DNA samples from all the men associated with Tammy who would allow police to swab their mouths, and he sent the samples to the Tennessee Bureau of Investigation (TBI) to try to match them to sweat stains on the collar of the polo shirt. In April 2002, he got the call. The CODIS database had revealed that the sweat came from a frequently homeless man named John Albert Harris, who had a long rap sheet. Police located and arrested Harris. He plea-bargained for twenty-three years in prison with no chance of parole.

Advancing DNA technology gave hope that the Trimble case might eventually be solved. From 1990 to 1996, police had tested approximately seventy young men who lived in the Trimbles' neighborhood in 1975. By 2004, the number was closer to one hundred. So far, the semen stains from Marcia Trimble's clothing had not identified her killer.

Captain Mickey Miller had never given up on the Trimble case. In 2001 and 2002 he was still attempting to find young people who were children in the Copeland-Dorcas area in February 1975, to obtain blood samples. Many of the families had left the neighborhood in the first few years after Marcia's death. Captain Miller made contacts as far away as Canada, but some of the young men and women still lived at home. A number of them had been in and out of mental institutions. Miller re-interviewed Rhonda Allen, who had first told investigators about the neighborhood children's participation in "sex games." Following that interview, Sergeant Postiglione went to Turney Center to follow up with one of the boys from the neighborhood who was in prison. The young man added some information about the "sex games," saying it was mostly boys who performed oral sex on one another, and that the little boy who accused Jeffrey Womack of molesting him was actually molested by several of the other neighborhood boys.

Several activities related to the case took place in the spring of 2002. Virginia Trimble submitted to hypnosis once again, to try to recall more facts about the evening Marcia disappeared, but nothing of significance came from the hypnosis.

But around the same time, it appeared there might be some progress in the case.

Captain Mickey Miller contacted Dr. William Bass, a forensic scientist who spent most of his professional career at the University of Tennessee, Knoxville, in the Department of Forensic Anthropology. Best known for establishing the legendary "Body Farm," Dr. Bass spent many years researching the decomposition of dead bodies and consulted with police departments all over the nation. Captain Miller asked him to review the autopsy report on Marcia Trimble and render an opinion on time of death.

The time of death had always been a troubling issue for police. Dr. Jerry Francisco's final autopsy report stated that Marcia Trimble died shortly after she disappeared, though his earlier estimate had put the time of death at just a few days before her body was found. Time of death was one of the issues Jeffrey Womack's attorneys hammered when he was charged with the murder in 1979.

Dr. Bass divided the thirty-three-day period from February 25 to March 30 into three segments and counted the number of days the temperature was 32 degrees and below and the number of days the temperature was 52 degrees and above. The temperature reached 52 degrees on ten days at the end of the month, only ten days when blowflies would have been active, causing the beginnings of decomposition. The autopsy report stated there was minimal decomposition, meaning, in Dr. Bass's words, "the eggs of blowflies were about to hatch or had just hatched."

Dr. Bass pointed out the temperatures he was using were outside temperatures, and it would have been even cooler inside the Thorpes' storage building, in the dark corner where Marcia's body was found. He reviewed the autopsy report that stated there was minimal decomposition, clean clothing that "did not appear to be worn for a week or a month," and livor mortis that suggested the "body was not moved but was consistent with the location and position where she was found." His findings regarding blowfly activity supported Dr. Francisco's report. Dr. Bass stated: "It is my professional opinion that she was in the shed the entire 33 days."

It should have been settled: Marcia Trimble was killed shortly after she disappeared. But not everyone was satisfied. The question remained: How did searchers miss finding the body?

In 2004, Detective Pridemore and Sergeant Postiglione were immersed in the Janet March case, one where DNA science could not help—the case with no body, no crime scene, no cause of death. Her husband, Perry, the only viable suspect from the time she disappeared in 1996, was now in Mexico. Pridemore and Postiglione put their energies into the case. Months later, ADA Tom Thurman decided that at last he could secure a conviction based upon the circumstantial evidence that the Cold Case detectives had assimilated. Thurman obtained a grand jury indictment against Perry March. March was extradited from Mexico in 2005. He was tried and convicted of second-degree murder in 2006, ten years after the crime. No body, no cause of death, no time of death—securing a conviction in such a case was an extraordinary accomplishment for Tom Thurman and the Cold Case detectives.

In January 2004, Nashville mayor Bill Purcell named Ronal S. Serpas as the new police chief for the city. Former chief of police Emmett Turner had retired after thirty-four years on the force. Serpas came from the state of Washington where he'd served as director of the State Patrol. Serpas, distrustful of Turner's assistants as well as the experienced veterans on the force, quickly implemented a reorganization plan, with an emphasis on traffic and patrol.

In a shocking move, Chief Serpas canceled the agreement with the district attorney's office, whereby the Cold Case Unit was under police auspices but located in the district attorney's office. By that time, Terry McElroy and Grady Elam had retired. Sergeant Postiglione consulted with the Cold Case Unit but was not full-time. Al Gray was reassigned to the district attorney's office. Bill Pridemore, the only detective left to investigate cold cases exclusively, was transferred back to Homicide and instructed to work on the old cases when he had time. The move outraged several victim advocacy groups. The *Nashville Scene* reported the decision by Serpas in February 2005 and quoted several citizens who still hoped the murderers of their family members would be found. Virginia Trimble said, "If somebody had information that could help solve Marcia's case, who would they call? There is no Cold Case Unit for them to call."

The advocacy groups put pressure on Serpas, but the chief initially refused to budge until finally, after intense pressure from citizens, he relented and reformed the Cold Case Unit. Pat Postiglione was still in charge as the sergeant, and Bill Pridemore was senior detective. The Cold Case offices were on the first floor of the Criminal Justice Center, in the rear of the building. The Homicide/Murder Squad office became the Homicide/Cold Case Unit.

Captain Mickey Miller was another veteran officer affected by the new chief's reorganization plan. In 1990, Chief Kirchner had put Captain Miller in command of the Personal Crimes Division of Criminal Investigation, the division responsible for homicide, rape, and robbery. Miller's work on the Trimble case during the 1990s may have angered the public, but within the police department, he'd made significant strides, stepping up to assistant chief of police. The new chief had other plans for him. In 2004, Captain Miller's new assignment was commander of the West Precinct. He moved from the Criminal Justice Center downtown to the outlying precinct on Charlotte Avenue. Officially, he was no longer involved with the Trimble investigation. But the case had become personal for Mickey Miller. He had talked with Virginia Trimble regularly since he began to review the case in 1990. He continued to work on the case on his own time, and he still hoped Virginia would have justice for Marcia. Justice, Miller believed, meant that Jeffrey Womack would someday be nailed for the crime.

Chief Serpas was not finished with his plans for the department. Consistent with his emphasis on traffic patrol, he instituted "Mission One," mandating that once a month, every non–field officer in every division had to work a weekend night riding on patrol. This required the detectives to actually put on their uniforms. Many questioned whether the "old heads"—as the younger guys called the veteran detectives—could physically perform the job. The "Weekend Patrol" disrupted their schedules and proved to be a terrible blow to the morale of the Nashville police force. Detectives sometimes spent all day in court on Friday and then that night on "Mission One." Bill Pridemore began to check out his options for retirement.

But by spring 2007, Sergeant Pat Postiglione and Detective Bill Pridemore were hot in Nashville, coming off the successful work in the Janet March case, which had resulted in the conviction of her husband, Perry March, for murder despite the absence of a body. The two men were the toast of the city. Their faces were found on covers of local magazines and the detectives had received top honors for their work in the March case. Their peers recognized them as "Investigators of the Year." The *Nashville Scene* had named the detectives, along with ADA Tom Thurman, "Nashvillians of the Year."

Still, Pridemore and Postiglione had their feet and egos grounded. The March case was over. It was time to get back to work, to focus on the shelves of three-ring binders that represented old, unsolved cases.

They did not anticipate that they'd be turning their attention to cases from 1975.

25

A Profile

Things were quieter in Bill Pridemore's world after the successful conclusion of the Perry March trial. All the grueling preparation had paid off, but Pridemore was glad for a few months when his workday didn't always extend into the night. Finally he'd been able to take a little time off. He was still thinking about retirement in the not-too-distant future. It was spring now, April 2007. He played golf most weekends. What a life it would be if he could go to the golf course every day. It might be a good thing to retire on a high note—while he could still relish in the Perry March conviction, while he could still think about his part in helping to find justice for Janet March's family.

On a bright, warm day in the first week of April, Sergeant Pat Postiglione stuck his head in Detective Bill Pridemore's office. The offices of the Homicide/Cold Case Unit consisted of three rooms. One was a meeting room. Another was the main office area, a brightly lit room where the other detectives worked in six cubicles. As senior detective, Pridemore had his own larger, private office in the back room. He spent a lot of time in his office, so he'd made it a pleasant place to be. He'd brought in lamps for soft light. He had a lava lamp next to his chair. His wall was decorated with photos. The personalized office was the envy of his fellow detectives.

The unit had received a call from a friend of the Sarah Des Prez family inquiring about the status of the case. Often, where there had been some publicity in the newspaper or on TV about the Cold Case Unit, family members or friends would call about various other cold cases.

Postiglione was carrying a large black three-ring binder. He dropped it on Pridemore's desk with a thud. It was the case file of Sarah Des Prez, the Vanderbilt coed murdered in February 1975.

"What do you think?" The sergeant stared at the detective. Working together for so long, the two experienced partners and close friends could almost read each other's thoughts.

Pridemore glanced at the file, then back up at Postiglione. Both detectives nodded at the same time. It was time to take a fresh look at the Des Prez file.

Pridemore took the Sarah Des Prez file and spread it out all around him. He went through every report, every letter, every document. He studied the copies of newspaper articles. On unsolved cases, he always found it helpful to read the theories of the media and the public.

Bill Pridemore always tried to keep an open mind and not get tunnel vision. He had learned over the years to never rule out anything or anyone. He compiled a list of possible suspects: neighbors, students, everyone Des Prez knew or came into contact with. He studied every page of the case file and reviewed the officers' reports line by line. He made an outline of the entire case, noting every piece of evidence. The process took most of the month of April.

On April 26, 2007, Pridemore and Postiglione drove out to the Metro Police property room, located in an old building

on the outskirts of the city. Assisted by property room personnel, the detectives were able to locate a large, dusty box in
the back containing packaged evidence of the Des Prez case.
Smaller boxes with the return address stamped "Federal Bureau of Investigation" were inside the large box. Each piece
of evidence was wrapped in old brown paper and encased in a
thick layer of dust. Pridemore filled out the forms, checked out
the evidence, and carried it back to his office. He began going
through each piece, making sure he had everything that was
mentioned in the case file.

One afternoon as he worked through stacks of documents
near the bottom of the Des Prez file, Pridemore bumped into
something that grabbed him—a court order dated March 26,
1975, signed by Judge Cornelius. The order was based on an
affidavit by Detective Diane Vaughn requesting that she be allowed to obtain hair samples from Jerome Barrett so that the
FBI Laboratory in Washington, D.C., could conduct an analysis "in the interest of furthering justice."

Bill Pridemore remembered Detective Diane Vaughn, who
had died from cancer in the 1990s. He had personally known
Vaughn and was aware of her outstanding reputation as a professional, no-nonsense detective. Pridemore studied the order.
He also found a Metropolitan Police Department property re-
ceipt that listed three articles of clothing owned by Jerome
Barrett. Again, Diane Vaughn was listed as the officer deposit-
ing the evidence.

Detective Vaughn had been one of the lead detectives in the
Des Prez case. Why had she been investigating Jerome Barrett? Why had she included his name in this file?

Closing the file, Pridemore added Jerome Barrett's name to
the list of possible suspects.

Weeks passed, and Pridemore continued to pore over the
file. He placed crime scene photos of the Des Prez apartment

around his office. The photos helped him to immerse himself in the case. One afternoon, as he made his third pass through the file, a signature caught his eye: J. Sledge. He knew Detective James Sledge to be a top-notch professional. Sledge had actually worked the Des Prez crime scene on the night of the murder. Pridemore glanced at the report. He had seen the report before, but Sledge's name caused him to read it again, more carefully this time. He looked at certain notations Sledge had made:

> "Third floor apartment with exit from kitchen to fire escape. Kitchen door locked."
>
> "No visible signs of forced entry."

Officer Sledge's words spoke to the veteran detective.

From the crime scene photos, Pridemore began to visualize the scene. He saw it as a typical college student's apartment, cluttered, clothes lying everywhere. He pictured the victim entering her apartment and preparing for bed, and then the suspect entering the apartment, progressing into the bedroom. Studying the details of the crime scene, Pridemore imagined how the suspect forced himself on the victim, how she ended up in the final position—the way her father and brother discovered her—and how the suspect searched and ransacked the room before finally exiting. Pridemore viewed the crime photos carefully, again and again, thinking about items that could be considered evidence now, items that were possibly overlooked in 1975.

The veteran detective was convinced that when Sarah Des Prez climbed the steps to the third floor, someone had been waiting for her in the shadows, and it wasn't a drunk college boy.

Pridemore was especially interested that the report mentioned *9 Negroid pubic hairs*. The hair evidence was so encouraging that Pridemore got a little ahead of himself. On

Thursday, May 3, 2007, even before he located the evidence, he prepared an official examination request and called a private forensic lab he had used on several cases in the past to ask if they could examine the hair evidence. He had a good working relationship with the manager of Orchid Cellmark, a private forensic lab headquartered in Texas, with satellite offices across the nation, including Nashville. It was once the only lab besides the FBI Lab that could perform many of the DNA analyses. If he needed results quickly, Pridemore would submit a request to the Metro Police Department to spend the money for the lab services. Sometimes if the Nashville Police Department didn't approve enough money for the services, the Orchid Cellmark manager would cut a deal with Pridemore.

The following Monday, May 7, he contacted the FBI Lab and asked about evidence that the Metropolitan Police Department had sent to the FBI in 1975, specifically evidence taken at the Des Prez crime scene.

He waited. Pridemore knew he was onto something. The days dragged by.

On Friday, May 11, an FBI records supervisor in Washington called him. The news came as a blow. All of the records concerning the Des Prez case had been destroyed in 1995. It was a day for bad news. Within hours, the Metropolitan Police Department property room called, saying that no one had been able to locate the pubic and head hair samples.

But Bill Pridemore took the news in stride. Bad news and no news were two of the hallmarks of working cold cases. He continued to push, looking for anything that might turn into a lead. With the help of the district attorney's office, he began searching through old 1975 Davidson County criminal cases, trying to find any possible connection to the Des Prez case. He was unsuccessful in locating even a cold trail.

Pridemore decided to approach the case from a different angle. He contacted the fingerprinting experts to find out if they could review the latent print files and determine if any others were found. He was notified on May 11 that some of the prints taken at the Des Prez crime scene were suitable for identification.

After receiving the bad news from the FBI, Pridemore turned to science to apply to the Des Prez case. He and Postiglione had been successful in using DNA in other cold case files. He wondered if it was possible to use DNA analysis in this case. Pridemore glanced over at the Des Prez file. The Metro Police Department had sent the FBI evidence from the Des Prez crime scene in April 1975. At that time, there was no DNA testing available. Was it possible that there were still some traces of DNA on the Des Prez bed quilts and sheets he had picked up from the property room? He understood the larger question: Even if there were samples of semen, would there be enough to create a DNA profile? He knew that PCR testing made it possible to amplify and copy even a small amount of DNA, but he also knew that as years went by, if evidence was not preserved properly, the samples could become degraded. No case he'd ever heard of used DNA evidence that had been around for thirty-two years.

He put his plan into action on May 21, 2007. He carried the victim's pillows, blanket, comforter, and blouse, along with photographs of the crime scene, to the TBI Lab in Nashville and completed a request for examination. Pridemore knew these were items that had never been examined or tested. In the section above his signature line, Pridemore wrote:

"Examine items for DNA evidence. If positive, examine for possible profile."

Meanwhile, Pridemore requested that the Metro Police Department compare the fingerprints found in the Des Prez crime scene with a Jerome Sydney Barrett, OCA (offender classification allotment) number 58410, based on Detective Vaughn's previous investigation.

During the next few weeks, Detective Pridemore spoke

many times with Chad Johnson, a scientist classified as a special agent with the TBI. On June 28, 2007, Pridemore took photographs of the crime scene to the TBI Lab. Agent Johnson, who had reviewed everything submitted, looked at the photos and asked for additional items from the scene. The next day, Pridemore carried Des Prez's bed sheets and a bed quilt to the lab, once again requesting examination for a possible DNA profile.

He continued working the Des Prez file along with his regular caseload. He knew that if the lab results revealed no DNA or if the DNA was too degraded for even the advanced PCR method to utilize, then the case was almost at the end of the line. But he had a feeling about it.

Bill Pridemore checked his voicemail on the afternoon of August 27, 2007. It was a typical busy Monday, and Pridemore was only half listening when the voice came on. It was Special Agent Joe Minor from the TBI Lab.

Minor said, "Bill, we're sending a report to your attention. You should get it tomorrow. Call me if you have questions."

The next day Pridemore found on his desk a large official envelope with a return address of the State of Tennessee, Tennessee Bureau of Investigation. There was a large red stamp marked "Confidential" on the outside of the envelope and the address was to Detective Bill Pridemore, Metro Police Department.

He sat down at his desk and opened the envelope. The three-page document was entitled "Official Serology/DNA Report," dated August 26, 2007. Victim: Sarah Des Prez. Pridemore scanned the first page of the report, which listed the exhibits he had provided to the lab. He dropped down to results. "Examination revealed the presence of semen." The report explained that the DNA was isolated and analyzed through the PCR technique and a gender marker established.

This meant they had determined the contributor was a male. There was a note below.

"The above male (unknown) DNA profile has been added to the CODIS Data Base for forensic unknown samples."

The TBI Lab tests determined that nearly all of the evidence—Sarah's blouse and all the bedclothes—contained the presence of semen. The report noted, "Each DNA profile was consistent with the male profile contained in the first exhibit."

The detective sat there and looked at the report. A DNA profile was like a fingerprint. Though the male suspect was still unknown, he had left his DNA fingerprint, and sooner or later, it would be identified. Bill Pridemore smiled to himself. The Des Prez case had gone from cold to hot.

26

Case Number 75-30512

The end of summer 2007 found Nashville in a brutal heat wave. August highs hit upper-90s most afternoons, with temperatures often spiking to over 100 degrees. Along with the heat came drought. Less than an inch of rain fell during the month of August. September was typically a cooler month, with gentle rains and hints of fall in the air, but the first week of September 2007 was sweltering, with temperatures still in the 90s and no significant rainfall.

Even in the midst of the heat wave, Bill Pridemore would have been happy to be on the golf course. He was one of those crazy golfers. But he had plenty of work to do in his air-conditioned office.

Following up on the TBI report, he was busy with the Des Prez case, attempting to eliminate suspects. His task now was to find all the males mentioned in the files, anyone connected with Sarah Des Prez, and try to obtain DNA samples. He started a new list of potential suspects and began the process.

* * *

Every state has one agency that acts as coordinator of the CO-DIS database, the DNA index system. In Tennessee, the TBI was the one agency that could enter names into CODIS. Every week the TBI matched unsolved murder files with new profiles in the computer system. In the event the computer located a match, the FBI physically double-checked the match and sent a letter to the local State law enforcement officials.

On Monday, October 1, 2007, Special Agents Joe Minor and Chad Johnson of the TBI Crime Lab called Pridemore. They had huge news. The FBI had contacted the TBI Lab with information that they had obtained a CODIS cross hit on the DNA profile from the Des Prez case.

The news got better.

"The profile matched another unsolved murder profile," Joe said. "Case 75-30512. That's Marcia Trimble."

Pridemore felt a rush of adrenaline. He tried to wrap his mind around the idea: *FBI scientists and the CODIS database have confirmed the same DNA profile on Sarah Des Prez and Marcia Trimble. How amazing was that!* After a minute, he realized that it made sense. Although Marcia was nine years old, and Sarah was a college student, both victims had been sexually assaulted and murdered, and both crimes took place in February 1975.

But the news was totally inconsistent with the work of the Nashville Police Department over the last thirty years.

The agents were not emotional-type guys. They were passing on the official information from the FBI, but Pridemore detected the uncharacteristic note of excitement in their voices. They wanted to know what his next move would be. Pridemore didn't have an immediate answer. Agent Minor volunteered the TBI's assistance.

The detective finished his conversation with the agents and wasted no time calling Sergeant Pat Postiglione to tell him about the Trimble match. He enjoyed being the bearer of the news.

And then for another moment Pridemore let himself think about the possibility that he could see both of these cold cases solved before he retired—Sarah Des Prez and Marcia Trimble. It was almost too much to imagine.

On the following day, Tuesday, October 2, Pridemore and Postiglione met with Deputy DA Tom Thurman and Captain Mickey Miller to discuss the similarities between the Des Prez and Trimble cases. They determined that one of the similarities was Sarah Des Prez's younger brother, Walter. The Des Prez family lived on Estes, one block from Copeland. Walter, who spent time in a mental institution, had committed suicide in San Francisco in 1990, but San Francisco Police retrieved a blood sample from the autopsy.

The detectives and Thurman ended their meeting with plans to begin the process once again of reviewing the Trimble file. Pridemore reviewed a portion of the file and determined at once that DNA samples from Walter Des Prez and other individuals associated with the case should be submitted to the TBI Crime Lab.

The next day, Pridemore went to the Metro Police Department evidence room and obtained DNA samples for individuals who were previously investigated in the Des Prez file. He submitted DNA from four males to the TBI Crime Lab.

On October 9, Detective Pridemore obtained a search warrant for Benjamin Blanton. Blanton had been a good friend of Sarah Des Prez and had actually stopped by her apartment on the night she was out with Trammell Hudson. Several days after the murder, police detectives had observed Blanton with scratches on his left and right forearms. Sergeant Postiglione went with Pridemore to the Blanton residence in Green Hills. Benjamin Blanton, tall and thin, wore a denim shirt and blue jeans. His graying hair was pulled back in a ponytail. A throw-back to the 1970s, Pridemore thought. Blanton glared at detectives through his round glasses and spoke in a deep voice that managed to be very loud. "This is an invasion of my rights as a U.S. citizen! I went through this in 1975." The detectives explained that they were not arresting him, that he was just one of many people being interviewed in connection with Sarah Des Prez's death, but he ranted on about police harassment. "This is highly irregular. You are interrupting my day." Finally, the detectives said if he didn't trust them, he might want to talk to Tom Thurman. He said, "I'll go see this Tom Thurman."

Blanton met with the assistant district attorney and explained that he did not trust the validity of DNA or polygraph, but he agreed to cooperate and give a blood sample. After Blanton gave the sample, Pridemore brought Blanton back to his residence. He was calmer on the way home. He talked about the burden of caring for his parents for twenty years. Pridemore noted that although Blanton had argued with and berated the two detectives, he had not required the execution of the search warrant.

That same day, the detectives obtained a DNA sample from Dr. Roger Des Prez, Sarah's elderly father. Although they had to go through an attorney first, Dr. Des Prez was cooperative. His wife did much of the talking. Sarah's father was quiet, reflective, as if remembering happier times with her.

On Thursday, October 11, Pridemore went back through the Des Prez file and reviewed the documents that Detective Diane Vaughn had generated, including those on Jerome Barrett and Charles Mintlow, an African American who'd lived in the same apartment building as Des Prez and had admitted to visiting the victim. Mintlow made sense, and though Pridemore still couldn't understand exactly why Vaughn had been investigating Barrett, he followed up on her findings. He requested that the TBI conduct a search to determine if Bar-

rett's and Mintlow's DNA standards had been included in the
CODIS database. Special Agent Connie Howard of the TBI
said Mintlow was in the national CODIS database but Barrett
was not. She advised Pridemore to call the Memphis Police
about the status of Jerome Barrett.

Pridemore called Sergeant Pride of the Memphis Police
Department sexual offender registry. She had some important
news. Barrett was in compliance with the requirement of being on the registry and was scheduled to report for a meeting
in December 2007. Pridemore asked, "Since he's on the list,
does that mean he's required to provide a DNA standard?"
Sergeant Pride didn't know. She referred Pridemore to the
state administrator of the sexual offender registry, Pam Beck.

Ms. Beck had more information. She said, "Anyone who
was placed in the Tennessee Department of Corrections prior
to 1996 is not required to provide a DNA standard." Bells
went off in Pridemore's head. Barrett had been convicted and
served time for the Judy Porter rape at Belmont—twenty years
before the 1996 date, in February 1976. In 1996 he was in
prison. That was the reason he was not included in the CODIS
registry.

Pridemore got busy. On Monday, October 15, he called
Sergeant Tim Helldorfer in Memphis, explaining that he was
trying to locate Jerome Barrett and obtain a DNA sample,
and that he would need to obtain a search warrant for Barrett's DNA. Sergeant Helldorfer agreed to assist Pridemore.
Whenever Nashville was ready, he would help in obtaining
the warrant.

The two officers scheduled a meeting in Helldorfer's office
for Wednesday, October 17.

27

Memphis

Detective Pridemore had work to do before his trip to Memphis. He had to prepare a search warrant and detailed affidavit. Pridemore had taken DNA samples in other cases. He knew the process.

Based upon years of experience, he also knew there was a good chance the search warrant would later be challenged on legal technicalities. In the affidavit for a warrant, he included the facts about the Des Prez murder, specifying that evidence from the sexual assault was found with African American pubic hairs and semen. He explained that there had been a rash of rapes and sexual assaults in the same general area where the victim's body was located. He stated in the affidavit: "The pattern of the assault is consistent with a white female being assaulted in a dorm room or apartment." He added that Jerome Barrett had been arrested and charged with committing at least two rapes and one attempted rape in the vicinity of Des Prez's residence, and that he was later tried and convicted for rape in

Davidson County Criminal Court. Once he was convicted of Judy Porter's rape, the others were not prosecuted.

The last thing Pridemore did was pick up sterile gloves and cotton swabs from the police supply room to take on his trip to Memphis.

Memphis, the largest city in Tennessee, is located on the Mississippi River in Shelby County. Founded in 1819 on the bluff above the river, it relied upon agriculture, specifically cotton, and grew to become the world's largest cotton market. Since the cotton economy depended on slave labor, Memphis also became a major slave market.

During the 1960s, the city was in the center of the civil rights movement. Martin Luther King Jr. was assassinated on April 4, 1968, at the Lorraine Motel in Memphis. The river town was also home to the famous Beale Street. Many notable entertainers got their start in Memphis. Music legends such as B. B. King, Johnny Cash, Jerry Lee Lewis, Roy Orbison, and Elvis Presley recorded for Sun Records in the 1950s, and Elvis purchased Graceland mansion there. The famous Peabody Hotel, located in downtown Memphis near Beale Street, was one of the finest hotels in the South; it was said, "The Mississippi Delta begins in the lobby of the Peabody Hotel."

There was another side of Memphis, a dark side. It had been ranked in the top four most dangerous cities in the United States for several years. In 2006, the metropolitan area of Memphis-Shelby County was ranked the second most dangerous in the nation. The Memphis Police were still reluctant to patrol certain areas of the city unless they had backup.

Early Wednesday morning, October 17, Detective Bill Pridemore picked up Sergeant Pat Postiglione outside the Criminal

Justice Center and headed west for Memphis. Postiglione normally liked to meet early in the morning with his detectives and discuss their cases, as well as check his e-mail, prior to going on any trips. However, the sergeant understood the need to get on the road this morning. The detectives would have to go to court in Memphis and obtain the judge's approval and signature prior to actually trying to track down Jerome Barrett. Sometimes the court process could take hours or even days—and Barrett might not be easy to locate.

The veteran officers were quiet on the first part of the trip out of Nashville. They cruised on I-40, heading west through gently rolling terrain. The trees were at peak color. It was a fine October day, a good day for a road trip. As the detectives approached the exit sign for Highway 50, Postiglione remarked, "How many of those inmates at Turney Center do you think we're responsible for?" The Department of Correction Turney Center prison was located off of Highway 50, near the Duck River.

Pridemore shook his head. "It's a nice morning and I don't want to think about those jerks." On a lighter note he said, "I have a friend who has a farm on the Duck River. This is beautiful country."

The detectives didn't say anything else about their previous work.

As they approached Shelby County, the detectives began discussing their plan. Sergeant Helldorfer had been very helpful. He already had it arranged for them to get the warrant.

Postiglione and Pridemore had followed many leads in many cases for years and had made many trips like this. They didn't let their expectations soar too high. A valuable part of the process was eliminating suspects, and that's what they expected to do. As they neared Memphis, they talked about who they would contact next. The two veteran detectives who often joked that they could read each other's minds didn't have to put into words their other thought: *It was great to be getting*

*one more shot at solving this case—and solving one meant
solving two.*

Pridemore called Sergeant Helldorfer's cell phone. Helldorfer told them to park in the garage across from police headquarters and the courthouse.

At 9:45 A.M., the two detectives met Helldorfer on the sidewalk by the south entrance of the square high-rise building. The sergeant was a small, dark-haired man who wore a shirt and tie. Helldorfer took the men inside and led them down a long connecting hall to Division 8 of the Shelby County General Sessions Court. During a break, Helldorfer went up and whispered to the assistant district attorney. The district attorney announced to the Court that there were detectives from Nashville here asking the Court to consider issuing a search warrant.

Judge Tim Dwyer had Bill Pridemore sworn in as a witness and asked him several questions. Pridemore explained the history of the Des Prez case and why they needed the DNA. After a short hearing, Judge Dwyer agreed to issue the search warrant allowing the detectives to obtain DNA samples from Jerome Barrett. At 10:50 A.M., Judge Dwyer signed the warrant. The officers walked back to the police station to Sergeant Helldorfer's office.

Helldorfer drove the detectives to the address listed for Jerome Barrett, a modest brick home on Eldridge Avenue. He was not there, nor was he at their backup address on Pecan Circle. There, they spoke to a woman who advised them that Jerome Barrett's father lived at this address. The father was disabled, and the woman was apparently his caregiver. Pridemore assured the woman that Barrett was not in trouble, but they needed to speak to him.

"He has a grass cutting business," the woman said. "He's out working."

Sergeant Helldorfer gave her a business card. "Would you have him call me?" he said.

They thanked the woman and left. They waited another hour, hoping Barrett would call. Helldorfer took them out for some good old Memphis barbecue.

At 1:00 P.M., Pridemore and Postiglione decided to return to Nashville. Sergeant Helldorfer assured them that he'd try to locate Barrett later in the evening.

Pridemore drove toward the interstate and decided to stop for gas before starting the trip back. They were still at the service station in the downtown area when he received a call from Helldorfer. "Barrett called and left his phone number," the sergeant said.

Postiglione punched in the number. Barrett answered.

"Something has come up in Nashville," Postiglione said. "We'd like to talk with you."

"I'm working," Barrett said. "I don't want to meet the police around any of my customers."

Postiglione kept his voice calm and courteous. "We'll meet wherever you want."

Barrett suggested they meet at his father's home, where the detectives had gone earlier in the day. Postiglione immediately called Helldorfer back and told him about the conversation. The Memphis sergeant insisted that he and another detective meet with the Nashville officers and escort them to the location. "That's a rough part of town," Helldorfer said.

The detectives waited at the service station for the Memphis Police Department squad car. At approximately 1:45 P.M., the officers drove up to Barrett's father's house on Pecan Circle. As they got out of their cars, a tall black man walked down the driveway toward them. He was wearing army fatigue pants, an army jacket, black work books, and a knit cap.

"I'm Sergeant Helldorfer of the Memphis Police Department," the sergeant said. "Are you Jerome Barrett?"

"Yes," Barrett said.

"Do you have identification?" Postiglione asked.

Barrett produced his driver's license. The photo ID showed him with a fuller face. Postiglione looked at him, checked the picture, and looked back at him. Barrett volunteered that his weight loss was due to religious fasting.

"Mr. Barrett, this is Sergeant Pat Postiglione and Detective Bill Pridemore from Nashville," Sergeant Helldorfer said. "They have a search warrant for you, sir."

Barrett said nothing while he studied the detectives.

"Please read this search warrant, Mr. Barrett," Pridemore said as he held out the warrant. Barrett took it and read the whole document, and handed it back to Pridemore.

"That's not me," he said, without emotion. Then Barrett began to ask questions. "What specific facts did you tell the judge to get this warrant?" It was clear to Pridemore that the man knew the system.

Nevertheless, Barrett went to the Memphis Police cruiser without objection. He climbed into the backseat, and Pridemore took a sample from the inside right side of his cheek with one cotton swab and the inside left side of his cheek with another. Afterward, the men stood in the yard, and Pridemore told Barrett that his DNA samples would be compared to the evidence in the case.

"If they don't match, you'll never see us again," he said.

As the Nashville detectives got in the car, Barrett snarled, "Well, I won't see you again."

Pridemore thanked Barrett, and the two Cold Case detectives headed back to I-40 and Nashville. On their way, they called Sergeant Helldorfer and thanked him for his effort in the case.

The main purpose of the trip had been to obtain DNA samples to eliminate Barrett as a suspect, and the detectives had done their job. Driving back, both detectives admitted they didn't know much about Jerome Barrett, but that he had "been around the block and knew the system." Pridemore commented, "I think Diane Vaughn had figured him out."

On Thursday, October 18, Pridemore submitted the DNA samples of Jerome Barrett to the TBI Lab, along with a form requesting that the samples be compared to the DNA evidence in the Sarah Des Prez and Marcia Trimble cases.

28

Making the Case

Other cases besides the Sarah Des Prez case demanded Detective Bill Pridemore's attention. The detective was accustomed to working several cases at once, but the Des Prez murder was never far from his mind. He thought about the Trimble murder, too, and the DNA evidence that connected both of the cases from February 1975. It was still mind-boggling to think that the same perpetrator could have committed both crimes. The question remained, *Who?* Pridemore knew it was possible that the DNA profile might never be identified, that the killer might get away with the murders, even with the DNA "fingerprint" on file, but he had a gut feeling that wasn't going to happen.

Toward the end of October, Pridemore spent significant time attempting to track down students who had lived in Mims Hall during fall and winter of 1974–1975. It was good to be out making calls, out from behind his desk where files looked like smokestacks. The low humidity was a welcome change from the past weeks. The sun gave off a pale gold light. Indian summer in Nashville. But he hit a dead end; Vanderbilt security notified Pridemore that they were unable to locate any of the Mims Hall residents from 1974–1975. The university had destroyed all admission records from 1979 and before. This was another frustrating aspect of working cold case files; over the years, records were destroyed. A search of Sarah Des Prez's high school yearbooks turned up no new information, either.

Pridemore also investigated individuals who had dated Sarah Des Prez during that time period. He learned there was a rumor going around that Sarah had dated a freshman football player while she was working at Mims Hall and that Sarah had "put him down hard." Desperate for any new lead, the detective scheduled an appointment with Anna Chytil, who had been a friend of Sarah's and was thought to have information about the football player. In the interview, Anna said she and Sarah shared an apartment for a short time. She knew there was a football player in Sarah's life; he often came over to Mims Hall when Sarah was working. But she did not know his name.

Another lead that led to a dead end.

Late Tuesday afternoon, October 30, Pridemore received a phone call from Special Agent Chad Johnson of the TBI Crime Lab. He wanted Pridemore to meet with him on Thursday. Pridemore confirmed the appointment and wrote it on his calendar. Johnson didn't mention the purpose of the meeting, but Pridemore expected more questions in the Des Prez case.

Thursday morning, November 1, Pridemore worked several different files. At 10:00 A.M., he left his office and the Cold Case Unit to go to the TBI Crime Lab meeting. He planned to return to the unit in time for an 11:30 meeting with other Cold Case detectives. He drove his undercover car east of downtown to the TBI building on Ben Allen Road. The Consolidated Facilities of the TBI was a modern building that housed several laboratories, as well as administrative of-fices of the Tennessee Bureau of Investigation. After passing through security at the entrance, Pridemore was met by the young scientist, Agent Johnson, in the lobby of the building. Johnson's manner was guarded, and his expression was one the detective couldn't quite make out—a suppressed smile? Pridemore wondered what was up.

Instead of going into the small office the scientists used, adjacent to the laboratory, Johnson led the way to an elevator, and they went upstairs.

"We're meeting in another office that has more room," Johnson said,

"Sure," Pridemore said. Generally, they would make con-versation as they walked to a meeting. But today something was different.

Johnson and Pridemore entered a spacious conference room. The room was adjacent to the office of the TBI direc-tor, Mark Gwyn. It had a large conference table and a dry-erase whiteboard. The TBI emblem hung on the wall. It was a typical government-sanitized conference room, but what was not typical was the fact that the room was full. In addition to Pridemore and Johnson, Agents Joe Minor, Laura Bose, and Connie Howard were sitting at the table, along with Assistant Director Wilder and Director Gwyn. Questions were buzzing in Pridemore's head, but he didn't think this was going to be a *bad* meeting. The atmosphere seemed congenial enough. He took a seat by the director.

Everyone made introductory comments concerning the weather and crime in Nashville. "I guess you're wondering why we brought you up here," Director Gwyn said, finally. "We have the results of the DNA test concerning Sarah Des Prez."

Pridemore waited. He was a little impatient, but he man-aged not to squirm. Everyone around the conference table was silent, their attention fixed on the director.

Gwyn said, "Based on the preliminary results, there is a match between the evidence and profile established at Sarah Des Prez's apartment with a one Jerome S. Barrett."

It took a minute for the fact to sink in, the reality that they'd actually cracked the more than thirty-year-old case. "That's good news," Pridemore said. "Excellent work, everybody." Several agents nodded, murmuring agreement.

Director Gwyn also nodded and smiled. Pridemore's adrenaline started kicking in. Exciting as it was to solve the Des Prez case, he realized that wasn't the only reason he had been called to this meeting with all the agents and the director.

"We also have a match in another one of your unsolved murder cases," the director said. Clearly, he wanted to make the most of this moment. "In 75-30512, we have a match with the evidence provided in that case and with Jerome S. Barrett. That's the Trimble case, of course."

For a minute, no one said anything. Pridemore could scarcely believe what he'd heard. Though he already knew that the profile matched evidence in both cases, to have a name, to say *Jerome Barrett's DNA is a match in the Marcia Trimble case*, was incredible. The case that had become the ultimate murder mystery in Nashville finally had a link to solid evidence.

Director Gwyn leaned forward. "Bill, everybody in this room has worked on it one time or another. That's the reason we all wanted to come to this meeting." No one at TBI headquarters had ever called Pridemore by his first name. The director slid a large file across the table. "We've assembled Jerome Barrett's record and everything we could locate on him. Each agent had an assignment. It's all there." He indicated the file. "This is top priority. Anything the TBI can do for you, let us know."

Pridemore looked at the file and back at Director Gwyn. "Thank you, sir. We really appreciate it," he said.

Pridemore noticed that the agents, all well-respected professionals, were beaming. It had taken a while for their crime lab to build a reputation. The TBI Crime Lab was about to hit a new level based on their work on the Des Prez and Trimble cases.

For the next forty-five minutes the agents discussed Jerome Barrett's record. When the meeting was over, Pridemore spoke to every individual agent and the TBI director personally. "You're just as much a part of the cold case team as I am," he said.

Director Gwyn shook his hand as they left the conference room. "Good luck on this one, Bill."

"Thank you, sir. Thank you for your work and the work of this Bureau."

Pridemore walked to the elevator. When he reached his car, he sat in it and looked over the file. Jerome S. Barrett. He thought about Barrett's hard words: "I won't see you again." As Pridemore thumbed through the file, he thought about all the work the police department had done on the Marcia Trimble case, all the pain Virginia Trimble and the family had suffered for so long.

"Yes, I'll be coming to see you again, Mr. Barrett," he said. He closed the file and started the engine. And then he was struck by the thought: *How the hell are we going to place him on Copeland?*

29

Dark Overcoat

Although Detective Bill Pridemore and Sergeant Pat Postiglione remained quiet, the news of the DNA material on Des Prez and Trimble shot around the Nashville Police Department. Pridemore was surprised that a number of veteran officers dismissed the results of the DNA in regard to the Trimble case and continued to maintain that Jeffrey Womack was Marcia Trimble's killer.

At the same time, though, Bill Pridemore continued to plan his retirement for the following year. After thirty-five years of police work, he was tired. Tired of murder and murderers. He'd known too many men who wore themselves out on the job and spent their retirement years in doctors' offices. Pridemore was in good health. He wanted to retire while he could still enjoy life. He would work on his golf game, but he wouldn't spend all his time on the golf course; he'd do more volunteer work through the church. He and his wife Denise were active in the Hermitage United Methodist Church.

Deputy DA Tom Thurman called Pridemore and asked him

to review the Des Prez case file in preparation for testifying
before the grand jury. As a part of that review and preparation,
Pridemore had to confirm that no statement or evidence had
been overlooked. Excitement mounted in the Cold Case Unit.
Bill Pridemore couldn't think too much about his retirement yet.

In 1975, the state medical examiner had been Dr. Jerry Francisco, whose office was located in Memphis, but some years
later Davidson County hired its own medical examiner, Dr.
Charles Harlan, who was also chief medical examiner for the
State. In 1985, during Dr. Harlan's tenure, Nashville built
the Forensic Science Center on Hermitage Avenue, down the
street from the old General Hospital. The current medical examiner was Dr. Bruce Levy.

The November 12, 2007, meeting with Dr. Levy brought
Pridemore's perspective on the case back down to earth. All
cases had problems, and this one was no exception. Dr. Levy
told Pridemore the good news first, that his office had located
most of the medical reports from February 1975. However, the
medical reports from the first week of February were missing,
and the ones they did have did not include those of Sarah Des
Prez.

Pridemore recognized the significance of the missing medical reports. In a trial, the Court would've allowed Dr. Levy
to testify from the Des Prez medical reports since Levy's office had created them, but without the reports his testimony
would be limited, since he had not actually participated in the
medical examination of Sarah Des Prez's body. In short, the
missing records could present a huge roadblock for the prosecutors. There had to be evidence of a homicide before the
DNA results could be effective or even admitted into evidence.

But this wasn't Pridemore's first rodeo. He knew there was
another way around this issue. He asked Dr. Levy to examine the photos of the body and read the initial police reports.

Pridemore waited for about twenty minutes while Dr. Levy completed the task.

When Dr. Levy finished, he looked at Pridemore and nodded. After reviewing the reports and studying the photographs of Sarah Des Prez's body, Dr. Levy stated that in his medical opinion Sarah Des Prez had been viciously and violently attacked, raped, and murdered.

Pridemore thanked the doctor for his time. "We'll be in touch when we're getting closer to a trial date," he said. Dr. Levy promised his staff would keep searching for the mysteriously missing records. As Pridemore drove back to police headquarters, he felt better about the case.

The next day Pridemore continued digging through Jerome Barrett's file. He called TBI agent Jeri Powell and requested Barrett's prison records with the Tennessee Board of Probation and Parole for the period around August 14, 1974, the date Barrett was paroled the first time. Pridemore wanted any information about where Barrett might have been after his release from prison.

The following week, Pridemore was called to testify before the Davidson County grand jury concerning the murder of Sarah Des Prez. Pridemore testified for forty-five minutes about his investigation. Two days later, on Monday, November 19, 2007, the Cold Case office received a phone call from the district attorney's office. The grand jury had issued a two-count indictment against Jerome Barrett for the murder of Sarah Des Prez.

Pridemore made immediate plans to drive to Memphis and arrest Jerome Barrett.

The news of the indictment brought the February 1975 case into focus for Pridemore. The Court would be setting a trial date soon, and the detective had a lot of work to do before the trial. Suddenly, the date he had set for his retirement, September 30, 2008, seemed very distant. His goal: convictions in the Des Prez and Trimble cases.

* * *

Pridemore and Postiglione lost no time setting out for Memphis again. After they left Nashville they called Sergeant Helldorfer of Memphis Homicide and told him of their plans to arrest Jerome Barrett that day. The sergeant told them to call back when they were approaching Memphis.

When the detectives were about forty minutes out of Memphis, Sergeant Helldorfer called and advised that the Memphis Police Department had Jerome Barrett in their custody and were transporting him to Homicide at the downtown station. It was very welcome news for the Cold Case detectives. They had been dreading the hassle of driving the streets of Memphis looking for their murder suspect, wasting an entire day.

As they parked in the Memphis Police parking lot, another car stopped nearby. Four men in fatigues got out of the car, followed by a large black man. It was Jerome Barrett. Pridemore and Postiglione glanced at each other. They waited until the group had entered the police station before they headed that way. Their experience in such matters had taught them that there was an appropriate time to speak with the suspect, and it wasn't in the parking lot. Nor was it in the elevator. As luck would have it, they came up behind the four-man team and Barrett at the elevator. The doors opened, and the others entered. "We'll get the next one," Pridemore said.

They went up to the Homicide Division and were met by Sergeant Helldorfer. After thanking him for his work, they followed him down a long hallway. He stopped at a door that had a one-way mirror in it. Pridemore peered through the window to see Jerome Barrett sitting alone at a table, handcuffed. His hands were huge and rawboned. His eyes were fixed in a blank stare on the wall in front of him.

Pridemore and Postiglione went into the interview room and advised Barrett that they had a grand jury indictment for his arrest for committing a homicide in 1975. He gave a short burst of disgust. Pridemore began reading him his Miranda rights. Barrett sneered. "You got the wrong man. I ain't saying nothing. I want a lawyer."

Pridemore handed him the indictment. He read the whole thing and slammed it on the table. "Two counts, two counts of murder?"

"Sometimes they'll include that on the indictment," Pridemore said, "but it is *one* victim."

"One victim, two victims, it's still false," Barrett said. "DNA will exclude me, the DNA will exclude me," he kept saying, over and over. He looked up at the detective. "You got the wrong man," he said again.

Sergeant Postiglione shook his head. "You didn't waive your rights. We can't talk to you about this case any further." He nodded toward Helldorfer, and the sergeant motioned to two uniformed officers who were standing in the hallway. They came to get Barrett and walked him to the men's room, then they escorted him to the Nashville detectives' car.

During the three-and-a-half-hour drive back to Nashville, Pridemore asked Barrett if he wanted something to eat. Barrett shook his head. He didn't say a word.

The victims' statements were consistent about one point. They all said Barrett ranted and raved about being their God, their Lord. Pridemore wanted to make the point that he knew the details of the rapes. He turned to Barrett and asked, "Who is your God?"

Barrett gave the detective a hateful stare. "God is good. He is my Lord and Savior," he said. He refused to speak after that. He stared straight ahead for the rest of the trip.

Finally arriving at the police headquarters in Nashville, Pridemore escorted Barrett to the booking office. After Barrett was booked, Pridemore allowed him one phone call. He dialed his mother in Memphis. After the call, Barrett was turned over to the sheriff's deputies at the Davidson County jail.

Exhausted, Pridemore reflected on the day's events as he

drove to his Neely's Bend home. He had been with Jerome Barrett for five hours and not once during that time did Barrett ask who the victim was or anything pertaining to the facts of the case. Barrett knew his business.

On November 20, the Metro Police Department issued a press release announcing that Jerome Barrett had been indicted and arrested for the brutal murder of Sarah Des Prez on February 2, 1975. The press release gave details of the arrest in Memphis and noted that Mr. Barrett was being held without bail preceding the preliminary hearing.

The press release further stated: "Barrett was convicted in 1976 of the February 17, 1975 rape of a Belmont student. He was sentenced to sixty years imprisonment [but] released in 2002."

"Sarah Des Prez's death was not forgotten," Chief Ronal Serpas said. "I am very pleased that scientific advancements, along with the diligence of Cold Case Detective Mr. Bill Pridemore, have now resulted in a murder indictment."

In a *Tennessean* article, a spokesperson for the TBI was quoted as saying that before this DNA match, "the latest profile we ever had was from the early 1990s."

Along with the break in the Des Prez case, the media reported the possible link to Marcia Trimble. Once again, the Trimble case was back in the headlines. Blogs were full of memories about Marcia's disappearance and the discovery of her body. One blogger wrote: "Everywhere you go, 'old Nashville' is talking about it." Explaining to newcomers why the Trimble case was so "huge," the blogger said, "Quite simply, her disappearance cost Nashville its innocence."

The public was anxious for charges to be filed in the Trimble murder, but Detective Bill Pridemore, Sergeant Pat Postiglione, and Deputy DA Tom Thurman wanted to take their time and consider all the evidence.

Speaking to the media, Postiglione insisted that it was "routine for investigators to look at cases with similar circumstances, that were so close in distance, and that happened around the same time."

John Hollins, Jeffrey Womack's lawyer, told reporters the DNA match was real. "It's not a rumor. I'm sure of that," he said. He had it from "people involved in the investigation."

"Is it really over?" was the question posed by Nashville Post.com headlines, the question the entire city was asking.

The DNA match in the Trimble case was significant evidence, but more investigative work was necessary before an indictment could be issued.

They wanted to get it right this time.

Inmates who made telephone calls from the jail knew that their calls could be monitored. Pridemore sometimes listened to Barrett's telephone conversations, as a matter of due diligence. Jerome Barrett talked with his daughter, Jackie, who was taking care of his finances. With her, he often sounded domineering, and the focus of the conversations was Barrett himself, not the daughter or her family. Once she told him that she'd seen on TV about the Trimble case, and that the police were looking at him for the murder of the little girl. She asked him questions, but his only response was, "Um, um, um, mercy. Nine years old."

Reviewing the files of the February 1975 rapes and murders, and specifically Detective Diane Vaughn's investigation, Pridemore came upon the name of Evan Bailey, who had shared a room with Barrett in 1975. Evan was now a convicted felon, but after several weeks of research and phone calls, Pridemore finally located him living in Memphis. He called Evan and set up an appointment for Tuesday, December 4, 2007.

Once again, Sergeant Postiglione and Detective Pridemore drove to Memphis. They met with Evan at his sister's home. Evan Bailey Jr. was a slightly built African American, about fifty-five years old. The detectives thanked him for agreeing to visit with them. Postiglione asked Evan to tell how he came to know Jerome Barrett.

"I'd known him since 1970. Met him in the Shelby County jail," he said. "In 1974, I got released from prison. Got me a small place [on] Jefferson Street [in Nashville]. First of March, I ran into Barrett at the Temple. He asked me if he could stay with me. I told him all right and he moved in with only the shirt on his back."

The detectives remained silent, letting Evan take his time. He continued, "It was just for a few weeks. I went for days without seeing him. He was always alone, didn't have no visitors, no women or men, either. Didn't have no car, just rode the city bus or walked. He never worked as far as I know, just raised some money for the nation of Islam."

Evan Bailey paused again and stared at the wall, as if trying to remember. After a minute he said, "Next thing I know, some little lady detective comes and asks to search the apartment, look at Barrett's things. I was on parole, so I said sure. Didn't want no trouble with the law. Nothing I could do to stop 'em anyway."

He looked at the detectives. "That's about all I got," he said.

Postiglione asked, "Did you know he had been arrested?"

"The lady detective told me," Evan said.

"Did you see him again?" Postiglione asked.

Evan Bailey studied a moment, then nodded. "I saw him in 1984. We was both inside The Walls [the main prison in Nashville]. I had TB so I was in the hospital. Barrett sent word by another inmate that he thought I betrayed him." Evan emphasized, "*Betrayed* him, he said. Because I let police search the apartment." He glared at the detectives. "I watched my back after that."

The detectives asked if there was anything else. "That was the last time I had anything to do with him," Evan said. "I'd forgot he even lived in Memphis. Sure would hate to bump into that dude in a dark alley."

The Trimble case file included a peculiar report of a call from the Tennessee Highway Patrol in West Tennessee, the night after Marcia disappeared. The THP had stopped a white car driven by Phillip A. Wilson, in response to a BOLO, a call alerting law enforcement that the car was "wanted for kidnapping." The twenty-two-year-old Black Muslim, a student at Tennessee State University, was driving from Nashville to Memphis. When the THP sergeant contacted Nashville Police in the middle of the huge search for Marcia Trimble, the police had no information on the BOLO. Wilson drove away.

Subsequent investigation by Pridemore revealed Wilson never went back to TSU to finish school, he had taken the name Taqiyy Mohammed, and he now lived in Chattanooga. Detectives were able to talk to him on the phone, but when Detective Pridemore went to meet him in Chattanooga, he was a no-show. Months later, the same thing would happen to Sergeant Postiglione and Captain Miller. Finally, in a conversation with the detectives, he told them he was not going to help them, and they would never find him.

Larry Brinton had been a *Banner* reporter in 1975, and in 2007, he was a commentator for "Word on the Street," on WSMV Channel 4. In his commentary on December 5, Brinton recalled how the sorrow over Marcia Trimble's death had torn Virginia and Charles Trimble apart. "She turned her sorrow to religion; he turned his to the bottle," Brinton said. He told of introducing Virginia to Frank Ritter, the well-respected *Tennessean* reporter, and how "last year, there was a ray of sunshine: Virginia and Frank were married." In the wake of the news that police might have found her daughter's killer at last, Virginia was also dealing with several other big life changes: shortly after her wedding to Frank Ritter, he had suffered a series of strokes and seizures, leaving him totally deaf; she had retired from her job at American Constructors; and they were in the midst of planning a move to Kentucky to begin restoring a 130-year-old home.

"Life has been a long and bumpy trail for Virginia Trimble Ritter," Brinton said. Virginia's comment was: "You deal with what happens. I had faith in God."

As Jerome Barrett and his attorney, G. Kerry Haymaker, stood before Judge Steve Dozier on December 12, 2007, entering a not guilty plea, Detective Bill Pridemore was busy dotting i's and crossing t's on the investigation, which had to be rock solid. During December 2007 and January 2008, Pridemore attempted to track down witnesses and victims from the 1975 crime spree. He went to Property and Evidence to retrieve the two swabs taken from Barrett's cheeks. He packaged them and sent them overnight by FedEx to Gary Harmor, a forensic serologist at Serological Research Institute in Richmond, California. The lab still performed DQ alpha typing. DQ alpha, the first PCR-based test that many forensic labs used, was no longer used by most labs, but it was important to get a similar comparison, conducting the test on the swabs the same way they had conducted the original analysis on Marcia's clothing.

In mid-January, Harmor called Pridemore with his results. Barrett's DQ alpha profile matched the DNA profile found on the victim's jeans by CBR Lab. This meant that 8 percent of the general population would have the same genetic profile—a statistic that was, in itself, not conclusive, but it was useful in that it didn't eliminate Barrett.

* * *

On Monday, January 28, 2008, Deputy DA Tom Thurman called. He wanted Pridemore to meet and interview with him an inmate who had spent time in prison with Jerome Barrett. Thurman and Pridemore met in the hallway outside the U.S. attorney's office.

"You know this could be another wild-goose chase," Thurman said, with a smile. Pridemore liked the State attorney. If Tom Thurman said something, you could count on it. Thurman did not run his mouth or crow about his victories in the courtroom. Away from the office, the two were fierce competitors on the golf course. Tom Thurman also was an excellent triathlete who trained constantly. He was a gentleman, but tough. People respected Thurman.

Ronald Cauthern was on death row at the Riverbend Prison in West Nashville. Pridemore and Thurman went to the U.S. attorney's office on January 30, 2008. Inside, they were introduced to an attorney, Mr. Bruno, and his client, Ronald Cauthern. He was about five feet ten or eleven inches tall and very pale; not remarkable, as inmates on death row didn't get much sunshine. It was rare to meet a death row inmate anywhere but behind prison bars. Pridemore wondered what it was like for Cauthern to be in an office in downtown Nashville, like an ordinary citizen.

Cauthern stated that in 1987 and 1988, he had been incarcerated at The Walls, the main prison in Nashville. There, he'd met and was befriended by Jerome Barrett. Cauthern later became a Muslim and changed him name to Rasul Abdul Jihad. Cauthern said that because he became a Muslim, Barrett trusted and confided in him.

Pridemore and Thurman listened as Cauthern told of his conversations with Barrett. "Barrett said that once he was released from prison, he was going to build a dungeon on his father's land in Memphis," Cauthern said. "Barrett planned on holding white women in the dungeon. He would breed them whenever the mood hit him."

The inmate looked at Pridemore. "Barrett gave the impression that he'd raped at least three or four women. Once he said a girl had disrespected him. He said, 'I had to take her out.' He bragged about it. But I never asked him no questions. Didn't want to know." Cauthern recalled that Barrett repeated over and over that if a girl showed discipline and respect, he would not hurt her. He bragged about how he liked to stalk white college girls because they were naïve. He expected the white girls to be subservient; he always had to be in control. He said he didn't perform oral sex on the girls; it was beneath him. But he demanded it from them.

Pridemore and Thurman questioned Cauthern for another thirty minutes, but the inmate could not recall any more of Barrett's statements. The detectives thanked him and his attorney for meeting with them. As they started to leave, Cauthern thought of one more thing. "After he raped the women, Barrett gave them instructions about not watching him leave. He would walk out of the room and wait to see if they followed him or cried out."

As Thurman and Pridemore left the building, Pridemore said, "I think Cauthern was telling the truth. Barrett is bad."

Thurman nodded and pointed out that "Cauthern talked to us without any deal. Our office couldn't help him. I couldn't even get him an extra dessert on death row, much less a reduced sentence."

Throughout February and March 2008, Pridemore worked on preparing for the Sarah Des Prez murder trial. One afternoon he drove around with Postiglione and Thurman to the locations where the other incidents had taken place thirty-three years earlier, in February and March 1975. They determined that Sarah Des Prez lived less than two-tenths of a mile from the Vanderbilt campus, and that the Judy Porter, Charlotte Shatzen, and Dianna McMillan crimes all occurred less than one mile from the campus. Marcia Trimble lived just over five miles from Vanderbilt, and Judy Ladd's Berry Hill apartment was located just under three miles from the campus. The distances were measured by roadways, though Pridemore noted in his report that "if one would walk the routes taking advantage of the open areas, the route and distances would be more direct and shorter."

Regarding witnesses, Pridemore had two different issues. One was locating missing witnesses who had not been contacted in thirty-three years. The other applied to all witnesses. He had to "touch" them again, review their statements, and refresh their memories of the case.

Pridemore was immersed in the Des Prez case, but late one afternoon in March 2008, he decided to take a break from Des Prez and work on the Marcia Trimble file. Through years of experience, he had learned that sometimes it was productive to "let a case brew in his mind."

Bill Pridemore's wife Denise had a meeting at their church that evening, and Pat Postiglione was speaking at a civic group's supper. The other Cold Case detectives had left for the day. Pridemore spread parts of the Trimble file across the conference room table.

He placed Barrett's prison file on his left and Diane Vaughn's February 1975 files on the table. On the blackboard, he wrote:

FEB 2	Sarah Des Prez murdered
FEB 12	VU security arrests Barrett at girl's dorm
FEB 16	Judy Porter raped in her dorm room at Belmont
FEB 23	Charlotte Shatzen assaulted and neck cut with knife at her front door
FEB 25	Marcia Trimble abducted

MARCH 9   Dianna McMillan assaulted and raped

MARCH 12   Barrett arrested while attempting to break into
             Berry Hill apt. even though he knew he had been
             seen twice!! Twice!

Then he pulled out the memo prepared by veteran Homicide detectives in 1990–1991. It was entitled "Review of Marcia Virginia Trimble Homicide Investigation 75-30512." The document basically continued to focus on Jeffrey Womack. He turned a page he had marked: "It should be pointed out that there were no unsolved crimes of this nature around the time of area that Marcia was raped and killed. There was no indication of a multiple rapist loose on the community."

Pridemore looked at the blackboard and shook his head.

He read part of the Judy Porter case file. Diane Vaughn's note commented on how brazen the criminal was to remain in Porter's room for almost one hour. Judy Porter's statement was very clear: The rapist had given her specific instructions on what to do when he left. Dianna McMillan's statement contained almost the exact instructions.

The rapist had called Judy Porter and Dianna McMillan "white bitches" over and over.

Pridemore took a swig of cold coffee and opened Jerome Barrett's criminal file again. Barrett had been released from prison in August 1974. In December 1974 and January 1975, he had been arrested around Nashville four separate times for unlawful trespass and solicitation, all while still on probation. Pridemore also noticed Barrett had not bothered to show up for court on any of the four arrest warrants.

After thirty years of police work, Bill Pridemore knew exactly what Jerome Barrett was doing. He was supporting himself with burglaries and break-ins. On the weekends at night, he would hunt young white women.

Pridemore looked at the crime scene photos of Sarah Des

Prez and Marcia Trimble. The rapes and murders in both cases were violent. Barrett terrorized his victims. He choked them or stabbed them in their necks. He took his time, toying with them.

It had been there all the time, right in front of the Nashville Police Department. Barrett's own words, his detailed confession in the Porter case: "I was always searching for that unlocked door or open window."

Ronald Cauthern, the inmate Pridemore and Thurman interviewed, had stated that Barrett bragged about stalking white college girls and giving his victims detailed instructions and orders. Cauthern's account of Barrett matched the victims' statements. It was all consistent. Pridemore read the victims' statements again. In each case, the victim's description of the rapist included a long dark tweed overcoat. Jerome Barrett had also been wearing a long dark tweed overcoat at the Berry Hill apartment the night he was arrested.

Pridemore flipped through the witness statements in the Trimble file. He searched until he found Marie Maxwell's statement. She was the Trimbles' neighbor, the last witness to see Marcia Trimble alive. Marie stated that she'd peered through the hedge and saw Marcia Trimble with her cookie box, and she'd also seen a tall dark figure wearing a long tweed overcoat.

Pridemore opened the transcript of the Judy Porter rape case and found Detective Vaughn's testimony about her investigation of the Des Prez murder and the Porter rape. He read silently. Then he read it again out loud.

Question: *"Did you alert people at the police department about the facts of your investigation?"*

Answer: *"Yes sir, I did. At that time I had an all points bulletin put out with the description of the suspect, and from that I continuously informed other officers of the description of the suspect and what it was in connection to."*

The veteran detective stared at the blackboard. It became clear to him what happened thirty-three years ago in Nashville, Tennessee—the mystery, the crime that had haunted Nashville for so many years. Detective Vaughn had been on the verge of tying Jerome Barrett to the entire crime wave, including Marcia Trimble.

But then the Marcia Trimble case had blown up. It became media driven. The explosion caused the good ol' boys in Homicide to ignore their law enforcement experience. It became a race to make the arrest where the detectives were relentless and played by their own rules. They wasted thirty-three years trying to pin the Trimble murder on a teenager who passed numerous lie detector tests and whose DNA never matched the victim's evidence in any test, by any lab.

And in their haste, the investigators had ignored Detective Diane Vaughn's work.

Bill Pridemore closed the file and stared at the blackboard. He understood.

30

Who Is Jerome Barrett?

Detective Bill Pridemore continued his intensive research into Jerome Barrett's background, digging for any clue or trace that would contribute to the Sarah Des Prez or Marcia Trimble case.

Born in Memphis on April 6, 1948, Jerome Sydney Barrett was the son of Charles and Grace Barrett, and the oldest of four children. He was a product of the Memphis City school system. By his own admission, he could read "fairly well." He'd attended the all-black Geeter High School and graduated in 1967. The school, which closed in 1973 as Memphis began implementing court-ordered bussing to integrate the city's public schools, had been built on land donated by the Geeter family, great-grandparents of Tennessee congressman Harold Eugene Ford Sr., the first African American to represent Tennessee in the U.S. Congress.

Around the time of his graduation, Barrett was investigated for burglary, but not charged. In July of that year, Memphis Police held Barrett two days as a prime suspect in a murder, but again charges were dropped. In 1968, he was charged in a string of burglaries, but he was not convicted.

Though so far he had managed to stay one step ahead of police, Memphis did not hold much of a future for the twenty-year-old. The military looked more promising.

Jerome Barrett enlisted in the U.S. Army, and after basic training, he completed helicopter maintenance repair school at Fort Eustis, Virginia. Fort Eustis, a nine-thousand-acre training facility, is the home of the U.S. Army Transportation Corps. The Vietnam War had escalated, with over sixteen thousand U.S. casualties in 1968, the highest number of any year of the war. Barrett was headed into the thick of the fighting.

In September 1969, he left for Vietnam. He served as a crew chief for a Cobra U.H.I.G. helicopter. The Cobra was the army's first attack helicopter and was heavily armed with rocket launchers, miniguns, and a twenty-millimeter cannon. While in Vietnam, Barrett was prosecuted for going AWOL. In spite of this blemish on his record, from all indications, he was an effective helicopter mechanic. He was awarded the National Defense Service Medal, the Vietnam Service Medal, and the Vietnam Campaign Medal. After completing one tour in Vietnam, Barrett returned to the States where he was hospitalized for mental trauma he claimed he'd suffered during the war. He was treated with a course of drugs and eventually released. In 1971 he received an honorable discharge.

Barrett returned to Memphis in August 1971 and apparently plunged directly into a life of violent crime.

Growing up, Barrett had earned a reputation in the tough streets of Memphis as a fighter. Now the tall, rawboned twenty-three-year-old, hardened by war, began entering fights for cash. These fights were brutal affairs, though Barrett would later describe himself as a prizefighter. He continued to clash with police, as he had done prior to joining the service. In 1973, he was arrested for attempted rape and stabbing of the victim. The Memphis Police Department report stated that

Barrett was running away from officers and had blood on his face and mouth when arrested. Somehow Barrett again dodged the judicial system and was never convicted of the crime.

However, later in 1973, his luck finally ran out. He was arrested and convicted of several sex crimes in Memphis, including carnal knowledge of a minor, and assault. He was sentenced to ten years in the state penitentiary. The main prison in Nashville, The Walls, looked like a fortress out of the Middle Ages. Jerome Barrett became inmate number 73179. The prison psychiatrist who made an initial psychological evaluation of Barrett reported: "The prognosis for treatment is considered poor due to the resident's rigid beliefs and attitudes."

When Barrett came to The Walls, he was an unknown to the Nashville law enforcement officials. It was his first incarceration. He attended meetings of the Nation of Islam.

In 1974, he applied for parole. The Parole Board granted Barrett's request for freedom, and in August he was released after serving only one and a half years of his ten-year sentence. The board noted that Barrett "will be suitably employed in self-sustaining employment." In truth, Barrett had no real employment potential, but he did have a skill: burglary.

The board also stated in the certificate of parole that "the release of this prisoner is not incompatible with the welfare of society." That was far from the truth. When the State released inmate number 73179 to the streets of West Nashville, it unleashed a rapist, a robber, an accomplished street fighter, and now, an ex-con. He was a terrorist, waiting to descend on Nashville and inflict a plague of crimes upon the unsuspecting city.

"Solicitation of the public" was prohibited in many areas of Nashville in 1974. That law, like many others, meant nothing to Jerome Barrett. In the fall of 1974, he was arrested repeatedly for unlawful solicitation and trespass. He was arrested in Donelson, on West End Avenue, and on the Vanderbilt University campus while soliciting funds for the Nation of Islam. He treated the system with contempt and failed to appear at Court hearings.

Detective Bill Pridemore reviewed the string of assaults, rapes, and murders that took place in Nashville, Tennessee, in February and March of 1975, including the rape of Belmont coed Judy Porter in her dorm room on February 16. On March 12, Judy Ladd reported a break-in at her Berry Hill apartment. Upon their arrival, the police were shocked to discover that the intruder was still roaming around the apartment complex, armed with a loaded gun, wearing a ski mask, continuing to attempt break-ins. The intruder was Jerome Barrett.

Within days, Barrett was linked to three crimes. Charlotte Shatzen, who was severely injured when stabbed outside her Fairfax apartment on February 23, identified Barrett as her assailant. Dianna McMillan also identified Barrett as the man who had raped and terrorized her in her Acklen Park apartment on March 9. Police had searched Barrett's apartment and confiscated a number of items that they believed were stolen. Judy Porter was able to identify her personal property, making the connection to her attacker. Then, according to a police report, Barrett confessed. He stated that he "needed help and wanted to confess to the rape of the young white girl at the college." He said he was a messenger sent by the Nation of Islam, and he had been ordered to do what he did to the Belmont girl. He was arrested and charged with that rape and assault. A Nashville jury later convicted him of the rape and sentenced him to sixty years.

After Jerome Barrett's 1976 conviction for the rape of Judy Porter, he was transported from the Nashville-Davidson County jail to the Tennessee State Penitentiary. He had spent one and a half years at The Walls before; now, one and a half years later, he was back again. Since he'd been an inmate previously in the system, he was assigned the same number, 73179.

The Tennessee Department of Correction policy on inmate housing was based upon one principle: security. Long-term inmates were transferred frequently. The reason for the policy was that frequent transfers reduced the amount of time an inmate could prepare or plot to escape. Transfer also helped break up gang leadership.

In early 1977, Barrett was transferred to the Brushy Mountain state prison in Petros, Tennessee. In 1982, Barrett was sent to Fort Pillow state prison, located in the desolate river bottom near the Mississippi River. There Barrett joined the Black Muslims. Over the next few years, Barrett would be sent to other prisons across the state of Tennessee, including the Lake County and Bledsoe County regional prisons and the new main penitentiary in Nashville.

On the evening of October 14, 1986, guards at the Lake County prison were alarmed by a panic-stricken inmate named Timothy LeMay. When they calmed LeMay down, they learned that Jerome Barrett had vowed to kill LeMay the next morning. In January of 1987, Barrett was transferred back to the main prison in Nashville. He filed a petition in Chancery Court and had his name changed to Abdullah Jihad Abdul Jaami.

Barrett continued to pose a great security risk to the Department of Correction. In September of 1987, authorities discovered a dagger in his cell. Two months later, he was caught beating another inmate. Eventually he was placed in solitary confinement. His records were sprinkled with notations about disciplinary actions: "10 days punitive—forgery; 30 days punitive—possession deadly weapon; 15 days punitive—disrespect, RDO." RDO was a notation that meant the punishment would be set aside as long as there were no other offenses. It was an incentive for the inmate to stay out of trouble. It didn't work with Jerome Barrett.

Over the years, the Department of Correction compiled a list of a group of inmates that were "on Barrett's list." Barrett was eventually paroled and released in 2002.

During his time as an inmate in the Tennessee prison system, he had thirty-three disciplinary violations, including assault, threatening guards, and possession of deadly weapons.

Violence was Jerome Sydney Barrett's trademark.

31

Press Conference

On March 27, 2008, Judge Steve Dozier set October 6 as the date for the Sarah Des Prez murder trial. In April, Detective Bill Pridemore and Sergeant Pat Postiglione began meeting twice a week with Deputy DA Tom Thurman and the district attorney's office. The detectives and Thurman decided to request that the TBI Lab attempt to enhance the results of Jerome Barrett's DNA test; they hoped the lab could refine and retest with a goal of increasing the probability that the DNA was Barrett's. The current DNA reports were strong, sufficient to convict, but some of the matches were "partial profiles." Given the fact the case was so old, they wanted any extra evidence possible.

They continued to press the TBI for more assessments. Pridemore called Special Agent Johnson's office several times a week to see if the lab had been able to refine the results.

In the meantime, he went over each piece of paper in both the Des Prez and Trimble files to ensure that he had contacted every potential witness, examined every piece of evidence, and eliminated other potential suspects. He didn't know when the case would go to the grand jury.

Pridemore's attempt to learn as much as he could about Jerome Barrett led him to Yusuf Abdullah, who, like Barrett, had worked for the local mosque in 1975. The young Black Muslims had gone out in groups, selling Nation of Islam newspapers. Yusuf, born Clinton Joseph Moss, said Barrett "seemed to like white women and would make attempts to talk with them" as they went to various parts of Nashville. "I warned him that he had better leave the 'little Debbies' alone." A bus had left for Chicago on February 25, 1975, for a gathering to commemorate the day Elijah Muhammad died. Barrett "should have gone to the gathering," Yusuf Abdullah said.

Though many of the current officers in the police department were not old enough to have been on the force in 1975, most of them knew about the Trimble case. Rumors floated around the department on a daily basis. Even though Postiglione and Pridemore were working directly with the district attorney's office, it was necessary to inform and report to their superiors on the status of the investigation. It became practically impossible to maintain any sense of secrecy in regard to their work on both the Des Prez and Trimble cases. In major cities, the press has its own way of obtaining information. With police departments, the line used most often is "a source close to the investigation." The citizens of Nashville were especially interested in the Marcia Trimble case and the press understood that. Trimble was good for ratings. Trimble sold newspapers.

For the Nashville Police Department, the satisfactory prosecution of the Trimble case had become a catch-22. They were in business to reduce crime and to solve terrible cases such as Marcia Trimble's murder, but the idea that someone had been on a monthlong rape-and-murder spree just five miles from the Trimble neighborhood was a tough thing to swallow. Many of the older police officers continued to refuse to accept the idea that someone other than a neighborhood teenager killed the nine-year-old, fearing that if this were true, the work of the police departments for thirty-three years would seem wasted, almost foolish. The media understood that. They smelled blood.

Channel 4 News, the local NBC affiliate, ran a lead story about the Trimble investigation. But this time they put the FBI on the hot seat. The Channel 4 reporter interviewed Richard Knudsen, the top FBI agent in Nashville during the Trimble investigation, now retired. Knudsen was still reluctant to buy into the Cold Case theory that Jerome Barrett murdered Marcia Trimble. He said, "What are the chances that at that precise moment, he was cutting through the property and here comes Marcia selling Girl Scout cookies, and so then he assaults her. Sure it is possible. Yeah. Likely? Maybe no."

FBI agent Knudsen also continued to express doubts that Marcia's body was in the garage for thirty-three days. The piece pointed out that "no one thought she was in there the whole time except the experts who examined her body."

At the same time, Knudsen said he believed in DNA, and if the DNA matched Jerome Barrett, "I don't know how you defend that."

Commander Mickey Miller had worked on the Trimble case for nearly his entire career. He spoke with Virginia Trimble almost on a weekly basis. Virginia told reporters that on March 28, 2002, which would have been Marcia's thirty-seventh birthday, she'd visited Marcia's grave and promised her daughter that "Captain Miller is going to solve your case—soon."

Now, in a meeting with Pridemore and Postiglione, Thurman suggested that the only right thing to do was bring Miller into the loop as they moved closer to solving the Trimble case.

Miller, a veteran of the police force, had served as assistant police chief from 2001 to 2003 until he was reassigned by the new chief, Ronal Serpas, to command the West Precinct. Dedicated and well respected, Miller had spent years desperately trying to connect Jeffrey Womack to the murder of Marcia Trimble, even though Jeffrey passed several polygraphs and no forensic evidence ever linked him to the murder.

Mickey Miller set forth the "Evidence Against Jeffrey Womack" in the 1990–1991 "Review of Marcia Virginia Trimble Homicide Investigation." The document stated, "Whatever the reason, evidence shows that Marcia and March went with Womack through the backyard and into the garage." Yet there was, in fact, *no* evidence that Jeffrey Womack or March Egerton ever went up the hill behind Mrs. Howard's or into the Thorpes' garage. Nevertheless, Miller stood by the theory. Nothing changed his mind. Even during the weekly meetings on the Trimble case in 2008, Miller often implied that Jeffrey Womack still had something to do with the Trimble murder. He kept the "Womack Theory" on the table through May, and his theory continued to evolve: Perhaps Jeffrey Womack had stolen Marcia Trimble's cookie money and Marcia had chased him up the hill to the Geddes-Douglas Nursery on Estes where, according to Miller, Marcia then ran into Jerome Barrett.

Detective Bill Pridemore considered Mickey Miller a good friend, but he simply shook his head, smiled, and moved the discussion back to Jerome Barrett.

By the end of May 2008, the detectives and the DA's office had reached a decision: It was time to move forward with the Trimble case. Sergeant Pat Postiglione testified before the Davidson County grand jury regarding the Marcia Trimble murder.

Things were about to change.

On June 6, 2008, Davidson County DA Victor S. "Torry" Johnson and Metropolitan Police Chief Ronal Serpas announced the indictment of Jerome Barrett in connection with the February 1975 homicide of nine-year-old Marcia Trimble.

A Davidson County grand jury had heard the case against Barrett and presented the sealed indictment charging him with first-degree murder and felony murder. Barrett was officially served the charges by Cold Case Unit sergeant Pat Postiglione, Detective Bill Pridemore, and Commander Mickey Miller.

The press conference held at the district attorney's office to announce Jerome Barrett's indictment created a stir in downtown Nashville, and among the Nashvillians who watched the news reports on the local TV stations. "The murder of Marcia Trimble is one that affected the entire Nashville community," DA Torry Johnson stated. "It's a case that no one has forgotten. For the benefit of the Trimble family, I'm pleased to be able to make this announcement today."

Sharing the podium with Johnson were Chief Ronal Serpas, Deputy DA Tom Thurman, Pridemore, Postiglione, and Miller. Chief Serpas said, "For the past thirty-three years, more than two generations of police officers devoted thousands upon thousands of hours of investigative work to solving Marcia Trimble's murder. . . . I spoke to Virginia Trimble shortly after arriving in Nashville in 2004 and assured her that this department would never give up on Marcia's case or any other unsolved homicide."

He went on to say, "Today, I expressed my gratitude to Commander Miller, who, as a Homicide supervisor, spent a number of years pursuing leads in this case. I also thank Sergeant Postiglione and Detective Pridemore, both from our Cold Case Unit, for meticulously coordinating the crucial investigative work over the past several months. This is an important day for the Trimble family and Nashville as a whole."

A statement released by the police indicated that no further arrests were expected to be made in the Trimble case. Jerome Barrett would be arraigned on the new indictment in the coming weeks. He was already set to go on trial for the murder of

Sarah Des Prez in October 2008. Both cases would be prosecuted by Deputy DA Tom Thurman.

Virginia Trimble also issued a statement, in which she said: "It sounds as if this could be the next chapter in the life and death of Marcia Trimble." She thanked the Metro Police Department and the district attorney's office for their work, which she believed would "finally bring justice for Marcia and solve her murder that has haunted us all for 33 years." Later, she told reporters from WTVF Channel 5, "I wish Charlie could be alive to witness this day."

The news was the lead story on the three Nashville television channels that evening. The following morning the *Tennessean* headlines announced: "Arrest Is Made in Trimble Case."

The local ABC affiliate, WKRN Channel 2, interviewed retired lieutenant Tommy Jacobs regarding the indictment of Jerome Barrett. Jacobs said he was glad police never stopped looking for Marcia's killer and he hoped Barrett got the punishment he deserved, but the retired detective still had questions: "How did he get into the neighborhood? How did he get out of the neighborhood? How did he grab her?"

John Hollins, Jeffrey Womack's lawyer, said that when he told Jeffrey about the indictment against Jerome Barrett, Jeffrey's response was: "I'm glad they charged the right person."

For Detective Bill Pridemore, the indictment of Marcia Trimble's murderer was a high point in his career. He couldn't recall how many police officers, friends, neighbors, and citizens of Nashville had told him there would never be a conviction and that the mystery would never be solved. He was glad he hadn't retired, glad he had stayed the course until now. And more unfinished business remained before Bill Pridemore's retirement: a conviction of Jerome Barrett.

PART 5

Justice

32

The Process Begins

The sunny June day turned even brighter after the midday press conference. It was a splendid day in Nashville, and as print and TV reporters scurried from the district attorney's office, the news of Jerome Barrett's indictment was already spreading far beyond the city that mourned the nine-year-old blue-eyed girl. The Trimble case hit the national news with CNN's report, and the Associated Press story was picked up by dozens of newspapers, television and radio stations, and online news sources.

Teddy Bart, whose popular talk-radio show had been on the air in Nashville in 1975, commented on the case's ability to hold an entire city in its grip for over three decades. "It had all the elements: a beautiful little girl, a murder, a bungled police operation, fundamentalist religion, and a neighborhood where things like this aren't supposed to happen." The murder that haunted Nashville for so long was solved.

Or was it?

As the mild summer days passed, the public dissected the

Trimble case over and over, wondering, Had the police gotten it right this time? Would they be able to put Jerome Barrett at the Copeland Drive crime scene—a black man in the all-white neighborhood? And *why*? Why Marcia? Had Barrett targeted her or was their meeting a tragic coincidence? If he was one of the individuals in Mrs. Howard's driveway, who was the other one, and why had he not come forward?

Deputy DA Tom Thurman grappled with these questions, too. He knew he *had* to get a conviction in the Trimble case, the case that had remained in Nashville's consciousness all these years.

As the district attorney's office and police continued to strengthen their case against the ex-convict who had already served twenty-six years for the brutal rape of Belmont student Judy Porter, local television stations aired several news stories about Barrett's quiet life in Memphis since he was paroled in 2002. His neighbors were stunned by the charges against a man they knew as head of a community watch group and the son who helped care for an elderly mother in poor health. Barrett apparently had not known his daughter until after he was paroled. He had connected with her and worked for her husband in landscaping. Before his arrest on November 20, 2007, he had also had his own part-time landscaping business. One source said he hired young felons to work for him, to keep them out of trouble.

Demetria Kalodimos of WSMV Channel 4 interviewed Percy Cummings, Barrett's former cellmate from the state prison at Tiptonville. The fellow Muslim characterized Barrett as a spiritual leader, "the Imam." He said Barrett had admitted his guilt in the Belmont student's rape, the crime he was "locked up for," but he didn't confess to other crimes. Percy said, "The only thing that he would say at times was, you know, 'I done some wrong in my life.' " The cellmate said Barrett had terrible nightmares; he would wake up in a cold sweat. Percy didn't hesitate when asked if Barrett was capable of raping and strangling a nine-year-old girl. "Oh, yeah," he said.

Kalodimos called Barrett "a man with two different sides." Tom Thurman and the Cold Case detectives had spent their careers working to convict cold-blooded killers, and they were not surprised that Barrett's mother called him "a good son." Sergeant Postiglione would later say, "His whole life has been an act. He doesn't possess a conscience. He's been living a lie."

On July 2, 2008, Jerome Barrett, then sixty-one years old, appeared in Judge Steve Dozier's courtroom in Davidson County Criminal Court. Dozier was assigned to preside over the Des Prez trial, and now Barrett stood before him to answer charges in the murder of Marcia Trimble.

Judge Dozier, who grew up in East Nashville and graduated from Vanderbilt and the Nashville School of Law, was bright, scholarly, known for his well-reasoned judicial opinions, and considered a fair jurist. Dozier could immediately comprehend and decide complicated legal issues; he had a quick mind. His father had been a Nashville police officer for over fifty years. Judge Dozier had previously worked for the district attorney's office and successfully prosecuted the first murder case where DNA was used.

Jerome Barrett was going to be seeing a lot of Judge Steve Dozier.

Barrett pleaded not guilty to charges of first-degree murder and larceny. But first he was facing the Des Prez trial. He said he could not pay a lawyer. The judge ruled he was not indigent because he collected $29,000 a year from a Veterans disability pension. Judge Dozier appointed Kerry Haymaker, Barrett's attorney in the Des Prez case, to also represent him in the Trimble case and instructed Barrett to pay Haymaker $500 a month. Haymaker told the Court he was "not inclined to accept the appointment." Without divulging what would prevent him from representing Barrett, he implied there were reasons.

The judge noted it would be easier for everyone if the same attorney handled both cases, but he told Haymaker to file a sealed affidavit further explaining his concerns or get advice from the Board of Professional Responsibility, which oversees attorney conduct in Tennessee.

Deputy DA Tom Thurman, prosecutor for both Des Prez and Trimble, commented: "It is always easier to deal with one lawyer than two. There will be a lot of the same things addressed in both trials."

Haymaker was eventually removed from the Trimble case after he filed objections in a sealed affidavit. The judge appointed a public defender to represent Barrett in the Trimble trial.

Both sides prepared for the Des Prez trial scheduled for October 6, 2008.

On Friday, September 12, 2008, Haymaker filed a motion asking the Court for change of venue in the Sarah Des Prez case. The motion contended that every potential juror in Davidson County had probably been exposed to the media about the case. The motion stated that nearly a "hundred and seventy newscaster, newspaper articles in Nashville" had mentioned Barrett by name in the year. Haymaker stated: "It is obviously important to us, as it should be to anybody, that we get a fair trial where we pick juries who don't have a history of knowing about the Trimble case."

It was rare for a court to order a sequestered jury or an out-of-town jury in Davidson County. The expense for the court system averaged approximately $27,000 a week for hotel, transportation, and food costs for a sequestered jury. Most of the time a jury brought in to try a case in Nashville would be selected from a pool in Memphis, Chattanooga, or Knoxville. Tennessee death penalty cases by statute required a sequestered jury; this prohibited any access to local media and limited contact with anyone outside the jury. However, Barrett was not facing the death penalty, which had not been in effect in 1975. Under Tennessee law, a person must be charged with the penalties that were in effect at the time of the crime, which meant Barrett was only facing prison time.

The district attorney's office did not indicate whether it intended to oppose Barrett's change of venue request. Judge Dozier ruled on September 19 that an out-of-town jury would hear the Des Prez case. He also postponed the trial until January 26, 2009.

The State filed its own motion. The motion contended that Barrett was a violent sexual predator and that the jury in the Des Prez trial should hear about Barrett's previous arrests and crimes. Judge Dozier heard the arguments on September 25 and 26, 2008.

Deputy DA Thurman stated in Court, "I think it would be crucial for the jury to understand what was going on in this city back in 1975 as far as these vicious assaults and attacks on women, where he would be attacking them, raping them and robbing them. It also shows that when women didn't do what Barrett said, Barrett became particularly violent."

Defense attorney Haymaker argued that the evidence linking the other crimes did not satisfy the Tennessee Rules of Procedure, specifically that the crimes were too dissimilar. He noted, for example, that the evidence concerning what the attacker wore, said, or did was absent from the Des Prez case. He argued, "To let the Jury hear about the other charges would only prejudice them against Jerome Barrett."

Several women were present in court to give testimony about attacks by Jerome Barrett in 1975. Charlotte Shatzen glanced only briefly at the defendant before testifying that she was sure it was Barrett who came up from behind her early on that Sunday morning and grabbed her while she tried to close her umbrella. "I will never forget the eyes," she said. "I looked him straight in the face." She had picked Barrett out of a lineup some weeks after the attack. She said she could still spot him in the courtroom, decades later. "That's just something that stays with you."

Dianna McMillan, who had also identified Barrett as her attacker and had testified at the Judy Porter trial, told how he approached her in her garage and took her back into her apartment where he forced her to perform oral sex and raped her. He rifled through her apartment looking for things to steal while he brandished a pistol.

Sergeant Postiglione, who'd investigated the cold case with Detective Pridemore, testified that most of the crimes Barrett was charged with, with the exception of one, took place in the early morning hours of Sunday mornings. All the victims gave similar descriptions about what their attacker looked like, what he wore, and what he stole. Specifically, he called each of his victims a white bitch, repeatedly threatened to kill them, and wore a long dark tweed overcoat.

After hearing the proof and commenting on the law and the applicable rule of procedure, Judge Dozier declared that he would take the matter under advisement.

He would soon set the date for the Trimble murder trial. The trial that the media was calling "the trial for a generation" would be scheduled for July 13, 2009.

Detective Bill Pridemore left the hearing on September 26, 2008, knowing he wouldn't be back in court until he returned for the Des Prez trial. The time had arrived for his retirement. Tuesday, September 30, was his last day on the job. His colleagues threw a party to honor him, and Chief Ronal Serpas presented a plaque that recognized his thirty-three years of outstanding service. It was a good day, with plenty of reminiscing about the murders he had investigated. "I think I've seen every way—poisoned, stabbed, shot, drowned, burned on fire," he told a WTVF Channel 5 reporter who covered the celebration. He gave credit to Sergeant Pat Postiglione, his partner on so many cases. "My wife calls him my work wife," Pridemore said. He and Postiglione often disagreed on cases. "They've threatened to call domestic violence on us," he joked. But there was a certain chemistry. The partnership worked.

Pridemore said his good-byes, telling everybody he'd be seeing them. He'd be back to prepare for the Des Prez trial, and he'd stay in contact about the Trimble case. But now, after he cleared out his office, he was headed out of town for a golf tournament.

When Jerome Barrett walked into the courtroom for another hearing on Thursday, November 6, 2008, with his attorney in the Trimble case, James McNamara, he learned that his situation was becoming more problematic. The prosecution had two witnesses, inmates from the Davidson County jail, who said they'd heard Barrett make "self-incriminating statements." The State had to reveal the two informants because they were represented by the public defender's office, as was Barrett. Judge Dozier postponed a ruling on the conflict of interest. To protect the witnesses, their identity was withheld, but their statements would become part of the public record.

As the Christmas holidays approached, Barrett got a gift. The judge followed up on the motion filed by the State in September regarding prior bad acts, when the Court heard statements from the women who testified that they had been victimized by Barrett. Judge Dozier ruled that Barrett's past charges could not be heard at the Des Prez trial.

The new year arrived, 2009, marking thirty-four years since Sarah Des Prez and Marcia Trimble were murdered. As the first trial approached, both the district attorney and defense attorney struggled with critical issues that could determine the outcome of the case. Kerry Haymaker, Barrett's attorney in the Des Prez case, faced several difficulties. Barrett had spent time as a legal assistant in prison. That type of experience could create a situation where the client thought he understood the law better than his attorney. Furthermore, Haymaker knew Barrett could not testify. Even though Judge Dozier ruled that Barrett's previous convictions for sex crimes and rape would not be admitted into evidence, Haymaker would not allow Barrett to take the stand. To do so would open up his client to a blistering cross-examination. Plus, the case was thirty-four years old. Barrett had no witnesses Haymaker could use to place his client somewhere else. The standard alibi defense was not available.

In addition to those problems with his client, Haymaker faced the almost insurmountable issue that Jerome Barrett's DNA matched the samples found on the victim and at the crime scene. Haymaker was a smart lawyer. He knew the case should be settled, but his client refused to enter serious discussions to resolve the matter. Jerome Barrett was not interested in settling, because the Court, correctly following the law, had ruled that Barrett was not facing the death penalty. Because of his client's attitude and the fact there was no pressure of facing the death penalty, Haymaker was left with no options but to look for weaknesses in the State's case—and then try to punch holes in it.

The State's case was in excellent hands with Deputy DA Tom Thurman, who had made headlines in Nashville for the last twenty-five years for successfully prosecuting rape and murder cases. His accomplishments had earned him the name "the Thurmanator" among friends and foes alike. He was *the* attorney for the State. A native of Crossville, Tennessee, Thurman graduated from Tennessee Tech and the Nashville School of Law. He was an accomplished golfer and triathlete, a determined competitor. His father had been a B-17 bomber pilot in World War II, who once, after Nazis shot his plane, managed to get back to safety on one engine. Like his father, Thurman was determined to get the bad guys. His low-key style was firm and effective. His direct, no-nonsense approach connected with jurors. Attorney General Torry Johnson said of Thurman: "What sets Tom apart is he's extremely talented, meticulous in his preparation. He thinks of everything, pro and con, in a case and is prepared for any eventuality."

But Thurman was also plowing new ground in the Des Prez case. He had never tried a thirty-four-year-old homicide case. Many legal experts regarded this as the oldest case ever tried in Tennessee, if not the United States. Most witnesses' memories faded after a few months. And the State had a chink in its armor: the lost Des Prez autopsy report.

The week before the start of the trial, both legal teams had to adjust to new developments. First, Judge Dozier ruled that the jury in the Des Prez trial would not hear references to the Trimble murder or to Barrett's religion. Then the prosecution dropped the rape charge against Barrett, choosing to prosecute only the first-degree murder charge. Thurman said, "There is obvious proof of sexual assault, but he is not charged with that crime." In another pre-trial hearing, prosecutors argued that the jury should hear from inmates of the Metro jail who were prepared to testify that Jerome Barrett said he killed four people and would kill them, too. Judge Steve Dozier set a hearing to decide whether the informants could testify.

The last weekend in January 2009, as Nashville hunkered down against a wintry blast, the prosecution and defense teams made final preparations for the upcoming week.

It was time.

33

The Sarah Des Prez Trial

Judge Steve Dozier had ruled that because of the publicity surrounding the Sarah Des Prez case, it would not be possible to find an impartial jury in Nashville. To ensure complete fairness, the judge ruled that the jury would be selected in Chattanooga, a city located 120 miles southeast of Nashville, on the Georgia border. The prosecuting and defense attorneys and Judge Dozier traveled to Chattanooga on Monday, January 26, 2009, for jury selection in Hamilton County Criminal Court. Judge Dozier told the potential jurors that the attorneys had come to select an "unbiased group of people without knowledge of the high-profile case." After several hours of questioning, a jury of eight men and six women was in place. Three were black, and most were over forty years old. After being sworn in, the jurors were excused for the day. The next day, they were transported to Nashville and sequestered in the downtown Courtyard Marriott.

In a pre-trial hearing on Tuesday, Sheldon Anter, Barrett's former fellow inmate in the Davidson County jail, took the stand to testify that he'd heard Barrett say he killed four people. A small man with dark, brooding eyes, the inmate said Barrett confessed to killing white blue-eyed girls. Barrett's attorney Kerry Haymaker argued that the inmate was only trying to get a lesser sentence by making these statements. Deputy DA Tom Thurman argued: "Obviously, there is relevance to this." Judge Dozier stated that he would decide Wednesday morning whether the testimony could be used in court.

On a cold and cloudy Wednesday morning, January 28, 2009, the trial began in Nashville-Davidson County Criminal Court at the A. A. Birch Criminal Justice Building, named for Tennessee's first African American Supreme Court justice. The State's team entered the sixth-floor courtroom at 8:00 with a large cart of evidence. At 9:00 the jury came in. The dark-paneled courtroom was not crowded, though the much publicized trial was televised on WTVF Channel 5's cable station and Nashvillians were able to watch the proceedings on streaming video at their computers as well. The years had removed from Nashville the friends and classmates of Sarah Des Prez who were touched deeply by her death when they were all at Vanderbilt, but seated several rows back were Sarah's white-haired father, Dr. Roger Des Prez, and stepmother Patsy, Sarah's brother Roger, now a doctor in Tulsa, Oklahoma, and other family members who had waited thirty-four years to see justice for Sarah.

Jerome Barrett appeared at the defense table with his attorneys. Barrett wore a dark suit, yellow tie, and white shirt. His gray goatee was neatly trimmed. Standing beside Kerry Haymaker, he looked every inch of his six feet two inches.

As a preliminary matter, Judge Dozier ruled that Sheldon Anter could testify but could not use Barrett's words, "white bitches."

ADA Katy Miller, working with Deputy DA Tom Thurman,

read the indictment. A veteran prosecutor, Miller graduated from the Nashville School of Law and passed the bar while she was working for the district attorney's office in 1982, and she and Thurman had previously worked together on some of the most notorious murder cases in Nashville.

Opening statements by Haymaker and Thurman were short and to the point. Haymaker immediately set forth a theme for the defense. Where's the crime? Is this really a homicide?

Thurman countered with a hard-hitting two-prong attack: the medical examiner would testify that this is a case of homicide by strangulation, and Jerome Barrett's DNA had been found in five places in Sarah Des Prez's bedroom. He said, "There's nobody else in the world who matched the DNA."

The first witness to take the stand was the victim's brother. Dr. Roger Des Prez testified that he and his father had discovered Sarah's body after she failed to show up for her job at Mims Hall, a girls' dorm on the Vanderbilt campus. He described how they found her lying on her bed, nude from the waist down. Her face was bruised. He recalled for the Court that his father checked her pulse and tried to get her breathing again. "He covered her in a blanket and told me to call the police," Roger said.

The next witness, Thales Finchum, the first patrol officer on the scene, testified that he had secured the crime scene. He said Sarah's father, Dr. Des Prez, was "devastated."

George Trammell Hudson took the stand next. He had been a senior at Vanderbilt University in 1975. Now a gray-haired banker from Sarasota, Florida, and a former congressional candidate, he'd been on a date with Sarah Des Prez that Saturday night. They'd gone to a movie, to a nightspot on Elliston Place called Mississippi Whiskers, and to a frat party. He recalled that Sarah became ill while dancing, and he'd returned her to her apartment building at about 1:30 A.M. but had not walked her upstairs to her front door. "I asked her if she could make it to her apartment, and she said she could," he said.

"She walked up the steps, and that's the last time I saw her."
It was the last time anyone saw her alive—except her killer.

Lynn Redding, formerly Lynn Fussell, the neighbor who
had been watching Sarah's dog, testified that she'd gone into
the apartment for dog food the next morning and saw Sarah in
bed, but thought she was asleep. The dog went into the bedroom and "came out whining," she said.

As its next witness the State called former Metro Police
Department Identification Division officer James Sledge, who
had been working the midnight shift in February of 1975.
Detective Sledge was summoned to the crime scene, where
he took photographs. The Court allowed copies of the photographs of the body and crime scene to be introduced into
evidence. The room looked like a typically crowded college
student's room, with a record player, a wicker basket, clothes
strewn about. Sledge testified that the photographs were fair
and accurate as to what he saw. He also noted that the windows in the apartment were locked. The photos of Sarah Des
Prez showed a young woman, Caucasian, half naked in her
bed with a comforter over her feet. A close-up depicted her
badly bruised face and neck. When the photographs were introduced into evidence, the Des Prez family members left the
courtroom.

Detective Sledge then identified and showed to the jury
the evidence collected at the crime scene. Stored separately in
plastic bags, each was marked with a property tag. The mood
in the courtroom was somber as one by one he produced the
few items that remained from Sarah Des Prez's short time in
her little apartment: *a white comforter with tiny flowers, a
quilted bedspread, a gold-striped blanket.* The plastic crack-
led as he tore into it, calling out the name of each piece of
evidence: *striped bed sheet, pillow, the blouse she had on,
panties that were on top of locker, next to wicker basket.* The
identification of her personal effects went on and on: *brown
coin purse, her ID card, Christmas list with people's names*

and gifts, Red Cross donor card, library card, VU clinic card.
Sledge stated that no money was recovered from the scene. A
Metro latent print examiner testified that there were no fingerprints, and an FBI agent testified as to all the different places
where DNA was found.

Sheldon Anter took the stand and stated that he heard Barrett say, "I have killed before, and I will kill you."

Late in the morning, Detective Bill Pridemore testified
about his work on the case. The now-bearded Pridemore,
retired from the police department since September, slipped
easily back into his role. He stated that he had made it a personal priority to work on the Des Prez case. He reviewed the
exhibits and determined that the Metro Police Department did
not submit all the evidence for DNA testing in 1992. Pridemore took the evidence to the TBI Lab to test for DNA. He
requested that they enter into CODIS any DNA profiles they
might find.

Detective Pridemore explained that at first, family members were eliminated from the DNA search. Then they started
checking all the men around the apartments. After they were
excused, Jerome Barrett was identified as a possible suspect
because police could place him near the Vanderbilt campus
from November and December 1974.

After making several phone calls and researching police
data, Pridemore finally located Jerome Barrett in Memphis.
He and Sergeant Pat Postiglione drove to Memphis and served
Barrett with a search warrant for DNA. He obtained two
swabs of DNA from between Barrett's gum and cheek, one
from each side. The TBI Lab tested the swabs.

In 1975 the FBI had analyzed hairs found on the bed that
were consistent with a black person's hair, Pridemore said,
but those samples were missing. The FBI said they returned
the samples, but the police said they never received them. In
1975 property was sometimes returned to the detectives, who

then hand-delivered it to the property room. In any case, the samples had not been found.

Dr. Bruce Levy, chief medical examiner for Tennessee since 1998, was the State's last witness on the first day of the trial. Dressed casually, without jacket or tie, Dr. Levy gave the impression that this was all in a day's work. He poured himself several cups of coffee during the testimony. Dr. Levy testified that he had reviewed the written reports and found them acceptable. He had examined the crime scene photographs, police reports, lab reports, and newspaper articles at the time of Sarah Des Prez's death, and concluded that death was a result of asphyxia, by suffocation or strangulation. He studied photos of the victim's face and pointed out bruising and scraping, and petechia, red marks "like a red pen" in the area of the forehead, a marker for suffocation. Dr. Levy looked at another exhibit, photos of the upper body, and observed injuries from the neck, right breast, and right arm. Other photographs showed scrapes on elbows and bruises on legs. Although the original autopsy report was missing, he had a death certificate and a letter stating that there was no sign of drugs in the victim's system. Her blood alcohol was .07, equivalent to four drinks, below the level of intoxication, but it could have been higher earlier, Dr. Levy said. The medical examiner stated that from everything he'd examined, he concluded that Sarah Des Prez's death was indeed a homicide.

The first day of testimony ended. Pridemore, Postiglione, and Thurman commented on how well the trial was going. Maybe too well. They wondered where the knockout punch from the defense would come from.

The next morning, Thursday, January 29, 2009, the State played an audiotape recording from jail where Barrett made a phone call by using another inmate's PIN. In his conversation with an unidentified female, he said that he did not know Sarah Des Prez and that the DNA would not match.

On the heels of Barrett's own words, the prosecution followed up with testimony from Special Agent Chad Johnson, a serologist with the Tennessee Bureau of Investigation DNA Unit. Johnson's youthful appearance was deceptive. He stated that he had served as an expert witness between forty and fifty times, and he demonstrated his high level of competence immediately when he began to answer questions about DNA analysis. He explained the process for testing the DNA samples, including using a known standard from the victim and suspect.

Special Agent Johnson then explained his analysis regarding the death of Sarah Des Prez. He testified about the DNA that had been found in semen samples and in clippings taken from the victim's fingernails after she died. "DNA is a chemical and like all chemicals, over time, breaks down," he said. "In this case it did break down to some extent but there was plenty to get results from." He detailed the different samples he utilized, including those from the blanket, bed sheet, fingernail clippings, victim's blouse, and a pair of panties. He compared those with the DNA taken from the oral swabs from Jerome Barrett.

The special agent's next words sent a chill rippling through the courtroom: "There was more of Barrett's DNA under Sarah Des Prez's fingernails than her own."

Johnson concluded his testimony stating that while he found partial profiles on some items, there were four complete matches with Barrett's profile. He put it in layman's terms: The likelihood that the DNA belonged to Jerome Barrett exceeded the world population.

Defense attorney Kerry Haymaker did not cross-examine the special agent. He rested his case without calling any witnesses. It was still early in the afternoon when court adjourned.

* * *

On Friday morning, the attorneys presented closing arguments in the case. During closing arguments, Kerry Haymaker suggested to the jury that Sarah Des Prez got sick on that night and possibly suffocated on her own vomit; or perhaps she had suffered from a "mysterious disease." Facing the overwhelming DNA evidence, he implied that there was a possible consensual sexual relationship between his client and Des Prez. "He may not have wanted to disclose that he had been involved with somebody," Haymaker said. He ended his closing statement by saying that the State's case was built upon assumption after assumption, that there was a serious question as to whether there was an actual homicide, and the cause of death could not be determined.

Deputy DA Tom Thurman began his closing argument by displaying photographs of Sarah Des Prez, including a close-up of her face showing scratches and bruises and signs of a struggle. "Do you think that is a natural death?" he asked. "That is the face of a murder victim." Thurman immediately blew away Haymaker's argument by saying, "If Sarah Des Prez had a mysterious disease, why did she beat herself up?" He reviewed the DNA found at five locations and the fact that it was Jerome Barrett's DNA. He raised his voice when he pointed out to the jury again that there was more of Barrett's DNA than Sarah Des Prez's own found under her fingernails, yet the defense attorney did not mention that. Thurman discounted the idea that there was any kind of previous relationship between the two and pointed to the audiotapes, reminding the jury that Barrett had made a statement saying he did not know Sarah Des Prez.

Referring to the DNA analyst's testimony, Thurman reminded the jury that the victim "testified through Chad Johnson, just the same as if she sat on that stand and told you, 'Jerome Barrett is my killer.' "

Finally, Thurman showed photographs of Sarah Des Prez on PowerPoint. He turned back to the jury and said, "Sarah

Des Prez deserved a full life. Her family has now waited thirty-four years for justice in this case. That is a long time to right a wrong, but please have the courage to turn the proper verdict."

For about an hour, the judge charged the jury with detailed legal instructions concerning the evidence and burden of proof. The jury then retired to begin deliberations.

Friends and family members waited for the verdict. Attorneys on both sides waited. Reporters waited. The jury had gone out at 10:30 A.M. There was speculation that the jurors from Chattanooga would be back by the end of the afternoon, rather than continue into the weekend. Even so, the reaction all around was astonishment when, after a brief hour and a half, the clerk announced to the courtroom that the jury had reached a verdict.

Jerome Barrett returned to the courtroom with his attorneys. The jury filed back into their seats. After the courtroom settled, Judge Dozier asked the foreman if the jury had reached a verdict. The foreman said, "We have, Your Honor."

"What is your verdict?" the judge asked.

The Des Prez family and friends held one another, weeping, as the answer came.

"As to the count of first degree murder. Guilty."

After only ninety minutes of deliberation, decades of uncertainty came to an end.

Jerome Barrett showed no emotion as the verdict was read.

Afterward, Sarah Des Prez's brother, Roger, struggled through tears to read a statement. He thanked the prosecutors and detectives for all of their hard work. Deputy DA Tom Thurman stated that credit was due to all the people involved in the case for the successful prosecution after so many years. "We feel that justice has been served."

The afternoon following the conviction in the Des Prez murder trial, Pridemore and Postiglione had another reason to celebrate. They received the Investigative Services Bureau Investigators of the Year award for their work in solving the Des Prez and Trimble murders.

It was a huge honor, but Pridemore was thinking, *There's still one more trial.*

34

Challenges

Sarah Des Prez's murder was just as tragic as Marcia Trimble's. It crushed family members and shook the whole city, especially the Vanderbilt University community. So Jerome Barrett's conviction for her murder was big news locally. After thirty-four years, the jury's verdict brought a sense of relief and peace to the Des Prez family and friends, and it was a significant verdict for the city of Nashville.

For the Metro Police Cold Case Unit, the conviction also meant credibility. The Des Prez murder was the oldest homicide case ever solved in Nashville. The fact that a conviction was obtained without any witnesses who could put Jerome Barrett in Des Prez's apartment or even in the neighborhood was nothing short of remarkable.

But justice had not come full circle. There was a void in Nashville with one remaining missing piece of the puzzle. It was the Marcia Trimble murder mystery. No other case came close.

The last days of January 2009, Pridemore, Postiglione, and

Thurman quietly celebrated the Des Prez verdict. They had earned the right by hard work and perseverance. But even for a seasoned trial lawyer like Thurman, July 13, the date set for the Trimble trial to begin, seemed only weeks away.

Deputy DA Tom Thurman's experience had taught him that every case had problems and weaknesses. He recognized all too well the problems in the Trimble case. He had tried too many cases over the years to even begin to imagine that this one would be just a walk in the park.

The meetings between Thurman, Postiglione, and Pridemore continued over February, March, and April. The mood and structure of the meetings changed during these weeks and months. Thurman needed Bill Pridemore. Pridemore had an open mind, one that had not been tainted with the Jeffrey Womack witch hunt. Postiglione and Pridemore both had a fresh outlook on Barrett. They had been around Barrett, watched him, studied his criminal record, and understood that the man was capable of acts of horror and cold-blooded murder.

Now the intense pressure of the Trimble case shifted from the detectives and the police department to the district attorney's office—specifically to Tom Thurman. The media made the case the lead story, with articles, interviews, and commentaries. The Des Prez verdict added another major victory to his reputation, another notch on the prosecutor's gun. But a not guilty verdict in the Trimble case could stain an otherwise stellar career. It did not seem fair that one case could have such an impact on a reputation built on years of prosecuting the most vicious, dangerous criminals. Like it or not, Tom Thurman would be remembered for the verdict in the Marcia Trimble murder case.

The deputy district attorney did not have much room for error. Like the Des Prez case, with no witnesses who could put Barrett in her apartment, the State had no witnesses who could put Jerome Barrett at Mrs. Howard's driveway or in the

Thorpes' shed. DNA evidence linking the defendant with the crime scene would be the critical evidence. A jury's rejection of the DNA results could be fatal to the prosecution; Thurman's team had no fallback plan. Barrett's DNA was the State's evidence, and there was a problem: The original slides made from vaginal swabs during the Trimble autopsy at the medical examiner's office in Memphis had sparked controversy since the 1990s. When the autopsy was performed in 1975, forensic science did not have the benefit of DNA testing. But in the mid-1990s, with the rapid advance of DNA technology, the lab analysis of the slides had found multiple DNA profiles on the slides. The prevailing theory was that the staff at the medical examiner's office had left their own DNA on the slides while handling them; "touch contamination" occurred because certain precautions such as wearing gloves were not the standard of the day. But Thurman knew that the defense attorneys would be in attack mode and would use the contamination issue to contend that the State had not proved its case.

Though science was at the heart of the State's case, the prosecution had also identified Sheldon Anter as a potential witness. In March 2009, Thurman learned that Anter, who was in the country illegally, was facing deportation to Trinidad, since his sentence for a fraud conviction had been converted to probation. The district attorney's office tried to put a hold on Anter with a material witness bond, which would mean he could remain in Nashville until he testified. Thurman also entered a motion to do a video deposition of Anter, in the event that he was deported.

Earlier in the year, Judge Dozier had appointed the public defender's office to represent Jerome Barrett in the Trimble case. The Nashville Public Defender's Office enjoyed an outstanding reputation for top-quality attorneys, but it had constant budget problems and a small staff. Huge caseloads and low pay were the norm for public defender attorneys. James P. McNamara and Laura Dykes were assigned as Barrett's attorneys. McNamara, a graduate of the University of North Carolina School of Law, was a bright young attorney from Queens, New York, with an excellent legal mind. He had practiced law in Nashville since 1996. Dykes, a Crossville native like Tom Thurman, was a graduate of Vanderbilt Law School, had practiced law more than twenty years, and had tried numerous murder cases.

The defense had seventy-seven storage boxes of material in the Trimble case.

Like the prosecution, the defense faced challenges of its own in the Trimble case. For McNamara and Dykes, overcoming the results of the DNA would be almost impossible. They had no means to "explain away" the results.

In the middle of May 2009, the district attorney's office began reviewing all the evidence in the Trimble case. Because the investigation covered over thirty years, the case file was contained in fourteen 4-inch notebooks and storage boxes crammed with faded documents, newspaper articles, and other miscellaneous items from detectives who'd worked the case in previous years.

When he came across an audiotape, prosecutor Tom Thurman also realized that there had to be other tapes from the period that his office did not have. A search of the police archives led to an unmarked box with eighty audio- and videotapes, including telephone conversations between Virginia Trimble and friends, family members, and others in the community during the time the child was missing. Thurman immediately notified the public defender's office that these tapes had been discovered.

On May 20, Jim McNamara filed a motion for a continuance, asking that the July 13 trial be postponed to give his office more time to review the tapes. The request was based upon his heavy caseload and the fact that the trial was less than two months away. Judge Dozier denied the motion and suggested that the defense team work harder.

* * *

McNamara could not have been more disappointed to have his motion for continuance denied than was Detective Bill Pridemore.

Pridemore had known for months that his wife, Denise, would be receiving her doctorate from the University of Phoenix on Saturday, July 18, 2009. They would need to be in Phoenix, Arizona, the week previous to graduation day, the week of the trial. Denise was a professor as well as a post-graduate student. She had responsibilities. Whenever they talked about the conflict, her husband always told her there was a good chance the Trimble trial would be postponed. The Des Prez trial had been postponed. Postponements were not unusual.

But this trial was going forward.

A criminal defense lawyer's options were limited when evidence matched the accused to the crime scene or the victim. Barrett's attorneys recognized that a DNA match could be devastating, turning the credibility of their defense into shambles. One option available to the defense attorneys was to file motions, a legal pleading filed by one of the parties requesting the Court to grant certain relief. A hearing on a motion was conducted outside the presence of the jury. Motions could be useful weapons for attacking the State's main evidence from a number of different angles without the jury ever knowing it.

Jim McNamara filed a motion asking the Court to preclude the DNA test results from being admitted into evidence because the search warrant that allowed the State to take a sample from Jerome Barrett was unreasonable and illegal. Specifically, he argued that the search warrant the State had used to obtain the search warrant was based upon a false affidavit.

McNamara's motion was based upon two points: (1) the warrant did not contain any evidence linking Barrett to the murder of the Trimble girl; (2) the language in the police affidavit that the Court relied upon in issuing the search warrant was false.

Pridemore's affidavit contained a summary of Barrett's confession in the Judy Porter rape case at Belmont. Pridemore had said Barrett admitted during the confession that he would "enter buildings attempting to find unlocked apartment doors and then forcibly rape the victims."

McNamara argued that the affidavit was misleading. "On its face, the language in the affidavit is false." He noted that Barrett had confessed to only one crime, the rape of Judy Porter, but the affidavit implied that Barrett had confessed to multiple rapes.

The hearing took place on June 3, 2009. Deputy DA Tom Thurman went over the affidavit line by line. He explained in detail how the affidavit was accurate and argued that the Court was correct in issuing the search warrant.

Thurman called Detective Pridemore to the stand. Pridemore testified about his years on the police force and his experience in the Cold Case Unit. He stated that he developed Jerome Barrett as a suspect in the Trimble case based upon the results of the DNA tests as well as Barrett's involvement in the Des Prez murder, two rapes, one assault, and one burglary. During his investigation of the Trimble case, he had reviewed the transcript of the Porter case, including Barrett's confession.

"Barrett admitted he would enter apartment buildings trying to find unlocked doors," Pridemore said. Barrett, who had shaved his head since he was last in court, stared at Pridemore with hard eyes. Pridemore testified that he compared Barrett's confession with what occurred in the Des Prez, Shatzen, Porter, and McMillan cases. He told the Court he alone had prepared the affidavit for the search warrant.

McNamara, in closing, again stated that the affidavit was false on its face and requested that the search warrant be suppressed. Judge Dozier took the motion under advisement.

On June 17, 2009, Judge Dozier issued an order denying the defense's motion to exclude Barrett's DNA test results. The Court found that the search warrant and affidavit were sufficient and rejected the allegations that the affidavit was false.

Pridemore, Postiglione, Thurman, and the district attorney's office worked hard the next few weeks preparing for the trial. They called witnesses to confirm their attendance and to refresh their memories about the facts of the case. They spent time with the DNA experts from the FBI and the TBI.

The time came for Pridemore to decide: Would he miss Denise's graduation or would he miss the Trimble trial? It was a hard call. This was the biggest case of his career. He had continued to work on it during the nine months of his retirement. But he thought about all the late-night callouts, the social functions and family gatherings he had missed, and how much his wife had sacrificed for his job. He made his decision. During one of the strategy meetings, he told Thurman he would have to miss the trial. The deputy district attorney's expression didn't change. "You can't go to the graduation," he said. But then he gave one of his wry smiles. Thurman had been married a long time, too.

Sergeant Pat Postiglione would be the one to testify about the work of the Cold Case detectives.

* * *

On Wednesday, June 24, 2009, Jerome Barrett's attorneys filed a number of motions, some very broad and general, others quite specific. Among the defense's motions was a lengthy four-page motion addressing exculpatory evidence, asking the Court to require the State to produce certain information, including "the names and addresses of any witnesses whom the State believes would give testimony favorable to the defense in regard to the facts alleged in the indictment."

This was revealing because there were rumors circulating around the courthouse and the police department that some of the older officers still maintained that Jeffrey Womack had killed Marcia Trimble. Was it possible some of these officers would actually testify for the defense in the Trimble case?

Additionally, several detectives who had worked the initial crime scene and the investigation into Jeffrey Womack still clung to the theory that Marcia Trimble's body had been returned to the garage by the murderer. This theory implied that the medical examiner's findings were inconsistent and incorrect.

Another motion dealt with the State's witness Sheldon Anter, who had overheard Barrett bragging about killing "four people" while they were both incarcerated in the Davidson County jail. The defense's motion stated, "With respect to Mr. Sheldon Anter, a jailhouse informant, who has been identified as a potential witness for the State: (a) Information regarding any compensation that has been promised or provided to Mr. Anter, including but not limited to, any assistance that the district attorney general has provided to Mr. Anter with respect to his pending immigration case; (b) Information about any other cases in which Mr. Anter offered information to the district attorney general that proved unreliable; (c) Any demands for compensation that the witness has made of the State in exchange for their cooperation."

If the defense could discover that the State had promised

compensation in exchange for Sheldon Anter's testimony, they could attack Anter's credibility before a jury.

Barrett's attorneys filed a number of motions in limine.* One of the motions addressed the tainted DNA slides. The attorneys took a creative and unusual position for a defendant in a major criminal case. They contended in the motion: "There are adequate witnesses available to demonstrate an unbroken chain of custody." Normally the State has the burden of proving chain of custody, but the defense attorneys hoped the tainted slides would create doubt in the jurors' minds. Maybe there were others involved in the case that the State had not identified. Accordingly, McNamara requested the Court to allow the slides to be admitted into evidence.

The defense, in addition to facing the fact that their client's DNA matched the DNA found at the scene of the crime, had serious problems regarding their client's criminal record. It would be devastating for a jury to learn of Barrett's lengthy, violent criminal record. This was especially true concerning Barrett's murder and rape rampage during February and March of 1975 in Nashville. Barrett's attorneys filed another lengthy motion and memorandum of law asking the Court to exclude any evidence of other crimes and bad acts under Rule 404(b) of the Tennessee Rules of Evidence, which governed the admissibility of evidence related to crimes, wrongs, or acts committed by a defendant other than one for which the defendant presently stood trial. Courts have allowed proof of

---

* "In limine" is a Latin phrase that means "on or at the threshold; preliminary." Motions in limine are routinely filed within a couple of weeks before a trial. Courts appreciate them for they can narrow down the legal issues prior to the actual trial. The motions are also argued outside the presence of the jury. A motion in limine can be a weapon that cripples or destroys the opposition. Lawyers who fail to prepare for the issues raised in such a motion can see their case eviscerated before even starting the case.

another crime to address such issues as identity, motive, common sense, or plan and intent, but the State was not allowed to use evidence of other crimes to prove the character of a person.

Barrett's attorney contended that the other crimes that the State intended to introduce did not establish a common scheme or plan to the Trimble case. In other words, the modus operandi of the other crime and the crime on trial was not unique enough to serve as proof the defendant committed the other offense. The defense attorneys included in their motion the famous analogy applicable to the examination of a defendant's previous crimes: "Many men commit murder but when Jack the Ripper used his knife in a manner so peculiar that when his crimes were viewed together, there could be little doubt that they were committed by the same man."

In the memorandum of law, Barrett's attorneys then compared the specifics of the Trimble case with the murder of Sarah Des Prez, the assault of Charlotte Shatzen, and the statements made to Sheldon Anter about multiple people Barrett had killed.

During the Sarah Des Prez trial, the Court found that the similarities between the Shatzen case and the Des Prez case were sufficient to establish the relevance as to the issue of identity. Barrett's attorneys struggled to make a legitimate argument that the facts in the Trimble case were inconsistent with the facts in the Des Prez and Shatzen cases.

On Wednesday, July 8, 2009, Judge Steve Dozier ruled that the vaginal swab samples taken during the Trimble autopsy that were placed on the slides would be admitted into evidence in the trial. The judge also ruled that the jury would be allowed to hear evidence from Trimble's autopsy examination. This was important because it would provide the jury with facts showing that Marcia Trimble was in fact murdered, and would provide insight into how she was actually murdered.

At the same hearing, the prosecution introduced a new theory about why Jerome Barrett was in the Trimbles' neighborhood. Charlotte Shatzen testified that she was twenty-four years old when she was attacked outside her Fairfax Avenue apartment on February 23, 1975. She identified Jerome Barrett as her attacker after he was arrested at the Bransford House Apartments on March 12, 1975. "I looked right into his face," she said. When Barrett was convicted of the Belmont raping, charges for the attack on Shatzen were retired. Charlotte Shatzen was just under five feet and weighed just over one hundred pounds, not much larger than Marcia Trimble, Sergeant Pat Postiglione testified.

Postiglione also told the Court that Charlotte Shatzen's parents lived on Dorcas Drive. Their yard backed up to the Trimbles' yard on Copeland. The theory the prosecution now offered was that Jerome Barrett was in the neighborhood looking for the woman he had attacked just two days earlier. The prosecution believed he found her name on her mailbox, but she was not at her apartment; she was in the hospital recovering from the injuries Barrett inflicted. He'd found another "Shatzen" in the phone book. Charlotte's parents were the only other "Shatzens" listed in the telephone directory.

Judge Dozier called the coincidence "ironic," but ultimately ruled that the jury would not hear evidence of the Des Prez or Shatzen case. The prosecution could not bring in their version of why Barrett was in the Trimbles' neighborhood. He noted that "there's just no proof" to support the theory that Barrett had been out looking for Charlotte Shatzen. The judge ruled that the evidence of the other crimes would prejudice the jury. However, the Court did rule that Sheldon Anter could testify. Anter said he'd overheard Barrett claim to have killed Marcia Trimble. "He said he killed her but didn't rape her," Anter said. The Court found that Barrett's statements were "an admission."

After that hearing, Thurman met with the Cold Case detec-

tives and his staff for one final review of the case. Jury selection would begin on Monday morning. Jerome Barrett had
requested that this jury come from Nashville. Disappointed
with the outcome in the Des Prez trial, Barrett believed the
Chattanooga jurors had arrived at their guilty verdict because
they were an "older" jury, which he felt made them more conservative. It was true that the average age of the Chattanooga
jury had been sixty-eight. Barrett believed he'd have a better
chance with a younger jury, even if they came from Nashville.

The city was gearing up for the trial. In an article in the *City
Paper*, Ken Whitehouse wrote that "the sights and sounds,
fears and suspicions of 1975 that changed how Nashvillians
forever lived their lives, will resonate once again" when the
crime was first explained to the jury. "It won't be called a 'trial
of the century,'" he said, "but in many ways it will be the trial
for a whole generation of Nashvillians."

Considering the problems inherent in a case that was over
thirty-four years old, there was not much more to do. The witnesses were ready. The DNA experts were all confirmed and
ready to testify next Wednesday and Thursday. Virginia Trimble was also ready to go forward with the case.

It was up to Deputy DA Tom Thurman to do what he did
best: try the lawsuit. A jury would finally hear the Marcia
Trimble case.

35

Voir Dire

Deputy DA Tom Thurman stayed busy over the weekend. He went on a bike ride with his wife Debbie, did chores around the house, and played with the family's three dogs.

Jerome Sydney Barrett's attorneys had notified the district attorney's office at the last minute that they might call a witness who would testify on their client's behalf. Supposedly, the potential witness would provide Barrett with an alibi. Thurman spent time on the phone tracking the man down and finally reached him in Memphis. The man's story was weak. Thurman felt he could deal with the man if he testified.

Thurman also practiced his opening statement. He wanted to insure that it included the critical facts and issues in a logical way. It needed to flow, not sound like jumbled notes off a legal pad. Thurman had a reputation for connecting with juries, but he wasn't one to rest on his laurels. He was an athlete, and in many ways trying a large lawsuit was similar to participating in a major athletic event. A lawyer who has worked the case and is thoroughly prepared has a great deal

of pent-up energy prior to the start, like a football player going into a big game. Once the ball is kicked and contact is
made, the player feels much better. Tom Thurman was restless. He was ready to go.

"Voir dire" is an old French-Latin term that means "to speak
the truth." In Europe and Great Britain the term was used to
denote a preliminary examination in which the Court examined a witness, party, or juror to test competence or interest
in the case.

In the United States, over the years, the term "voir dire" has
come to mean the selection process for jurors. In a Tennessee
criminal case, after the Court has given a brief summary of
the case and asked the potential jurors if they can be impartial
and if they can serve, the district attorney will first question
potential jurors. Then the defense will have the opportunity
to ask questions. If a juror's response to questions establishes
that there is a "cause" and that juror could not be fair, he or
she will be excused. Examples of "cause" for which the Court
would excuse a potential juror from serving would include
bias, prejudice, or an interest in the case.

Both the district attorney and the defense attorney have the
right to "challenge for cause." The attorney must state a reason
for the challenge, but there is no absolute right to have a juror
excluded. The judge will rule on the attorney's challenge and
ultimately decide whether a juror is competent and qualified
to sit on the jury.

In both civil and criminal cases, the selection of the jury is
one of the most critical aspects of the trial. For trial lawyers,
the jury qualification process is almost a rejection rather than
a selection process. One cannot become an expert in select-
ing juries by attending law school or seminars, or watching a
TV crime show. Choosing jurors is not a science; it is an art
acquired after years of trying lawsuits.

The skilled attorney knows it can be fatal to allow a person to serve as a juror if that person's views oppose those of his client. So a good attorney tries to be thorough, asking questions to flush out the juror's true feelings and opinions. Despite the attorney's preparation, the process is not a hundred percent. It is not extraordinary for jurors hostile to the client's position to slip through the cracks and sit on juries. For the most part, hostile jurors are not too difficult to spot during the actual trial. They will ignore the attorney, look or act bored, or refuse to make eye contact with the attorney.

The State and defense also have "preemptory challenges" to remove a potential juror, without the necessity or requirement of explaining cause. To a trial lawyer these preemptory challenges are precious and he tries to save as many as he can until the very end of the selection process. It is basically a right that is codified in the Tennessee Rules of Criminal Procedure. A preemptory challenge might be appropriate if a potential juror has experience in law enforcement or family members working in the field. That would not be grounds, in and of itself, for a removal for cause. However, someone steeped in the law enforcement culture would probably not be the type of juror a lawyer would want if defending a serious criminal charge.

In the case of *State of Tennessee v. Jerome Barrett*, each party would have eight preemptory challenges.

On Monday morning, July 13, 2009, the court's clerk called the case, and the attorneys for both parties announced they were ready to proceed. Virginia Trimble and her family sat in the courtroom. It was her first time actually seeing the man accused of her daughter's murder.

After the jury pool numbering about 125 jurors was brought in, Judge Steve Dozier gave a short summary of the case, including when it occurred and details about the victim. Then he began the process of voir dire.

He said, "If anyone has knowledge about the case, please raise your hand." Several responded. The judge then asked these people about their specific information and whether their knowledge would prevent them from serving on the jury. Judge Dozier explained that this jury would be sequestered at night during the trial. He asked the entire pool of jurors if serving would cause a hardship on them. He also asked them if they could be fair and impartial. Judge Dozier questioned eighty-three jurors. Ten of them were dismissed because of hardships. Another ten were dismissed because they conceded they could not be impartial. One woman burst into tears and told the Court, "I don't know if I can be fair." She was dismissed.

One potential juror, Marva McCord, told the Court that when she was eight years old she had gone to elementary school with Marcia Trimble, and Marcia had once given her a pretty bracelet. Marva was relieved when the Court dismissed her from the panel because she said she didn't think she could have endured the trial and the crime scene photos of the little girl.

"That's not how I remembered her, or how I want to remember her," she said.

Another woman stated she remembered the day it happened. "My son was the same age as Marcia. It changed the lives of a lot of people," she said. She went on to say that it had affected nearly every parent in Nashville. The woman was dismissed outright because she could not presume Barrett was innocent.

The Court asked a number of questions about publicity and how much exposure the jurors had to the news of Jerome Barrett and the Trimble murder. A male juror stated that he had followed the case for years and knew about Barrett's criminal record. He was dismissed after he told the Court he thought he could not be fair.

A number of jurors testified they knew Barrett was actually serving prison time for his conviction in the murder of Sarah Des Prez, which had occurred around the same time as Trimble. Several jurors testified that they did not watch much news or that they only recently moved to Nashville. Judge Dozier specifically asked each juror, "Would you be able to look at the graphic evidence in the case, including photos of the body of Marcia Trimble at the crime scene?"

On Tuesday, attorneys began questioning potential jurors, asking about their occupations, habits, acquaintances, life experiences, education, and families, as well as specific questions about where the jurors had lived in 1975 and their perception of the 1970s. Barrett's attorneys were searching for people who were intelligent and understood the system. They were not interested in a person who assumed "if there's smoke, there's fire." They did not want jurors with rubber-stamp personalities who believed whatever the prosecutor said just because he said it.

"Beyond a reasonable doubt" was the burden the State of Tennessee had to prove to prevail in the case. Barrett's attorney pounded the point that this was a heavy burden. Each juror said that he or she understood that beyond a reasonable doubt did not mean "possible" or "probably."

Deputy DA Tom Thurman had to deal with a different issue. The murder had happened thirty-four years ago in a dark garage. There were no witnesses that could give direct evidence such as "I saw Barrett in the garage" or "I saw Barrett yanking Marcia Trimble up the Thorpes' hill toward the garage." The veteran prosecutor was forced to prove his case with circumstantial evidence, defined by Tennessee law as "proof of collateral facts and circumstances which did not directly prove the fact and issue but from which the fact may be logically inferred." This rule and law required the jury to find that all the essential facts were consistent with the hypothesis of guilt.*

Thurman spent time questioning the jurors about the concept of circumstantial evidence. This would be important when the State's experts testified concerning the DNA evidence that inferred that Jerome Barrett was in the garage with Marcia Trimble on February 25, 1975. The jurors indicated that they understood. Finally, they all told Judge Dozier that they could render a fair verdict in the trial. On Tuesday afternoon the twelve-person jury with two alternates was accepted. Nine members of the panel were white; three were black. Nine of the twelve were fifty years or older.

Opening statements would begin Wednesday morning.

---

* There's an old country story that Tennessee lawyers use to explain circumstantial evidence: It is snowing very hard. A farmer is standing on the bank of a creek by a bridge. He looks up and sees a fox standing on the other side of the bank. The farmer then sees fox tracks in the snow on the bridge. Now that farmer did not actually see the fox walk across the bridge. His belief that the fox walked across the bridge is based upon circumstantial facts and under Tennessee law this circumstantial evidence would be admitted into evidence. Men have gone to the gallows based upon circumstantial evidence.

36

Trial for a Generation

Deputy DA Tom Thurman had been making opening statements for more than thirty years.

The opening statement is typically the first real opportunity for an attorney to visit with the jury and to tell the story of the case. It has to be concise and articulate. With the opening statement, jurors get their first chance to evaluate the lawyer and his client. First impressions are critical. Many legal experts would say the opening statement is the most important part of the trial. A good lawyer should start thinking about his or her opening statement many months prior to trial. Thorough preparation will transform a jerky mishmash of facts and theories into a smooth-flowing stream of common sense coupled with a clear theme.

There are two cardinal rules for effective opening statements. First is to address the weaknesses in the case up front. A skilled lawyer will look directly into the jurors' eyes and tell them about the problems with the case. It is essential to disclose any problems as soon as possible. If an attorney hides the bad facts or just skips over them, a worthy opponent will immediately recite the facts and coat them with "Mr. Attorney failed to tell you this," making the attorney and his client appear less than truthful, thereby injuring their credibility for the remainder of the trial.

The second rule is not to overstate the case. If the lawyer made a promise in an opening statement that he couldn't prove later, the opposing attorney would make sure in the closing argument that the unfulfilled promise came back to bite.

On Wednesday morning, July 15, the dark-paneled courtroom on the sixth floor of the A. A. Birch building began to fill. Virginia Trimble Ritter and her family and friends made their way through a maze of TV cameras, lights, cables, and reporters that lined the marble hallway. Virginia, her husband Frank Ritter, her forty-six-year-old son Chuck, tall and broad shouldered with a dark beard, and the group of supporters, mostly women, entered the courtroom and filled several rows.

The prosecutors spoke to Virginia and others in the courtroom before taking their seats and straightening their papers. Deputy DA Thurman was dressed in a navy suit, his hair close cropped. He was joined by ADA Katy Miller, her dark hair clasped at the nape of her neck, and ADA Rachel Sobrero. Sobrero, a graduate of Colorado College and University of Denver Law School, was a slender young woman dressed in a conservative light-colored suit.

Court officers brought Jerome Barrett into the courtroom. He wore a dark suit and white shirt. His beard was turning gray. He towered over his defense counsel, attorneys Jim McNamara and Laura Dykes.

Judge Steve Dozier took the bench, and the jurors entered the jury box. The judge asked if both sides were ready to proceed.

ADA Katy Miller read the indictment that set forth the

specific charges against Jerome Barrett. When she finished, defense attorney McNamara stood and announced that Barrett pleaded not guilty.

Tom Thurman walked to the center of the courtroom and faced the jury. In a quiet, conversational tone, the distinguished-looking prosecutor introduced himself and Katy Miller to the jury. He projected an air of confidence, with no hint of apprehension. The heart of his case was DNA evidence, and Thurman planned to put on expert after expert to testify about DNA analysis. The jurors were not scientists, and it was reasonable to believe they might find it difficult and confusing to follow the complex scientific explanations. Thurman's opening statement had to simplify the issue, to make the jurors understand why DNA was such powerful evidence against Jerome Barrett.

The prosecutor began by painting a picture of the 1970s. *Jaws* was the number one movie in 1975. Children played in their neighborhoods without fear. Gently pacing, Thurman related the events that occurred on the afternoon of February 25, 1975. He described nine-year-old Marcia Trimble and the fact that she was excited about delivering Girl Scout cookies. Neighbor Marie Maxwell saw Marcia Trimble standing in the Howard driveway talking to two individuals, he told the jury.

From her front-row seat, Virginia Trimble watched intently as Thurman described how the Trimble family became concerned when Marcia failed to return home, and the search for her began that night and expanded over the following days and weeks. Thurman acknowledged that it was not clear if the different divisions of the police department were sharing information, but police never gave up, working the case for thirty-three years before Jerome Barrett was indicted.

Thurman named the witnesses and told what their testimony would be. One of the witnesses, Sheldon Anter, and Barrett were inmates at the Davidson County jail. Anter overheard Barrett say that he killed Marcia Trimble but did not rape her. Anter said that Barrett got into a fight in jail and threatened another inmate by saying, "I've killed before and I will kill you." Thurman said the State had not compensated Mr. Anter for his testimony.

At the defense table, Barrett shook his head.

The prosecutor described how the evidence in the case would show that tests on the semen stains found on Marcia Trimble's blouse isolated a definite DNA profile. After a search warrant was issued by a Memphis judge, the police took DNA samples from Jerome Barrett.

Tom Thurman paused and looked at the jury. Every eye in the courtroom, including Virginia Trimble's, was on the solemn prosecutor. He said in a quiet voice, "The DNA samples taken from Marcia Trimble's blouse matched the sample taken from Jerome Barrett." He told the jury they would hear from the FBI and TBI and other DNA experts who would confirm the match. He said, "They will testify that this calculated match is rarer than one in six trillion, or more than the population of the world."

He concluded by saying, "The evidence will be clear and beyond a reasonable doubt that Jerome Barrett killed Marcia Trimble."

There was some restless shifting in the courtroom as Thurman returned to the prosecutor's table. Then defense attorney Laura Dykes walked to the jury box. She made eye contact with them and said, "The question is: Who killed Marcia Trimble?"

She said that there were a number of other questions the State's proof would not answer. She began reviewing the evidence and witnesses. First, there was Marie Maxwell who, Dykes said, saw Marcia Trimble and two *white* individuals standing in the Howard driveway. Who were those individuals? Dykes said, "The prosecution and the police to this day do not know who was standing there with Marcia Trimble."

She continued the story, stopping to interject questions along the way. The night Marcia disappeared, police searched with police dogs, Dykes told the jury. She noted that during the initial search of the Thorpe garage, the police saw fertilizer bags stored in the back of the outbuilding. The police were satisfied with their search of the garage. Then thirty-three days later, Marcia Trimble's body was found on top of the fertilizer bags. Had the murderer brought the body back there? Dykes contended that the State could not answer that question.

She pointed out that in 1990, Lieutenant Jacobs and Captain Miller had reviewed all the evidence in the case, and at that time, police continued to maintain that the main suspect was a neighborhood boy.

She made a surprising admission, stating that Jerome Barrett was arrested and in custody from March 12, 1975, on. The defense attorney pounded the fact that Marcia's body had been discovered on March 30. "Was Marcia Trimble killed on March 30?" she asked. If so, it certainly could not have been by Jerome Barrett.

Dykes came to the end of her opening statement, posing the questions, *Who were the two people with Marcia Trimble in the Howard driveway? When did Marcia Trimble die? Where did she die? Did she die in the garage or somewhere else? Whose DNA was in her vagina?* She looked at the jury and said, "With all due respect, the State of Tennessee cannot prove that Jerome Barrett killed Marcia Trimble on February 25, 1975, beyond a reasonable doubt."

Laura Dykes said, "When you have heard all the evidence, you will have more questions than answers." She returned to the defense table.

It was time for the evidence.

Everyone in the courtroom leaned slightly forward as the State's first witness, Virginia Trimble, took the stand. She wore a white blouse with a black jacket and pearl necklace.

Her blond hair was short. The eyes behind her glasses were wise, and—in spite of everything she'd gone through since February 1975—kind.

She testified that she now lived in Kentucky and was married to Frank Ritter, known to many for his outstanding career as a journalist with the *Tennessean*. She said that Charles Trimble, her former husband and father of her children Marcia and Chuck, was deceased.

"Is it OK if I call you Mrs. Trimble?" Katy Miller asked. Virginia said yes.

In 1975 the Trimbles lived on Copeland Drive, in the Green Hills area. "Children played in the streets, lots of children," Virginia said. At that time she worked half days at Westminster Kindergarten and was also a Girl Scout leader.

Katy Miller passed her a photograph and asked her to identify it. Virginia's voice quivered as she said, "That's my Marcia." She said it was the last photograph of Marcia taken while she was alive. Miller asked questions about the neighborhood and where Marcia was allowed to go. "Pretty much anywhere on Copeland and Dorcas," Virginia said. She identified photographs on Copeland Drive, as well as aerial photographs of the entire neighborhood.

Virginia Trimble testified that on the afternoon of February 25, 1975, Marcia had come home after school between 3:30 and 4:00. A snack after school was normally fruit, such as apples and pears. She also ate a powdered doughnut that afternoon. Virginia's mother-in-law, Marcia's grandmother, came to the home around 5:00 and gave Marcia $5 for Girl Scout cookies. At about 5:20 Marcia said she was going to deliver cookies to their neighbor, Marie Maxwell. Her mother told her to put on a coat, but Marcia said she didn't need one because she'd be right back. Virginia said Marcia walking out the door to go to the Maxwells' house was the last time she ever saw her daughter alive. Marcia had had about $20 in her

Girl Scout cookie box, and she was wearing a blue and white checked blouse, jeans, "and little black patent leather boots she bought with her Christmas money."

At around 5:45 it was time for dinner. Virginia said she went outside and called for her daughter. When she saw their family dogs across the street, she knew Marcia had been there. The Maxwells lived on that side of the street. Virginia came back inside and called Marie Maxwell, who told her she had seen Marcia in Mrs. Howard's driveway but that she never came to her house to deliver the cookies.

Virginia told the Court that her husband called Sergeant Sherman Nickens of the Metro Police Department, a friend of the Trimbles. Nickens made other calls, and uniformed police officers came out and filed a missing person's report. Virginia said, "I excused myself and went into Marcia's bedroom and started praying, and I never have stopped since."

She described the massive search that began that night. Police cleaned out Charles and Virginia's bedroom and established a command post, which remained there for the next ten days. Virginia identified the police's diagram of the neighborhood, which showed the Trimble house, the Howard driveway, and the Thorpe house.

Prosecutor Katy Miller asked the court officer to pass Virginia a package. "Can you identify the contents?" Miller asked. Virginia choked back tears. "Yes, this was the blouse Marcia was wearing at the time she delivered the cookies," she said. Marcia had worn the blouse the previous Friday to a birthday party. Virginia said, "I had washed it, and it was clean." She described the days that her daughter was missing as terrible, but said she'd continued to have faith that Marcia would come home.

Thirty-three days later, on March 30, 1975, the Trimbles were at church for Easter. One of the Youth Guidance officers assigned to the Trimble family came to them and said they needed to go home. When they arrived at their house, they were met by Sergeant Sherman Nickens. Police Chief Joe Casey was also there. Sergeant Nickens said, "I have news about Marcia." On the stand, Virginia Trimble wiped away tears again. "I knew automatically that it was not good news." She told Nickens she wanted to go to the living room, so they all went inside. Sherman Nickens told her, "We found Marcia's body and she's dead."

The courtroom was silent as Virginia Trimble cried softly. Katy Miller told the Court she had no more questions.

Defense attorney Jim McNamara stood up. Many legal experts thought a lawyer trying to cross-examine Virginia Trimble, who had suffered so much for thirty-four years, would be on thin ice, but McNamara began questioning. Virginia stated that then ten-year-old neighbor boy March Egerton, a classmate of Marcia's, had helped her deliver cookies that afternoon and later played basketball with Chuck. She said there had also been four boys playing basketball across the street. In the end, all the cross-examination provided was a few more details for the jury without clearly establishing any foundation for McNamara to use later in his defense. Virginia Trimble went back to sit with her family and friends. She hugged her husband.

The State called Harry Moffett, who'd been the one to actually find Marcia's body, as its next witness. Harry, with silver hair and a deep tan, said he now lived on St. Simons Island, Georgia. In 1975, he had been thirty-three years old, living in Memphis. His wife's sister, Marie, was married to John Thorpe, and on Easter weekend, Marie's two sisters and their families were all visiting the Thorpes. Harry Moffett had come home from church. Between 10:30 and 11:00 A.M., he went into the Thorpes' garage to find a boat motor, and had noticed something in the back corner. "I saw a little girl's face looking up at me," he said. "I was in a bit of a state of shock."

He went to the house and quietly asked his brother-in-law, John Ed Fuller, to come out with him. John Ed went to the back of the garage, saw the little girl, and touched her arm with a broom. Neither man smelled any odor about the body. They went inside and called the police.

Harry Moffett identified photographs showing the inside of the outbuilding and the front opening, looking out of the garage from the back wall. The State also introduced a photograph of Marcia Trimble's body in the back corner of the garage.

In the brief cross-examination, Harry said that "standing at the end of the garage, if you knew where to look, you could see her."

After a short break, the State's next witness was Captain Tom Cathey. The retired captain, a small, wiry man with steel gray hair and a strong jaw, had been in charge of the Homicide Division in February 1975. At that time, he had been in Homicide for thirteen years. Cathey testified he was not really involved when Marcia Trimble disappeared, but he went to the scene immediately after the body was discovered and took charge of the crime scene. He described the garage as an open-ended, all-wooden structure facing north. When Cathey arrived, he immediately ordered the front entrance of the garage secured and boards placed on the dirt floor. He had photographs taken of the inside and outside of the garage, and of the body.

Tom Thurman passed Cathey a number of photographs of the garage and Marcia Trimble's body. Cathey identified the photos and testified that Detective Tommy Jacobs, who would go on to become lead detective on the Trimble murder, had assisted him in the crime scene investigation. Cathey had worn rubber gloves and dictated notes to Carol Lawrence of Youth Guidance regarding his findings and measurements.

Captain Cathey testified that he could not see Marcia Trimble unless he was within three feet of the body. He said, "She was well concealed." Using a diagram that the ID officers had made of the garage, he testified that the girl's face was toward the east wall. Cathey said when he'd first arrived and stood at the entrance of the outbuilding, he could not see the body.

Her clothing was "all in place," Cathey said. He told the Court he was extremely careful in removing all the evidence at the crime scene, including her boots and socks, blue jeans and blouse, placing each in a separate bag. He'd then placed her body on a sheet on a table, before putting it into a crash bag. The funeral home came to remove her body. "That was the normal procedure then," he said.

Cathey looked at wrapped packages and identified them as containing Marcia Trimble's clothing, evidence that was sent to the FBI. He said he'd attempted to have prints developed, but there were "no prints of value."

Since Nashville did not have a medical examiner at the time, Cathey left Nashville at 6:00 P.M. that night and flew with the body to Memphis, to the state medical examiner's office. There, Dr. Jerry Francisco asked him to obtain dental records for Marcia and weather records for Nashville from the time of the disappearance to the time the body was discovered. After the investigation became a homicide, Cathey said his detectives began canvassing the neighborhoods with forms, asking if the neighbors had seen anything unusual.

In defense attorney Laura Dykes's brief cross-examination, Cathey said he'd left the Homicide Division in February 1976 and had not worked on the case after that.

The State's next witness was Dr. Jerry Francisco. White-haired Francisco, now a retired professor of pathology from UT Medical School, testified that from 1971 through 1989, while he was the medical examiner for the State, he performed thousands of autopsies and had testified as an expert in hundreds of cases. Judge Dozier ruled that he was an expert in this case. Dr. Francisco performed the autopsy on Marcia Trimble in UT Medical Center in Memphis. He said she was four feet seven inches and weighed approximately seventy-two pounds, noting that the human body loses weight during decomposition.

Responding to Tom Thurman's questions, Dr. Francisco said cause of death was "asphyxia due to manual strangulation." He noted wounds on the skin of the neck, fracture to the thyroid cartilage, which would take "considerable pressure," cyanosis or blueness of lips, and petechial hemorrhages, tiny pinpoint red marks indicating asphyxiation. He said there was no injury to the vaginal area and the hymen was intact.

The doctor answered that the time of death was "at or around the time of the disappearance on February 25, 1975." He gave the basis for his findings. First was the minimal decomposition. "If you know the temperature, you can get a good idea," he said. He also based his conclusion on the larvae present and on the body's lividity, the settling of blood due to gravity. He stated that Marcia Trimble's body had been in the same location from the time of her death to her discovery. Finally, he said the presence of a fragment of pear in Marcia's stomach indicated that she'd eaten it just before death.

Dr. Francisco testified regarding the slides that had been prepared and tested in the Memphis lab. Explaining the mixture of DNA profiles on the slides, he said there had been no precautions taken in the lab to prevent the transfer of DNA because at that time they didn't understand how easily DNA could be transferred. The slides prepared from vaginal fluids were kept in the slide drawer in the Memphis Medical Center Laboratory. The transfers by lab staff of the slides contributed to the compromise and contamination.

During defense attorney McNamara's cross-examination, Dr. Francisco stated that Marcia Trimble's body had been found in the first stage of decomposition. He had studied the temperatures during the time period she'd been missing and noted that it would be even colder inside the storage shed. He restated his position on cause of death and time of death. In response to McNamara's probing questions, Dr. Francisco admitted it was possible the body could have been moved from another location, but "with all circumstances, it is more reasonable to say it was in the garage for thirty-three days." The former medical examiner was adamant; he restated his opinion that the contamination of the slides had occurred by "touch," as other people handled the slides in labs. At that time "no care was taken in the storing and handling of the slides," he reiterated. "That is the best explanation for multiple profiles."

McNamara was unable to successfully attack Dr. Francisco's findings. Deputy DA Thurman announced to the Court that they did not need to redirect. Dr. Francisco was excused, and the judge halted the proceeding for a recess for lunch.

After lunch the State called an expert in the field of forensic anthropology. Dr. William Bass, retired professor at the University of Tennessee, Knoxville, and internationally renowned founder of the "Body Farm," explained that forensic anthropology is a science where law overlaps with science, and that the major factor in decay of a body is temperature. On the Body Farm, he worked with donated dead bodies placed under certain conditions to gain scientific evidence.

Responding to Katy Miller's questions, Dr. Bass testified that he had been asked to look at the Marcia Trimble autopsy report in 2002 to give an opinion on how long the victim had been dead. He subsequently wrote a two-page report that contained his opinion in the case. Dr. Bass testified that, with a reasonable degree of scientific certainty, Marcia Trimble had been dead from the time she disappeared.

Of all the witnesses so far, the dapper-looking Dr. Bass was the most animated, the most passionate about his field. He described the impact that temperature has on the decaying process. Looking at the jury with keen eyes, falling into the teaching mode of his years as a college professor, he explained that flies lay eggs in orifices, including eyes, nose, and ears. Maggots will hatch, but if it's cold, it takes longer for the growth process to begin. Maggots have a three-stage growth process. Dr. Bass told the jury that based upon Marcia Trimble's body condition, the maggots and flies had not been there very long when her body was discovered.

He noted that in the autopsy report Marcia Trimble's fingers, lips, and skin were dry, the body was just beginning to dehydrate, and the body had not decayed much. Dr. Bass again agreed with Dr. Francisco's report regarding lividity and his conclusion that the body had not been previously moved from the garage.

Defense attorney McNamara tried to create confusion about which police records were actually provided to Dr. Bass in 2002, but Bass held his own during the cross-examination, and even when it appeared that the attorney might rattle him, he was congenial and genuine in trying to understand McNamara's argument. Clearly, the jury liked Dr. Bass. He was polite when the defense argued that the doctor's conclusion was not an "independent opinion," that it was based on Dr. Francisco's findings and on the information the police gave him. Maybe the police didn't give him all the facts. Dr. Bass's smiling eyes indicated that he realized the trap McNamara was setting for him. "You have to be careful," he said to no one in particular. "I have a couple of sons who are lawyers." He then reiterated his opinion that Marcia Trimble had been dead since the time she disappeared, because of the explanations he had given, and because the time she was discovered remained unchanged and unchallenged.

The State's next witness was William Gavin, retired FBI special agent, another expert witness. Gavin had worked in the FBI Crime Lab in Washington, D.C., for most of his career. He examined blood and other body fluids that local police found at crimes. He had testified as an expert in forensic serology in over 150 cases. Gavin said he had been working in the FBI

Lab on March 31, 1975, when he received a pair of panties, a pair of jeans, and a blouse from the Nashville Police in the murder of Marcia Trimble. He took cuttings from the different areas that appeared to be stained. These tiny pieces of cloth were then mixed with different chemicals to determine what the stain was. DNA was not available as a testing process, but they looked at blood groups A, B, AB, and O. They were unable to form blood groupings. Gavin's report of the test of the clothing was made an exhibit to his testimony.

Gavin testified that on the panties there was no blood and no semen. On the jeans the results were semen stains. Finally, on Marcia Trimble's blue and white blouse, the test results found the four different semen stains. There was also a stain on the blouse sleeve; it was human blood. Gavin examined each item of clothing handed to him and pointed out to the jury where he took cuttings and the location of his initials.

ADA Rachel Sobrero questioned Gavin, demonstrating that she had an extraordinary grasp of the complexities of DNA analysis. Gavin's testimony was an indication that the jury would need to digest some highly technical information.

During cross-examination Gavin explained about the FBI policy that was in effect in 1975 that did not have him sign the actual test result, but his lab code, "OJ," was included in his report. McNamara asked how he and others in the lab prevented contamination. Gavin was at ease explaining the procedures. "There *was* protocol to prevent contamination," he said, but no, he did not wear gloves in 1975.

To many who followed the Marcia Trimble murder investigation over the years, Marie Maxwell was the most interesting and mysterious witness in the high-profile murder case. In 1975, she was a bright, attractive housewife with two young children. Her family happened to live across from the Trimbles.

Tom Thurman had mentioned Marie Maxwell in his opening statement as the last person to see Marcia Trimble alive. In 1975, the police focused on the neighborhood boys, specifically Jeffrey Womack, as suspects. Frustrated with their inability to make a case against Womack, investigators pressed Marie Maxwell in numerous interviews. During several of the interviews a psychiatrist also attempted to hypnotize her as a commercial artist sketched a composite of a person based upon her statements. The composite sketch was of a white male, much shorter than six feet. For obvious reasons, the State did not want the composite sketch introduced to the jury. The defense did. Judge Dozier ruled that he would hear testimony from Marie Maxwell outside the presence of the jury, known as a proffer of evidence.

Marie Maxwell was a tall woman with short gray hair. Now the dean of students at Harpeth Hall School, located across from Copeland Drive, Mrs. Maxwell wore a tailored suit in a block design. Regarding the sketch, she testified that she had attended three or four hypnotic sessions with FBI agent Richard Knudsen. She said she'd tried to cooperate. "I don't really believe I was hypnotized," she said. "I concentrated as hard as I could."

Judge Dozier asked retired FBI agent Knudsen to come forward and testify about the sessions. Agent Knudsen stated that he thought Marie Maxwell was hypnotized and the psychiatrist was only trying to get her to relax to enhance the memory of the event.

Tom Thurman argued that the composite sketch drawing did not have a proper foundation; Marie Maxwell did not even think she was hypnotized. The defense argued that under the current case law the drawing was relevant evidence. Judge Dozier accepted Marie Maxwell's testimony that she was not hypnotized when the drawing was made but ruled that the composite sketch was relevant and would be entered into evidence. The judge said the jury could weigh and consider the composite drawing for what it was worth.

The jury returned, and the State called Marie Maxwell to the stand. She testified that she knew Marcia Trimble from seeing her play in the neighborhood. She recalled the events of the afternoon of February 25, 1975, when she drove up the driveway, parked her car, and walked around the car to get her daughter from the car seat. As she glanced toward her neighbor's driveway, she saw through the hedge three individuals standing in the driveway near the Howard house. She thought one of the individuals was Marcia, delivering Girl Scout cookies. She noticed nothing unusual. Marie took her daughter inside and went to get her checkbook to pay Marcia for the cookies. As she waited, she heard her dog barking at the back southeast rear of their fenced-in backyard. Later, Virginia Trimble called her, asking if she had seen Marcia. Marie told her she thought Marcia had gone to the Thorpes' house because her dog was barking in the back corner of the yard.

Tom Thurman asked questions about that instant when Marie saw the three individuals. She testified that it was becoming dark and she only looked through the hedge for four or five seconds. She recognized Marcia Trimble's cookie box on the ground. She was familiar with Marcia's size and height and said the girl was looking away from her at the time. Marie testified that their heads were not above the hedge and that the ground sloped up toward the Howard driveway. She identified photographs of her driveway and Mrs. Howard's driveway, as well as the photo looking up the Howard driveway. She pointed out that in the photograph of the Howard driveway, one could see the Thorpe garage in the distance. It was on the hill behind the Howard property. There were woods between the Howard property and the Thorpe garage.

Marie Maxwell told the jury she was ultimately interviewed some twenty times by police and FBI. She again said that she didn't believe she was actually hypnotized. "I did not believe the hypnotic sessions were helpful but I was desperate to help," she said.

In regard to the other two people besides Marcia, Marie Maxwell said the second person appeared to be a child. The third person was taller. Earlier descriptions had put that person at maybe five feet eight inches, based on her estimate of Marcia's height. She'd thought Marcia was about four feet tall, when, in fact, she was four feet ten inches. Marie said the taller person wore a long, dark, drab overcoat and long pants. She'd first assumed it was Mrs. Howard; perhaps that was why she'd also thought the taller person was white. Marie Maxwell said the person was dark complected and dark around the head. She did not know the race of the third person. She also said the hedge still had some leaves on it and she could not see the people clearly. Finally, she testified that she never saw the face of the taller person.

Tom Thurman asked her bluntly about the descriptions she had given over the years. They were "all over the place," he said.

"I've always been concerned about the reliability of my descriptions," she admitted.

On cross-examination, defense attorney McNamara asked her again about the 5:30 P.M. chronology and the instant she saw the three individuals. Marie Maxwell testified that she was interviewed by Detective Tommy Jacobs at her home, and at that time she told Detective Jacobs she did not know Jeffrey Womack. The defense attorney asked her to identify a photograph of Jeffrey Womack. McNamara introduced into evidence the composite sketch done during the hypnotic sessions. Marie Maxwell admitted the sketch was of a white person.

On redirect, Tom Thurman asked Marie about the hypnotic sessions and about the sketch. "I did not think I was under hypnosis and I never identified anyone," she said. "I didn't see the facial features of the tall person."

She testified that months later Jeffrey Womack knocked on her front door collecting for charity. She had thought: *He's a suspect. Why would he come to my door?*

Finally, Tom Thurman asked Marie Maxwell, "How does your testimony today jibe with the composite sketch?"

"The composite sketch does not have any value," she answered. "We had been deprived of the innocence of our neighborhood and the safety of our children. I tried everything I could do to help."

It was the end of the first day—a long day for everyone.

37

Exhibit 42

Thursday morning, July 16, began with Commander Mickey Miller as the State's first witness.

Miller testified that he was a captain with the police department and had worked as a police officer for thirty-two years. In 1990, while he was in charge of the Criminal Investigation Division, which included Homicide, he started a review of the Trimble case.

Miller testified he'd gone to Memphis, picked up the Trimble slides from the state medical examiner's office in 1990, and sent the jeans and clothing to the FBI Lab. In March 1992, he sent them to another lab, CBR Lab in Boston, for additional tests. He sent the same evidence to the TBI Lab in 2000 and to the FBI Lab in 2004. The reason for continued testing was advancing DNA technology. Miller testified that the police department obtained over a hundred DNA samples, including two from Jeffrey Womack. Captain Miller left Homicide in 2003.

Under defense attorney Laura Dykes's cross-examination,

Miller admitted that he and Lieutenant Tommy Jacobs had worked together on the Marcia Trimble case in 1990 and that Jacobs shared a number of theories with him. They reexamined the evidence and interviewed a number of people. When Dykes asked Miller about a report of other theories in 1990, Deputy DA Tom Thurman objected, claiming that the question would elicit hearsay. Judge Steve Dozier ruled that the report and Miller's testimony would be hearsay in response to the question. Miller told the jury that Jacobs did have information about the case based upon years of investigation. Dykes also got Miller to admit that when the police obtained blood samples, they had to explain to the Court the basis for why the person was considered a suspect in the case. Miller also said that all people he had blood drawn from, as well as all the people who were polygraphed, were white. Miller determined that Barrett was arrested on March 12, 1975.

On redirect questions by Thurman, Miller testified that Jeffrey Womack passed several polygraph examinations.

The State's next witness was Charles Blackwood, a private investigator who had previously been a crime scene investigator for the Metro Police Department. He was questioned by ADA Katy Miller and testified that he had used an ALS (alternate light source) to examine Marcia Trimble's clothing. His job was to determine if he could locate any stains, and indeed, he found five different stains on her jeans. He explained how he took cuttings and samples and made his initials on the clothing. He identified the samples of clothing.

The next witness was Michelle Ray, an investigator with the sheriff's office. She testified that security cameras were inside the jail, including the fourth-floor special segregation unit where Jerome Barrett was housed. She also identified a videotape taken of Jerome Barrett in the unit.

Finally, the State called Sheldon Anter. The small man with slick, dark hair wore a light suit. He told the Court he was from Trinidad, currently living with his family in Tennessee but facing deportation proceedings. He testified that he'd received no assistance or promises from the State. Anter testified that in the summer of 2008 he was in the Davidson County jail, specifically in segregation unit 4-A. Jerome Barrett was also an inmate in that unit, in a cell across from Anter's. In the showers, on the rooftop, and in the recreation area, Anter said that Barrett made various admissions regarding Marcia Trimble. He said his DNA was *on* her, not *in* her. Anter asked why, and he said, "I killed her but I didn't rape her."

Anter testified that Barrett had also had an altercation with another inmate, Frank White. White called Barrett a baby killer and Barrett responded, "I've killed before and I'll kill you." Anter reviewed the videotape previously introduced by the sheriff's investigator, which showed where Barrett charged into Frank White's cell to attack him. Anter testified that he did not report the incident, but the police came to him ten days after the fight. He said he did not request the meeting with the police.

On cross-examination, Anter gave the jury some insight into Jerome Barrett. "Jerome had good days, then flipped. He was up and down," Anter said. But the defense attorney's lengthy questioning had Anter sweating. McNamara probed his immigration status and pointed out that Anter could have seen Barrett's story on television.

Next, Detective Hugh Coleman of the police department testified he was a member of the Cold Case Unit in 2008 and interviewed Sheldon Anter. The detective testified that he, not Anter, had requested the interview. He said Anter cooperated.

Andrew Napper, another inmate in the same cellblock as Barrett, testified that he also heard Barrett make the statement "I killed her. I didn't rape her." McNamara emphasized Napper's lengthy criminal record and the fact that he had been a paid informant for the State. "This time you're cooperating for free?" McNamara said. Napper said yes.

* * *

From Phoenix, Arizona, Detective Bill Pridemore watched the trial when he was in his hotel room. At other times, he and Pat Postiglione exchanged phone calls and text messages. Postiglione had to wait in the victim/witness room, a lounge-type area on the fourth floor, until his time to testify. Pridemore asked how certain witnesses did on the stand and how the deputy DA thought things were going. The prosecutor's mood was a good barometer.

They were on the phone when Postiglione said, "Hey, they're calling me."

Sergeant Pat Postiglione was the State's next witness.

Postiglione testified that he was the sergeant at the Cold Case Unit; he had been a police officer for twenty-nine years, and a Homicide detective since 1987. He testified that he and Detective Bill Pridemore helped develop Jerome Barrett as a suspect in the Marcia Trimble murder. Postiglione participated in executing the search warrant to obtain DNA samples from Barrett. He identified the swabs that had been taken from Barrett and submitted to the TBI Lab. He testified that the DNA samples were also sent to a California lab for additional testing. After the TBI reported the results, a Davidson County grand jury indicted Jerome Barrett for the murder of Marcia Trimble. Postiglione and Pridemore arrested Barrett in Memphis.

During cross-examination by defense attorney Laura Dykes, Postiglione admitted that Jerome Barrett had been in jail from March 12, 1975, through March 30, 1975, and beyond. Marcia Trimble's body had been found on March 30, 1975.

The next witness was Janice Williamson, a DNA specialist. She had worked for CBR Lab, a biomedical research institute in Boston, from 1974 to 1997, specifically in DNA analysis during her last seven years at CBR. She explained the fundamentals of DNA, saying DNA was the "genetic code that makes each person an individual" and DNA is found in "any cell that has a nucleus," such as saliva, blood, roots of hair, semen, or skin. The Court ruled she was an expert for purposes of giving opinion evidence in this case.

Williamson testified that she took the cuttings from the Trimble clothing and tested them. She was able to isolate a profile from the cuttings. She then took the head hair of Marcia Trimble and tested it to create a profile, then compared the profile from the Trimble cuttings with Marcia Trimble's DNA. She testified they did not match. This was important testimony for the State, establishing that the stains on Marcia's clothing were not from Marcia herself.

Though the substance of her testimony was highly technical, Williamson made the DNA technology easily accessible. The defense did not attempt cross-examination of Janice Williamson. The Court recessed for lunch.

Thursday afternoon, Meghan Clement also testified as an expert in DNA analysis. Since 1994, she had worked at Lab-Corp, a medical diagnostic lab in North Carolina. Clement explained that PCR testing is now the preferred test to analyze DNA, and that an early type of PCR testing was DQ alpha. In 1994 LabCorp received evidence from CBR Lab—eighty-one vials of DNA and slides. They tested thirty-five different DNA samples from individuals in the Trimble case. The lab compared the DNA samples with the profile of Marcia Trimble and excluded all individuals. Defense attorney Jim McNamara brought up the "mixtures" on the five slides that came from the autopsy. But the point Clement made was that no matches occurred in the testing by LabCorp.

Taking a break from the DNA experts, the State called Officer Tom Lunn, a retired police officer from the Berry Hill

Police Department. Lunn said that on March 12, 1975, at approximately 8:30 P.M., he arrested Jerome S. Barrett at the Bransford House Apartments. At the time of the arrest, Barrett was wearing a ski mask and two pairs of gloves. But even more telling, Lunn described in detail the coat Barrett was wearing: "It was a full length topcoat down to the knees with dark brown tweed."

Lunn identified the mug shot of Barrett taken at that time. In response to Laura Dykes's questions, Lunn said Barrett told him at the time of the arrest that he was working for the Nation of Islam.

Joe Minor, the next expert witness, worked for the TBI as supervisor of the Forensic Science DNA Lab. He concurred with the FBI Lab's findings regarding the DNA profiles. He said they'd developed a strong male profile from the clothing, and he entered it into CODIS, but there was no match. He said the slides from the medical examiner's office were contaminated and did not match Barrett's DNA.

The State then called Gary Harmor as its next expert witness. A forensic serologist at Serological Research Institute in California, he testified that on December 12, 2007, he had received a package from Detective Bill Pridemore containing oral swabs taken from Jerome Barrett. His lab had used DQ alpha testing, an older type of testing, on the swabs. DQ alpha was still reliable but not as sensitive as today's methods. Harmor developed a profile from Barrett's swabs. "His type occurs in 8% of the population," Harmor said.

Defense attorney McNamara saw an opportunity. "If his type occurs in eight percent of the population, how many in the jury could have been a contributor?"

He finished his cross-examination, asking: "Are there some things that DNA testing can't tell you? When the DNA was deposited? How did it get there? Who put it there? Was it deposited directly or indirectly? How long had it been there?"

A good punch for the defense.

Chad Johnson, special agent for the TBI, testified next. Johnson, also a DNA specialist, testified he sent Barrett's DNA profile to the FBI Laboratory in Washington, D.C.

ADA Rachel Sobrero then called Jennifer Luttman. To the jury and others in the courtroom, here was simply another expert, but Sobrero knew how important this testimony would be. The prosecution had saved Luttman for the last witness in their case in chief.

Dressed in a black business suit, Jennifer Luttman appeared young, but she'd spent years working with the FBI, and she testified that she was chief of the CODIS Unit, and before that had been a DNA analyst for the Bureau. Many in the courtroom would later say she was the most impressive witness for the State. She testified she had worked on over a thousand DNA cases and lectured on DNA analysis around the world.

In a conversational manner, she explained that there were three possible outcomes from the stain evidence. One, the DNA profile from the stain was compared to a known reference sample. If they did not match, the suspect was excluded. The second possibility was that the outcome was inconclusive. Finally, if the DNA profile matched the reference sample, there was a match. If that happened, they then calculated the probability for such a match. "When it is rarer than one in six trillion," Luttman said, "we say a certain person is the source."

Luttman testified that the FBI Lab had the head hair from Marcia Trimble, as well as the cuttings from her jeans, panties, and blouse. She stated that the tests determined there was semen present in the stains on the blouse and jeans but not on the panties. A court officer passed her Exhibit 7, Marcia Trimble's blue and white blouse. Luttman held it up and showed the jury where the semen stains were on the blouse.

Luttman described the additional tests that had been performed. The tests were not able to locate DNA on the jeans, but additional tests on the blouse cuttings had revealed a DNA profile. Luttman referred to it as a major contributor. They compared Marcia Trimble's DNA with the DNA found on the blouse stains. These tests excluded Marcia Trimble as the major contributor of the DNA located on the stains. Luttman said they then submitted the unknown DNA profile into the national CODIS database.

Sobrero asked that a document be passed to the witness. Luttman identified it as the FBI report that contained the results of their testing. The FBI report was marked as Exhibit 42.

Referring to the report, Luttman testified that in October 2007, the FBI Lab received a suspect's DNA profile from the TBI. The suspect's name was Jerome S. Barrett. Luttman described in detail how her lab compared the profile of Barrett with the profile of the major contributor found on the blouse stains.

The courtroom grew quiet as Luttman continued: "The results of the comparison between the suspect's profile and the profile of the major contributor of the DNA contained in the stain on the blouse was a match."

She explained how they calculated the probability of the match. Sobrero asked, "What can you say about the calculated probability of the match?"

Jennifer Luttman looked at the jury. "I can say that the match was rarer than 1 in 6 trillion. The world population is 6 to 8 billion. I, therefore, can say that with a reasonable degree of science certainty that Jerome Barrett was the source of the DNA found in semen on Marcia Trimble's blouse."

On that note, prosecutor Sobrero said she had no further questions.

Defense attorney Jim McNamara cross-examined Luttman but was unable to do anything to weaken her testimony. After Judge Dozier excused Jennifer Luttman as a witness, Deputy DA Tom Thurman rose and said, "Your Honor, the State of Tennessee rests its case."

* * *

Luttman's testimony had been the final blow. It devastated the defense effort, for now. The undisputed and overwhelming DNA evidence put Jerome Barrett with Marcia Trimble.

Defense attorney Jim McNamara made a motion for acquittal outside the presence of the jury. This was standard practice at the end of the State's proof. Judge Dozier noted that based upon the medical examiner's testimony and findings that the cause of death was manual strangulation, and that at the time of death the victim was alive, the motion regarding premeditation was denied. He also noted that Barrett's admission to Sheldon Anter about the murder, as well as the video that showed Barrett attacking someone and making verbal threats, as well as the DNA evidence, was basis to allow the case to go to the jury. Judge Dozier commented that the DNA evidence "placed Barrett with Marcia Trimble." He said, "Therefore, I overrule the motion."

At 5:10 P.M. on Thursday, the defense stepped up to try to do some damage control.

The defense's first witness was Bill Fallati, a Metro police officer who took part in the search for Marcia Trimble in February 1975. He said that about two and a half weeks after Marcia disappeared, he searched the Thorpe garage. He went into the right side of the garage shed and walked around the walls. Fallati testified that he had not seen the body of a child on the fertilizer bags.

On cross-examination from Tom Thurman, Fallati admitted he did not write a report about the search. He admitted he'd told Captain Mickey Miller within the past week that he was not sure what he saw.

"Is it possible a child was there?" Thurman asked.

"I can't say one hundred percent," said Fallati.

On redirect, Laura Dykes asked, "Very possible or a slight possibility?"

Fallati fidgeted. "I don't think there was, but I can't say one hundred percent."

The next defense witness was E. R. Downs, a former police officer. With long hair, a beard and mustache, and a lined face that looked as if he'd lived a hard life, Downs was much different in appearance from the TBI, FBI, and police detectives who had so far testified in the case. He testified that he had been in the Police Academy at the time Marcia Trimble disappeared. He said the recruits were taken out to the Green Hills area to help in the search, and on Friday, February 28, 1975, he'd conducted a search of the Thorpe garage. He started on the right wall and followed it to the back, then came down the other side to the entrance. He specifically recalled seeing the swimming pool and the fertilizer bags. Downs said he did not see a child's body in the garage, but he testified he felt "strange" about the outbuilding and wrote a three-page report of his search. He also drew a diagram. The defense submitted that diagram as the next exhibit.

On cross-examination, Downs said he attended a large meeting of police officers the day after the body was found, and at that time, he didn't know she had been found. At the meeting, he raised his hand and said he had searched the garage and found nothing.

Thurman blistered the former police officer on cross-examination. He forced Downs to grudgingly admit that he had been suspended from the police force in August 1977 for lying to a superior officer. Thurman said, "You resigned from the police department after you were arrested for 'breach of trust.' Correct?" Downs did not deny it but said he would like to see the paperwork.

Thurman questioned him further about his search of the Thorpe garage, clearly trying to make the point that Downs didn't remember those details until he was taken back to the garage and asked to write a report and draw a diagram.

"Isn't it true they took you to the garage so you could see?" Thurman asked.

"That's a lie," Downs said.

Tom Thurman returned to his chair. At 6:15 P.M. the second day of the trial ended.

By Friday morning, there was a general feeling in the courtroom that the trial was almost over. But Tom Thurman's face revealed nothing. He had been a prosecutor long enough to know never to underestimate the opponent.

The defense called John Thorpe Jr. to the stand. Now forty-eight years old, Thorpe recalled life in his neighborhood in 1975. He'd lived with his father, mother (now deceased), and sister. He pointed out on a diagram the houses in the area and described the "big back yard" between the shed and the woods. Neighborhood children often played ball in the yard.

Thorpe said he had been fourteen, an eighth grader at St. Paul Christian Academy in Green Hills, in 1975. He had had basketball practice until 5:00 P.M., then came home, ate potato chips and drank a Coke, and went to the Egerton house to play basketball. He showed on the diagram where he passed by the garage. He saw nothing strange at the time. But he remembered, later, Charles Trimble coming out in his front yard, calling, "Marcia! Marcia!"

During Katy Miller's cross-examination, Thorpe said that there used to be a path from the back of his family's yard down through the woods to the Maxwell house, but after the Maxwells moved in, the path became overgrown. He said he went into the garage several times after Marcia went missing, since he kept his bike in there, but that he kept it up front.

The next witness for the defense was Larry Felts, now an attorney practicing criminal defense. Felts testified that in February 1975, he had been a police recruit. He'd partnered with E. R. Downs and together they'd searched the Thorpe garage on Friday, February 28.

Felts testified that he'd walked into the left side of the garage while Downs had walked down the right side. He described the inside of the building as cluttered, with a dirt floor, and he recalled items such as tools hanging on the wall, a jar, and a commode on the floor. He specifically recalled seeing a small swimming pool. Felts said he spent about two minutes searching the garage, and he testified that the body was not there.

Larry Felts said that during the meeting of recruits and police officers thirty-one days later, the sergeant asked if anyone had searched the garage. He said he and Downs held up their hands. The sergeant told Downs and Felts to go into another room and write out reports detailing their search of the Thorpe garage.

During cross-examination by Deputy DA Tom Thurman, Felts could not recall how many other sheds he may have searched during that time, though he said he remembered that particular building because there was no front door and it had dirt floors. He admitted that he did not write supplemental reports on his other searches, and the garage didn't have lights inside. Some areas of the outbuilding were darker than others. Felts did not recall anyone other than himself and Downs being there at the time of the search, but he said he wouldn't dispute it if someone else said he was there, too.

Thurman asked the witness if he was fired from the police department. Felts tried to wrestle with Thurman but had little success. Thurman came back with, "You were fired because you leaked information of a police raid to major gamblers." Felts tried to explain that he only gave incorrect information. Thurman countered: "You were dismissed because you lied to your supervisor both orally and in writing. And you did not appeal your dismissal." Felts had no response.

The next witness was Antonio Johnson of the Davidson County Sheriff's Office. The substance of Johnson's testimony was that Sheldon Anter had wanted to talk with him in August of 2008, after having seen news about Jerome Barrett's case on television. Thurman asked a few brief questions and returned to the counsel's table. The Court asked the defense, "Who is your next witness?"

Mr. McNamara rose and announced to the Court, "The defense rests."

There was a little stir in the courtroom. Judge Dozier asked if the State had any rebuttal witnesses. Tom Thurman responded that they had one witness, Billy Butler.

Billy Butler, a white-haired retired police officer, had served on the force for seventeen years and left in good standing. He said he'd been on the same search with Downs and Felts. Butler testified that he'd peered through a hole in the back of the Thorpe garage and saw Felts and Downs standing outside the front of the garage. Butler walked around to the front and saw the two officers walk inside. He remembered a commode but did not see Felts and Downs look under anything. He testified they were inside the garage for a couple of minutes.

At the meeting thirty-one days later, Butler told the sergeant that he had been on the search with Downs and Felts at the garage in question. Butler testified he was taken out to the Thorpe garage and asked to write a supplemental report and draw a diagram. While standing in front of the garage he wrote the report and drew a basic diagram.

On cross-examination, Butler testified he never went inside the garage. It was pointed out that his diagram did not include the commode or table.

Tom Thurman advised the Court that the State had no other rebuttal witnesses.

After the jury was excused, Judge Dozier asked Jerome Barrett and his attorney to come to the podium. The judge explained that under the law, Barrett had the right to testify and asked if he had waived his right to testify. Barrett said, "Yes sir." The Court continued, "And you understand and have agreed to waive your right to testify?" Barrett nodded and said he understood and agreed to not testify.

The State had the opportunity to start and finish the closing. In a close case this "last chance to speak to the jury" is critical. ADA Katy Miller faced the jury and talked about how much had changed in thirty-four years. She mentioned cell phones, computers, and science. "That community was in a different place then," she said. "Copeland Drive was a quiet neighborhood. Kids played up and down the street and there were no leash laws, no 'amber alerts' like there are today."

Miller commented on the witnesses the jury had heard. She reminded the jury how Marie Maxwell described the coat the taller person was wearing in the Howard driveway and said, "When they arrested Jerome Barrett, he was wearing that coat." She reminded the jury of the photos of the garage taken from the entrance and pointed out that Captain Cathey testified he could not see the body from the entrance of the garage. She praised Cathey for his thorough work at the crime scene and the fact he'd worn gloves while he took Marcia's clothes off of her body. Miller also commended Cold Case detectives Bill Pridemore and Pat Postiglione for their work in the case.

Miller walked to the counsel's table and picked up the blouse. It was on a hanger. During the trial, the blouse had remained in its shipping package except when identified by an expert. Now, Miller walked around, carrying the blouse on the hanger. It was effective and chilling.

She restated Dr. Jerry Francisco's testimony about how upon death, blood chills and settles because of gravity. She noted Dr. William Bass's testimony, which confirmed Dr. Francisco's analysis of time of death and the fact the body had been in the garage the entire time. Miller reminded the jury that the TBI and Metro Police had sent the DNA profiles of eighty neighborhood suspects for testing. Those suspects were *all* excluded from the DNA that was located on Marcia Trimble's blouse. She recounted how the DNA taken from the blouse was placed into the FBI's CODIS database in 2004.

Miller retold the story of how the DNA from the blouse and Barrett's oral swab were sent to the California lab for comparison. Those test results confirmed that only 8 percent of the population, including Barrett, would have had the same type DNA that was found on the blouse. Then Chad Johnson of the TBI sent the new profile of Jerome Barrett to the FBI Laboratory in Washington where Jennifer Luttman of the FBI compared the DNA found on the blouse with Barrett's profile and the tests confirmed a match. Miller told how Luttman then calculated the odds and found that such a match was "rarer than one in six trillion."

Katy Miller reminded the jury that they had heard direct evidence about Jerome Barrett murdering Marcia Trimble through the testimony of Sheldon Anter, who had heard Barrett say, "I didn't rape her but I killed her."

Miller faced the jury and held up the blouse. "Jerome Barrett's DNA is on this blouse. You know who committed this crime. Jerome Barrett strangled her and killed her. Use science to convict him in this case."

The courtroom was silent as Katy Miller turned and sat down at the counsel's table. Defense attorney Jim McNamara walked to the open area before the jury box. "There is a danger in this courtroom," he said. "A danger an innocent man may be convicted of a murder." The district attorney's office had a "fierce desire to solve this thirty-four-year-old murder," he said. "Fortunately, we have the jury system."

McNamara then reviewed facts that he contended were not

in dispute. The last person to see Marcia Trimble alive was Marie Maxwell. Marcia was standing in the Howard driveway, not far from the Thorpes' garage. The search started that night and included the Thorpes' garage. Jerome Barrett was arrested on March 12 and Marcia's body was discovered on March 30.

He suggested that it would be very difficult for the jury to reconcile the State's DNA evidence with the theory of guilt. "You must be able to reconcile all the evidence in this case," he said. The state's DNA evidence was weak, he told the jury. If the DNA proof was strong, the State would not have relied upon testimony of someone like Sheldon Anter.

McNamara said the eyewitness Marie Maxwell was a good person who was trying to help, but he urged the jury to consider what she said in February 1975. "That is the best evidence," he said. McNamara spoke softly. "Marie Maxwell's description of the taller person made in February of 1975 is inconsistent with Jerome Barrett."

As to the issue of whether the body was in the shed the whole thirty-three days, McNamara defended the former police recruits Downs and Felts. "The State said they are not credible. What reason would they have to tell anything but the truth?" he asked. McNamara ripped the testimony and credibility of Andrew Napper, driving the point home with questions: "If Napper knocked on your door, would you let him in? Would you leave your purse in a room alone with Napper? If he was standing on the side of the road, would you give him a ride? You know the answer to my questions. No." Jim McNamara slowed his pace again. "You have the power to determine credibility. You cannot trust Napper."

As to Shelton Anter, who corroborated Napper's testimony, McNamara pointed out that he was facing the loss of his family, loss of his entire home and life. "You should completely discount the word of Sheldon Anter," McNamara said.

"You will not bring justice to Marcia Trimble by convicting an honest man." Jim McNamara looked hard at the jury.

"If you use your reason, common sense and courage, your verdict will be one of not guilty."

Deputy DA Tom Thurman had fought for justice in countless unglamorous cases, convicting drug dealers, robbers, and dangerous criminals. He tried the types of cases where he might get a thank-you and hug from the victim's family, but he'd also received death threats. It was a hard job that wore a person down. But Thurman understood discipline and duty. As he listened to McNamara finish his closing argument, the weight of the years poured onto his shoulders. His experience had steeled him for this. Thurman was ready to face the pressure.

He walked to the center of the courtroom, thanked the jury for their service, and told them he knew how difficult it was for them to see the pictures and hear the terrible facts about what happened to the sweet little girl. "There is not any question this was a premeditated murder," he said. "Look at how her throat was crushed, how she was strangled. The issue is who did it."

He asked, "How did Jerome Barrett's semen get onto Marcia Trimble's blouse? Mr. McNamara didn't talk about that." Thurman defended Marie Maxwell, pointing out that she specifically recalled the coat the taller person in the driveway was wearing: a long dark tweed overcoat. "Barrett had on that coat when he was arrested on March 12 in Berry Hill," Thurman said.

He interrupted his stream of facts and common sense to give his own opinion. "I do think she saw Marcia Trimble in that driveway."

He recalled for the jury the testimony of the "two outstanding experts" on time of death. Both Dr. Francisco and Dr. Bass said she died shortly after she disappeared.

"Was the body in the garage?" He posed the question and answered, "The experts say yes." Thurman ripped at the defense's theory, asking, "Does it make any sense that he would bring the body back? Does it? No. And if it happened, what difference does it make? Jerome Barrett did it. Barrett's semen was all over her."

He took up the issue of the police recruits, arguing that they wanted to be on the police force, so they could not admit they had been goofing off and missed the body. He pointed out that they both were known to have lied to their supervisors and were later fired as police officers.

Thurman explained how the slides came to be contaminated with other DNA, referencing the testimony of each expert that told about the reasons for contamination. "But keep this in mind when you discuss the slides," he said. "Barrett's semen was all over her body."

He reviewed Sheldon Anter's testimony and reminded the jury that Anter did not contact the police; the police contacted him. Anter received nothing from the State in exchange for his testimony. He had no motive to lie. "But you saw it for yourself in the video," Thurman said. "You saw Barrett rush into Frank White's cell. You saw the anger." He said in a quieter voice, "Anter told the police Barrett said, 'I killed her but I did not rape her.'" At the time Anter told the police that, the TBI did not have a profile on Barrett. "How would have Anter made something like that up?" Thurman asked the jury. "He didn't. Barrett told him."

He stressed again that the defense never gave any reason why Barrett's DNA was on Marcia Trimble's blouse. "We will never know why or how Jerome Barrett got into that neighborhood," Thurman said. "But we know he was there by the DNA."

He said, "They talk about the pressure in this case." At that point, the photo of Marcia Trimble's body in the garage appeared on the court's full-length screen. Thurman pointed at it. "One in six trillion, that's the number." His powerful words echoed throughout the courtroom.

"Pressure of the community to close this case. It's not about that," Thurman said. "We still have children murdered here. All children's deaths are wrong."

He moved closer to the jury. "This case is about Marcia Trimble. It's about justice. Marcia Trimble never got to go to high school, college, she never got to fall in love, to marry, to have children." For an instant his voice betrayed his deep emotion. "It's about justice," he said. "It's time for justice."

Once again, Tom Thurman had done his duty.

The jury began deliberations at 1:40 P.M., Friday, July 17. By phone, Sergeant Pat Postiglione and Detective Bill Pridemore tried to estimate how long it would take the jury to reach a verdict. Neither believed it would happen like Des Prez—a guilty verdict in ninety minutes. Postiglione was always the pessimistic one: Would the jury trip up on the unanswered questions, like why Barrett was in that neighborhood? Pridemore believed the jurors would make a decision before the end of the day. He couldn't let himself imagine any verdict but guilty.

As the hours ticked away toward evening, the hallway near the courtroom grew crowded with press and media, as if they, too, expected a verdict before day's end. Jerome Barrett's family waited in the hallway as well. Finally, at 8:30 P.M., Judge Dozier sent the jurors back to their hotel and told them to resume deliberations the next morning. Nashvillians went home. Barrett's family returned to Memphis.

The jury went to work at 8:30 A.M. on Saturday, and there would be another two hours of waiting. At about 10:30 A.M. the word came: The jury has a verdict.

For Virginia Trimble, her family and supporters, for the detectives and the attorneys, the pressure was almost unbearable. Years of anguish, disappointment, memories—all hurtled into this packed Davidson County courtroom. The moment had arrived for those beyond the courtroom: Jeffrey Womack, March Egerton, and the other young men who had been suspects. The jurors filed into the jury box. The night before, they had looked exhausted. Today they looked rested, but it was anybody's guess what that meant in regard to the verdict.

A profound stillness came over the courtroom. Virginia Trimble's family held hands as the jury foreperson, Anita Clark, stood and read the verdict.

Guilty on two counts of second-degree murder.

The jury fixed his punishment at forty-four years in the penitentiary.

The long-awaited moment was electric.

38

Nashville Will Not Forget

It was the kind of unseasonably mild summer morning that sent Nashvillians outside, to work in yards and gardens, jog, ride bikes, play golf or tennis. Seventy degrees with a light wind—this was extraordinary weather for July in Nashville. Moments after the guilty verdict in the Trimble case was announced, the news spread via twenty-first-century technology throughout a city that had followed the murder case since well before the advent of personal computers. The changes Nashville had experienced over thirty-four years were phenomenal. This morning, conversations turned back to the 1975 incident that many would forever associate with the end of an idyllic era, a time when children roamed freely in their neighborhood and came home at dark. The conviction of Marcia's Trimble's killer, more than three decades in coming, marked another profound ending, but Nashville would not forget.

Jerome Sydney Barrett, whose expression remained impassive as he listened to the guilty verdict, began to show his delayed reaction as the judge gave his final comments. Barrett lowered his head and looked down; his shoulders sank. Moments later, as he was escorted from the courtroom through the side door, he paused and heaved a deep sigh. His family was not in the courtroom that day.

In Arizona, Detective Bill Pridemore was anxious. It was still early in Phoenix, but he knew that by now the jury in Nashville should have been back at work for a while. Surely they would reach a verdict that morning. He and Denise left the hotel to drive to the University of Phoenix Coliseum, where Denise would participate in the graduation ceremony later that same day. On the road, he got the call from Sergeant Pat Postiglione.

Pridemore could hear excited voices in the background. Postiglione was in high spirits. "It's over," he said.

The prosecutors, Deputy DA Tom Thurman and ADAs Katy Miller and Rachel Sobrero, as well as Virginia and Chuck Trimble, family and a host of friends, and detectives who had worked on the case all exchanged smiles, handshakes, hugs, and pats on the back as the media prepared for a press conference. A podium was set up in the aisle of the courtroom, and the intimate group gathered around.

Thurman was the first to speak, and in his typical reserved fashion, said he was "happy" with the verdict. It didn't matter that the jury convicted Barrett of second-degree rather than first-degree murder, he said. He believed the jury had "a problem with premeditation" due to the language of the 1975 law under which Barrett was tried. But "it was more about guilt or innocence, not punishment." After all, Jerome Barrett was already serving a life sentence in the Sarah Des Prez murder.

The questions reporters asked indicated that there were still many unknown or unexplained details. Asked if police had stopped looking for other answers once they had DNA evidence, Thurman said, "We've never stopped looking for other answers." He indicated that they'd "always grappled with who the other person was in the driveway." Why hadn't the dogs found the body in the Thorpe garage? Thurman said the smell of fertilizer and mulch masked any other odor, and the low level of decomposition meant the body did not have a strong smell. He talked about the theory that Jerome Barrett had been in the neighborhood looking for Charlotte Shatzen, whom he had assaulted two days earlier. Her parents' yard backed up to the Trimbles' yard. They were the only Shatzens listed in the phone book, and Barrett was a stalker. It was an "extraordinary coincidence," Thurman said.

There was also a chance that Barrett might have worked at Geddes-Douglas Nursery. Police found no records to prove that, but Barrett's parole officer frequently sent parolees to the nursery as day workers, paid in cash. Still, the prosecution couldn't verify those theories. Perhaps it was just a "terrible chance encounter," but nevertheless, DNA proved Barrett was there.

Thurman talked about what an emotional case this had been for him. "I've worked on the case since 1990," he said. "It is part of the fabric of Nashville." He was asked about the children in the neighborhood that police had pursued during the investigation. "They are victims, too," the prosecutor said. "There are a lot of victims in this case." He mentioned Marie Maxwell. She "felt so much pressure to help," he said.

It was clear reporters wanted to keep asking questions, but Thurman relinquished the podium to Virginia Trimble. Dressed in a black suit and white ruffled blouse, Virginia stepped up and began to pour out her heart to the city that had waited with her all these years.

Much of what she wanted to say focused on her gratitude to the police and to the public. "Nashville has shared my pain," she said, "and that has made my pain much softer." She recalled the outpouring of concern during the search. An authentic Southern lady, Virginia Trimble wrote thank-you notes to the groups and individuals who'd brought food and drinks and in other ways supported the searchers. She apologized to anyone she might have missed thirty-four years ago. "I am grateful for every strawberry," she said, triggering a ripple of laughter much needed by everyone in the room, on this emotional roller coaster.

She spoke about pleading for Marcia's return during the thirty-three-day search, when she was an object of criticism by some who didn't understand how she could face the media with a serene smile. "The police told me to be calm," she said. She did her crying in the bathtub, playing one of the records that Marcia liked, she explained. "Then I'd go out to the media," she said.

She recalled the day Marcia's body was found, mentioning each individual who had been in her living room when Sherman Nickens delivered the news. "Chief Joe Casey was there," she said. "He worked as hard as anyone did." By this time in the press conference, many in attendance had taken seats in the courtroom. Virginia noted Major George Currey, seated a few rows back. She thanked him for bringing "much comfort to us."

It was as if Virginia Trimble had anticipated this occasion for a long time and memorized her lines; it was her moment. She did not leave anyone out. She told the story of meeting Frank Ritter, reporter for the *Tennessean* for forty-five years, and marrying him. She thanked the victims' advocates, who had grieved with her and were still waiting to see justice for their own loved ones. And then she thanked Captain Mickey Miller, the detective who became a good family friend after he began working on the case in 1990.

"I have a surprise for Captain Miller," she said. She gave Miller a framed picture of three crosses, a picture Marcia drew not long before she died. Police had dusted the glass for Marcia's fingerprints. "See, it shows her little fingerprint,"

Virginia said. She related the story of Jesus on the cross, crucified between two thieves. One of the thieves said to Jesus, "Remember me in paradise." Virginia said Marcia knew "the truth of salvation." Commander Miller wiped his eyes as Virginia presented the picture to him. She said, "It is a piece of my heart." Miller was not the only one wiping away tears. But Marcia's mother maintained her composure, as she always had in front of cameras during those awful days in 1975.

Wrapping up after nearly an hour, Virginia said she would like the opportunity to speak with Jerome Barrett, to have the final pieces of the puzzle, to know what actually happened and exactly what time it happened. She wondered, "Was it when I was calling her to come to supper?"

Someone asked Virginia if she had closure now. She looked thoughtful and then answered. "I think today we got the truth." She added, "I don't know about closure. I'm on the other side of pain. I can go to Marcia's grave and say, 'Now I know.'"

After Commander Miller, Sergeant Postiglione, and retired Lieutenant Jacobs spoke briefly to the media, the news conference ended. It was like the end of a family reunion, when all are about to return to various locales and pursuits, and they wonder when they will see one another again. They were all a little hesitant to leave. Yes, there would be the formal sentencing date in September. Some would be back for that occasion. But there would never be another gathering quite like this.

Reporter Nick Beres, along with legal analyst Jim Todd, had covered the entire trial for Channel 5's cable station. Beres called the news conference "remarkable," unlike any he'd ever seen. About the time the commentators were signing off, Pat Postiglione was trying to call Bill Pridemore, but Pridemore was not answering. Postiglione sent a text message: "We're going to the Gerst Haus to celebrate." The restaurant near the Criminal Justice Center, with its beer hall décor, was a favorite hangout for the police and courthouse crowd. In Phoenix, Pridemore, waiting for graduation to begin, saw

Postiglione's message. He could almost smell the sauerkraut. He could almost taste the beer that came in frosty sixteen-ounce "fishbowls."

Have a cold one for me, he thought, but he didn't text back right then. He would call Postiglione later in the afternoon and get the whole story. Now it was time to think about the ceremony, to watch Denise receive her doctorate.

This was a day to remember.

In the wake of the guilty verdict, local and national TV analyzed the fine points of the trial and the case itself over and over again in the days to come. Commander Mickey Miller and Lieutenant Tommy Jacobs appeared on Nick Beres's news show, *MorningLine*. Beres commented on the "riveting" news conference Saturday morning. The detectives talked about the "emotional exhaustion" of this case. Several callers just wanted to reminisce, which seemed all right with Beres and the detectives. Most of the questions that hadn't been answered might never be answered. But when someone asked again, "How did police miss the body?" Miller explained that searchers had gone into more than a hundred garages and basements, and they were looking for a live girl. They called her name, and they left. Jacobs, who had searched the Thorpe garage, said he hated that they missed the body, but the fact was, the evidence showed that she had been there the whole time. The detectives who'd targeted Jeffrey Womack and pursued him for years were now on board with the DNA evidence and Jerome Barrett's guilt.

The Trimble case was the focus of truTV's *Courtside* with Jack Ford and *Best Defense* with Jami Floyd. Reporter Lisa Sweetingham was still in Nashville, interviewing Tom Thurman, who reiterated that the trial was all about "putting this case to rest." He explained that the jury got to set the sentence because that was the way it was done under 1975 law. Barrett, already serving a life sentence, wouldn't be eligible for parole for twenty-five years, when he would be eighty-seven years old. Judge Dozier would decide whether Barrett would serve his life sentence and his forty-four-year sentence consecutively or concurrently, but whatever the judge decided, it was very unlikely that Barrett would ever be a free man.

Why forty-four years? Thurman said he didn't know why the jury had chosen that number, but he added that if Marcia Trimble had lived, she would now be forty-four years old.

Friday, September 4, 2009, arrived. It was the beginning of Labor Day weekend and the date set for Jerome Barrett's formal sentencing. Detective Bill Pridemore was not about to miss this day. He joined Sergeant Pat Postiglione and Commander Mickey Miller at the Cold Case office, and they walked across the street to the courthouse. They spent a few minutes drinking coffee in the victim/witness room before it was time to go to the courtroom. The seats behind the prosecution filled up. The defense's side was practically empty.

The previous Friday, Sarah Des Prez's father, Dr. Roger Des Prez, had died. Waiting in the courtroom for all the participants to arrive, Pridemore thought about the white-haired man who'd sat through the January trial and heard the jury render a guilty verdict in his daughter's murder. He remembered the day Postiglione brought the Des Prez file to his office, and the case was so cold. The tough detective nodded to himself, pleased that Dr. Des Prez had lived to see justice for Sarah.

Jerome Barrett was not in the courtroom. Jim McNamara made the announcement that his client wanted to waive his court appearance. Judge Steve Dozier would not permit it. McNamara went back to the holding room. The door between the holding room and courtroom was open, and Pridemore, seated in the third row, could see McNamara and the correctional officers talking to Barrett, who was scowling, not at all pleased that he wouldn't be allowed to make his protest. A few minutes later, court officers brought Barrett into the courtroom, dressed in standard Tennessee Department of Correction blue jeans and loose blue shirt. In his TDOC attire, the convicted killer of Marcia Trimble presented a stark contrast to the starched-looking defendant who had previously come to court each day in suit and tie.

Barrett refused to sit down. He muttered, "This is a big charade." He addressed the judge with a smirk and said, "I knew it all along." The smirk also contrasted with his solemn expression during the trial.

Judge Dozier came back with a calm but stinging line: "Then maybe you know what the decision ought to be."

The judge then announced his ruling, that the Trimble sentence would run consecutively to the life sentence imposed for the Sarah Des Prez murder, meaning it would begin at the end of the life sentence. Dozier said the sentence would "lessen the likelihood [Jerome Barrett] will ever be released in the community again, and hopefully close Mr. Barrett's ability to hurt anyone else." As Judge Dozier delivered the sentence, Barrett turned his back to the judge, a defiant gesture that Tom Thurman later said "showed the disregard he has for the law." *That's the* real *Jerome Barrett*, Pridemore thought.

The sentencing proceedings did not take long. It was too early to go somewhere and celebrate. It was almost too early for lunch, but Pridemore, Postiglione, and Thurman went to the coffee shop in the courthouse for a sandwich. Next to their table sat Mickey Miller, Tommy Jacobs, and Dick Knudsen. Pridemore had never met the former FBI agent, though he was certainly familiar with his reports. He and Knudsen introduced themselves, then returned to their respective groups. There was not much conversation between the two tables. In the aftermath of the verdict and sentencing, there just wasn't much to talk about.

After a quick lunch, the men dispersed. Mickey Miller left with Pridemore, Postiglione, and Thurman. Outside, Thurman veered off toward his office. The others walked across the street. At the door of the Criminal Justice Center, Pridemore stopped.

"Guess I'll be seeing you," he said.

It was a strange moment for Detective Bill Pridemore—*retired* detective. He didn't know when he'd see Postiglione and Miller again. Retirement hadn't taken him out of the loop. The whole time, he'd been coming into the office, involved in preparation for the trial. Now it was over, and he had no reason to come back. He felt a sudden sinking in the pit of his stomach, something like the post-holiday blues.

"Aren't you coming in?" Postiglione asked.

Pridemore knew the routine. They'd go to the Cold Case office, reminisce, and decompress. They'd recall the sentencing, the trial, the investigation. He'd been there many times. It was hard to let go.

"Nah, I've got some things to do," Pridemore said. He smiled his broad smile and said so long.

"Stop by and see us sometime," Miller called back as he opened the door.

Pridemore didn't say if he would or wouldn't. Postiglione and Miller went inside.

It was a gorgeous day—blue sky, warm sun, low humidity—as Pridemore crossed the street at the corner of the old courthouse. He thought about his plans for Labor Day weekend, plans that included a lot of golf, and come Tuesday, he could go right back out to the golf course. There was something to be said for that.

A few minutes earlier, on the way back to the CJC with Postiglione and Miller, Pridemore had remarked on a light note, "Another one down the pike."

Postiglione, who often talked about retirement but kept postponing it, seemed to be in one of his pensive moods— maybe the same kind of letdown Pridemore was feeling.

"It never ends," he'd said. "There's always another one."

Mickey Miller had turned to Pat Postiglione and said, "Time for you and I to get to work on Kathy Jones." Kathy Jones, the twelve-year-old girl brutally murdered in 1969 near the skating rink in Woodbine, was just one of the hundreds of cold cases represented in the black binders in the Cold Case offices. The shelves ran floor to ceiling around the vaultlike room. That's what Cold Case detectives did when they solved one case that had consumed them for months or years; they went on to another one. That's how they kept the blues away.

The fourteen black binders that comprised the Marcia Trimble case file would be going to the Archives now, the building located behind the East Precinct on East Trinity Lane. Bill Pridemore had sent his share of case files to the repository for solved cases.

He'd had a good run.

His step quickened as he headed toward the parking garage. He didn't look back. The sun was warm on his face.

Authors' Note

People still talk about how the Marcia Trimble murder changed Nashville. The case that took over thirty years to solve was a fascinating mystery, with an investigation that had plenty of complexities, but we were most intrigued by the profound effects of the tragedy that reached far beyond Marcia's own family. In many ways, Marcia Trimble belonged to the whole city. We wanted to write about what the murder of the nine-year-old Girl Scout meant to her neighborhood, how it shook the police department, how the lives of innocent people were changed. And we wanted to show why Nashville lost its innocence, too. As we turned the clock back to February 25, 1975, and began our research, we expected it would be hard to find all the information we needed on the coldest of cold cases, but in the end, we could have filled another book.

Our deep gratitude goes to the individuals who were willing to talk with us about the case. Major George Currey, retired, who as Youth Guidance director responded to the missing child report that first night and remained on the case for many weeks, spent an afternoon with us recalling those poignant events. Marie Maxwell, who was interviewed by authorities many times, shared her memories one more time with us. We are indebted to Major Currey and Mrs. Maxwell not only for providing factual information and clarification, but for giving us a sense of the emotional tenor during the night of Marcia's disappearance and the difficult period that followed.

We wish to thank Deborah Faulkner, retired deputy chief of police, for her insight and commentaries on the workings of the Nashville Police Department and the investigative efforts of Detective Diane Vaughn. We are grateful to Detective Jim Sledge for adding information about Detective Vaughn's police work. A special thanks to Diane's sister, Deborah Sullivan, who was kind enough to share personal stories and a photograph for the book.

We gratefully acknowledge the cooperation of Deputy District Attorney Tom Thurman and The Honorable Steve Dozier who took the time to answer our questions. We extend our thanks to Assistant DAs Katy Miller and Rachel Sobrero, to Jim McNamara and Laura Dykes of the public defender's office, to defense attorney Kerry Haymaker, and to Sergeant Pat Postiglione, all of whom were willing to discuss the Trimble and Des Prez trials. Thanks also to Susan Niland of the DA's office for providing the photograph of the prosecutors for our use in the book.

Judy Ladd gave us an eyewitness account of the incident that led to Jerome Barrett's arrest at her apartment building on March 12, 1975. We appreciate how she recalled that experience for us and continued to read what we wrote until we got it right.

We are deeply indebted to the print journalists who covered the Marcia Trimble story every day for many weeks following her disappearance. Time melted away as we immersed ourselves in the *Banner* and *Tennessean* archives at the Downtown Public Library. Between the lines of facts and quotes, the mood of the city came through, thanks to the talented report-ers. The *Nashville Scene* and local television stations, as well as the *Tennessean*, provided background material for more re-cent developments in the case. We acknowledge Matt Pulle's fine work in his two-part retrospective on the Trimble case, published in 2001 in the *Scene*. Pulle's comprehensive article provided source material for several passages in the book, spe-cifically the chapters about Jeffrey Womack.

Police records and trial testimony formed the factual ba-sis for the story. We drew from witnesses' statements, detec-tives' reports, and other evidentiary material, and relied on the trial testimony of witnesses including Virginia Trimble, Commander Mickey Miller, Lieutenant Tom Catney, and the experts in forensics for many descriptions, details, and ex-planations. To write about a case that has spanned more than three decades, it was necessary to reconstruct certain scenes and passages of dialogue, based on all available documenta-tion, but we did so making every effort to faithfully present the events that actually occurred.

We are especially indebted to our friend, Detective Bill Pridemore, retired, for his valuable insight into the case. He shared his experiences, read passages of the book for accu-racy, answered hundreds of questions, and never lost his good humor. Always gracious, he took our calls even when he was headed to the golf course.

The stages that a book goes through from the time it is first conceptualized until it finds its way to bookstore shelves is long and tedious, and we were fortunate to have the expertise of outstanding professionals throughout the process. We thank our literary agent, Sharlene Martin, for her business savvy and hard work on our behalf, and we deeply appreciate our Berk-ley editors, Shannon Jamieson Vazquez and Faith Black, who were patient and thorough as they worked with us to develop the final manuscript.

Our colleagues in the Nashville Writers Alliance deserve

our deep gratitude for being great critics, asking the questions that needed to be asked, never letting us off the hook.

To the family and friends who are a continual source of support and inspiration, we are forever grateful. We are blessed to have extraordinary people in our lives whose encouragement and enthusiasm never waver. Some things, thankfully, do not change.